CHANGING SOCIAL

The Nordic welfare model in the 21st century

Edited by Jon Kvist, Johan Fritzell, Bjørn Hvinden and
Olli Kangas

REASSESSING
THE NORDIC
WELFARE
MODEL

First published in Great Britain in 2012 by

The Policy Press
University of Bristol
Fourth Floor
Beacon House
Queen's Road
Bristol BS8 1QU, UK
t: +44 (0)117 331 4054
f: +44 (0)117 331 4093
tpp-info@bristol.ac.uk
www.policypress.co.uk

North American office:
The Policy Press
c/o The University of Chicago Press
1427 East 60th Street
Chicago, IL 60637, USA
t: +1 773 702 7700
f: +1 773 702 9756
sales@press.uchicago.edu
www.press.uchicago.edu

Reprinted 2012

British Library Cataloguing in Publication Data
A catalogue record for this book is available from the British Library.

Library of Congress Cataloging-in-Publication Data
A catalog record for this book has been requested.

ISBN 978 1 84742 659 8 (paperback)
ISBN 978 1 84742 660 4 (hardcover)

Cover design by Qube Design Associates, Bristol
Front cover: photograph kindly supplied by www.alamy.com
Printed and bound in Great Britain by MPG Book Group

FSC
www.fsc.org
MIX
From responsible sources
FSC® C018575

Contents

List of tables and figures   v
Notes on contributors   vii
Acknowledgements   xi

one   Changing social inequality and the Nordic welfare model   I
          Jon Kvist, Johan Fritzell, Bjørn Hvinden and Olli Kangas

two   Anti-immigration attitudes, support for redistribution and party   23
          choice in Europe
          Henning Finseraas

three   Do we all (dis)like the same welfare state? Configurations of   45
          public support for the welfare state in comparative perspective
          Mads Meier Jæger

four   Eroding minimum income protection in the Nordic countries?   69
          Reassessing the Nordic model of social assistance
          Susan Kuivalainen and Kenneth Nelson

five   Equality in the social service state: Nordic childcare models   89
          in comparative perspective
          Gabrielle Meagher and Marta Szebehely

six   Welfare state institutions, unemployment and poverty: comparative   119
          analysis of unemployment benefits and labour market participation
          in 15 European Union countries
          M. Azhar Hussain, Olli Kangas and Jon Kvist

seven   Social inequalities in health: the Nordic welfare state in   143
          a comparative context
          Clare Bambra

eight   Income inequality and poverty: do the Nordic countries still   165
          constitute a family of their own?
          Johan Fritzell, Olof Bäckman and Veli-Matti Ritakallio

nine   Is immigration challenging the economic sustainability of   187
          the Nordic welfare model?
          Christer Gerdes and Eskil Wadensjö

ten   Nordic responses to rising inequalities: still pursuing a distinct path   201
          or joining the rest?
          Jon Kvist, Johan Fritzell, Bjørn Hvinden and Olli Kangas

Index   207

List of tables and figures

Tables

2.1   Linear regression: the dependent variable is support for equalisation of   30
      income differences
2.2   Percentage of the voters that jointly support redistribution and   31
      a restrictive immigration policy
2.3   Multilevel logistic regression: dependent variable is whether   34
      the respondent voted for a Left party
A-2.1 Descriptive statistics   44
A-2.2 Country-level data   44
3.1   Results from latent class regression   56
3.2   Time trends in levels of support for the welfare state   58
A-3.1 Model fit for different latent class models   66
5.1   Children in childcare, Nordic countries, 2009   92
5.2   Forms of care: proportions receiving care, average hours in respective   99
      forms of care and FTE/100 children in the age groups 1-2 years and
      3-5 years, 2008
5.3   Childcare systems, usage and outcomes   104
A-5.1 Forms of care among children 1-2 years old by parents' highest education   116
      in 2008
A-5.2 Forms of care among children 3-5 years old by parents' highest education   117
      in 2008
6.1   Characteristics of the employment systems in 15 European countries   125
      in the mid-1990s and late 2000s
6.2   Replacement rates in different income levels, 1995 and 2007, in   128
      15 European countries
6.3   Poverty rates for different labour market transitions   130
6.4   Correlations between unemployment protection generosity and   131
      poverty in different labour market status in the 1990s and 2000s
7.1   Infant mortality rates and life expectancy at birth for   149
      30 countries and six welfare state regimes in 2003
7.2   Summary findings of three welfare state studies of absolute and relative   154
      socioeconomic inequalities in self-reported health
8.1   Poverty rates of old and new risk groups in Europe in 2007   176
8.2   Poverty profiles of old and new risk groups in Europe in 2007   178
8.3   Poverty persistency, 2008   180

Figures

2.1   Percentage difference in Left-voting between voters who jointly support   33
      redistribution and a restrictive immigration policy and voters who jointly
      support redistribution and a liberal immigration policy

3.1   Conditional response probabilities for different welfare state   54
      support types, 2006

3.2   Marginal distribution of welfare state support types across countries,   57
      2006

A-3.1 Effect of education on welfare support types   67

A-3.2 Effect of family income on welfare support types   67

A-3.3 Effect of socioeconomic status on welfare support types   68

4.1   Levels of social assistance and minimum income benefits in   76
      US$ purchasing power parities and 2005 price levels, 1990-2009

4.2   Adequacy of social assistance and minimum income benefits   78
      (type-case data and averages of a single person, a lone parent and
      a two-parent family), 1990-2008

4.3   Means-tested benefit expenditure as a percentage of total social benefit   80
      expenditure in different countries, 1990-2008

4.4   Poverty rates among recipients of means-tested benefits at four-year   81
      intervals, 1990-2005

4.5   Percentage reduction of poverty attributed to means-tested benefits   83
      at four-year intervals, 1990-2005

5.1   Childcare coverage, children aged 1-5, Nordic countries, 1990-2009   93

5.2   Combinations of care for children aged 1-2 and 3-5, coverage, 2008   101

5.3   Formal care for children 1-2 years old by parents' educational   103
      background, FTE places per 100 children, 2008

6.1   Country-specific poverty odds-rates for the employed-unemployed   134
      and unemployed-unemployed in the 1990s and late 2000s

8.1   Relative changes of income inequality according to the Gini coefficient   170
      in the Nordic countries from around 1985-2008

8.2   Income inequality around 1985, 1995 and 2005, and cross-national   173
      variation of these inequality estimates

8.3   Relative poverty rates and cross-national variation in these rates,   175
      around 1985, 1995 and 2005

—

Notes on contributors

Clare Bambra is Professor of Public Health Policy, Wolfson Research Institute, Durham University, UK. She has three main areas of interest: work, worklessness and health; social policy and international variations health; and tackling health inequalities by addressing the wider social determinants of health.

Olof Bäckman is Associate Professor of Sociology at the Swedish Institute for Social Research (SOFI), Stockholm University. He is also Director of the research group on social exclusion and poverty at the Institute for Futures Studies in Stockholm. His research mainly concerns issues of social exclusion and poverty with a particular focus on the welfare state and the life course.

Henning Finseraas is Researcher at Norwegian Social Research (NOVA), Oslo, Norway. His research interests include the comparative politics of the welfare state, determinants of welfare state policy preferences and electoral behaviour.

Johan Fritzell is Professor of Sociology at the Centre for Health Equity Studies (CHESS), Stockholm University/Karolinska Institutet and affiliated as Senior Researcher at the Institute for Futures Studies, Stockholm. He has published on the determinants and distributions of health and welfare in Sweden, as well as on comparative income distribution and poverty.

Christer Gerdes is Assistant Professor of Economics at the Swedish Institute for Social Research, Stockholm University. Gerdes has published on various topics, including the implications of immigration for government spending.

M. Azhar Hussain is Assistant Research Professor at the Department of Economics at the University of Copenhagen. His main research interests include applied microeconomics, income distribution analysis (inequality, poverty, polarisation and deprivation), comparative welfare state studies and econometric methods.

Bjørn Hvinden is Professor of Sociology and Head of Research at Norwegian Social Research (NOVA), Oslo, and Leader of the Nordic Centre of Excellence in Welfare Research called 'Reassessing the Nordic welfare model', funded by NordForsk (2007-12). His research interests include comparative welfare research, disability policy, ethnic relations, Europeanisation, welfare governance, civil society and participatory policy making.

Mads Meier Jæger is Professor of Educational Research and Econometrics at the Department of Education, Aarhus University, Denmark. His research interests include intergenerational social mobility, political sociology and quantitative methods. He has published on these issues in peer-reviewed journals such as *Social Forces*, *Social Science Research* and *European Sociological Review*.

Olli Kangas is Professor and Research Director at Kela – the Social Insurance Institution of Finland. His research interests include comparative welfare studies, the institutional set-ups of welfare programmes, the political and structural factors behind the development of welfare states and the consequences of social policy in terms of income distribution, poverty, legitimacy and collective action.

Susan Kuivalainen is Professor of Social Policy at the Department of Social Research, University of Turku, Finland. She is the Director of the Social Insurance Expert Training Programme TOPSOS and President of the Social Policy Association in Finland. She has published on social assistance, poverty and anti-poverty policies.

Jon Kvist is Professor of Comparative Social Policy at the Centre for Welfare State Research at the University of Southern Denmark. Kvist is active in various research networks, boards and projects. He has published widely on the Nordic welfare model, the European Union and social policy, comparative labour market policy and social policy, and on issues in comparative methodology.

Gabrielle Meagher is Professor of Social Policy at the University of Sydney, Australia. Her research explores the impact of marketisation and personalisation on the way social care services are practised, organised, distributed, experienced and understood by participants with different stakes in the system. She has a keen interest in comparative social policy, with a focus on Anglo-Saxon and Nordic countries.

Kenneth Nelson is Associate Professor of Sociology at the Swedish Institute for Social Research, Stockholm University. He is the director of several comparative research projects focusing on social policy and poverty. Nelson has published on various topics, including the measurement of redistribution, the European social inclusion process, social assistance and social insurance.

Veli-Matti Ritakallio is Professor of Social Policy in the Department of Social Policy and Social Work, University of Turku, Finland. His research interests include poverty, income redistribution, income transfers, welfare state models, cross-national comparisons and the methodology of empirical social research.

Marta Szebehely is Professor of Social Work at Stockholm University. Her historical and comparative research examines care from a gender perspective. She is particularly interested in the shifting boundaries between the family, the state and the market as providers of care, and the intended and unintended consequences of policy changes for the everyday lives of people in need of care, their families and paid care workers.

Eskil Wadensjö is Professor of Labour Economics at the Swedish Institute for Social Research, Stockholm University and Director of SULCIS (Stockholm University Linnaeus Center for Integration Studies). Wadensjö is involved in many projects and networks and is member of a number of boards. He has published many books and articles on international migration, integration, labour economics and labour market and social policies.

Acknowledgements

The commitment to promote equality through state policies was perhaps the greatest legacy of the 20th century. Until recently the Nordic countries were broadly perceived as showing the greatest will to reduce inequalities, of making the greatest efforts to prevent and dampen inequalities and of achieving the greatest degree of equality between men and women and between poor and rich. Only a decade into the 21st century the will, efforts and capacity can be questioned, also in the Nordic countries.

If even the Nordic countries, well-known for their equality achievements are changing, we can only but expect that changing equality will be less of an issue globally. To assess the causes, direction, scope and impact of changes we therefore collected a strong team of scholars all experts in their fields. The common questions they address are whether the support for equality and egalitarian policies is diminishing, whether policies are more more inegalitarian and whether the policies are less able to reduce inequalities. Hence, all studies assess the situation today compared with that at the end of the 20th century and compare developments across countries.

As editors we would like to thank these experts for making their piece to the puzzle. We hope they are other readers find that the picture provided by their studies contributes to a better understanding of the what is going on.

We also thank participants in seminars in Stockholm and Copenhagen for comments and suggestions to individual chapters. We thank Jennie Bacchus Hertzman for organising the Stockholm Seminar. We thank Natalie Reid for excellent language consultation. Finally, we are grateful for the financial support provided by the Nordic Centre of Excellence for Welfare, 'Reassessing the Nordic Welfare Model', funded by NordForsk (2007-2012).

Copenhagen, Helsinki, Oslo and Stockholm,
October 2011
The editors

ONE

Changing social inequality and the Nordic welfare model

Jon Kvist, Johan Fritzell, Bjørn Hvinden and Olli Kangas

Introduction: inequality on the rise?

Nordic mass media regularly announce the end of equality in the Nordic countries – is it a reality or merely another example of journalistic dramatisation and myth-building? In this book we aim to clarify in what ways equality has actually characterised the Nordic countries and to what extent we now find less equality in earnings and disposable incomes, participation in paid employment and informal care, social participation, educational achievements and health and well-being. Assuming that we can confirm that there has been a shift away from equality, we should then be able to point to factors and mechanisms that have sustained a high degree of equality earlier on and similarly, to the factors and mechanisms that are now driving the Nordic countries toward more inequality.

Why is Nordic social equality changing? We take as our starting point the international trend of growing income inequalities. Although countries have become richer, at least up until the 2008 financial crisis (Atkinson and Morelli, 2010), affluence appears now to be more unequally divided, and the gap between rich and poor is widening. Whereas many countries have experienced different degrees and patterns of change in their distribution of income over the last three decades (see, for example, Atkinson, 2008; ILO, 2008; Kenworthy, 2011; OECD, 2008), we also find several commonalities. While a decreasing, or at least stable, degree of income inequality was the norm in the Western world for most of the 20th century, in the 1980s that norm suddenly started to change. The general picture has since become one of growing income inequalities.

But it is not only the overall trend of growing inequalities that is of interest. We now have ample evidence that the shift in trends has been particularly evident at the upper end of income distribution. The prime example is the US: in 2007, the year before the latest financial crisis, the share of the total income going to the top 1 per cent of the population was estimated to be around 23-24 per cent, or close to one quarter of the total (Reich, 2010). Interestingly, this share is matched only by that in 1928. Thus two general and difficult questions emerge. First, what are the causes of this upsurge of inequality? Second, what are the consequences?

Although aggregated economic indicators and the distribution of income and wealth are important, the concepts of welfare and social inequalities are broader.

In the European Union (EU), scholars and policy makers have sought to advance and promote new and better indicators and targets that are closer to individuals and more amenable to policy interventions (see, respectively Atkinson et al, 2002; Europe 2020, 2010). Such broader perspectives on welfare, well-being and social inequality are also highlighted in the 2010 Sarkozy report (see Stiglitz et al, 2010). Arguably, these broader perspectives on welfare, well-being and social inequality are not necessarily new but rather very much in line with the Scandinavian strand of welfare research that for four decades has emphasised the multidimensionality of welfare. In this book we build on the Nordic strand of welfare research in our investigation of how social inequalities are changing.

More than money: the Nordic welfare strand of welfare research

Despite no generally accepted definition of welfare, the Nordic strand of welfare research has drawn much on Richard Titmuss's (1958) concept of welfare as command over resources. One of the main founders of Nordic welfare research, Sten Johansson (1970, p 25), defined an individual's level of living as 'the command over resources in terms of money, possessions, knowledge, psychological and physical energy, social relations, security and so on by means of which the individual can control and consciously direct her conditions of life', while defining welfare as the living conditions in the areas influenced by politics.

This perspective has several important theoretical features: first, the perspective on welfare is explicitly actor-oriented. The good life is not directly defined. Empirically the perspective involves a focus on conditions promoting or constraining individual agency. Second, according to this perspective welfare is multidimensional, including both material and intangible resources, while making collective resources essential in many phases of life. Unlike many previous approaches, the perspective has not been limited to economic hardship but rather included other important aspects of well-being that must be taken into consideration when analysing well-being or the lack thereof (Johansson, 1970, 1979). Johansson proposed that one could measure and evaluate human well-being on nine components: health, employment, economic resources, knowledge and education, social integration, housing and neighbourhood, security of life and property, recreation and culture, and political resources. Johansson's conceptual map laid the basis for the successive Swedish Level of Living Surveys, later to be replicated in some form in all the Nordic countries. For example, in his comparative Finnish project, Erik Allardt shifted the focus from resources to the level of need-satisfaction described by the catchwords 'having, loving and being' (Allardt, 1975, 1993).

The Nordic strand of welfare research has a clear affinity to Amartya Sen's focus on the abilities of individuals to fulfil their own potential (see, for example, Sen, 1992). According to Sen's capability approach, much more than the elimination of the monetary hardship is at stake in debates about poverty. Non-poverty means not only that one has sufficient money to make one's ends met but also that one has the ability to function, that is, one has the resources and knowledge to make conscious life choices that one is capable of realising. While Sen (1985) puts stronger emphasis on freedom of choice in evaluating welfare than the Nordic tradition of welfare research usually does, Johansson also covered this dimension when he talked of the individual's capcity to 'control and consciously direct his living conditions' (Johansson, 1970, p 25). His most telling example is a comparison between two individuals who starve: one because of poverty, the other because he or she has made the deliberate choice to fast. That the welfare of the latter person is better than that of the former constitutes a reasonable assumption. Despite slight differences in emphasis, the basic theme of the Nordic approach is a very wide concept of welfare that is always multidimensional and that includes the quality of life aspect (for a more elaborate discussion of the Scandinavian welfare concept, see, for example, Fritzell and Lundberg, 2005).

Equality means different things to different people. Hence, one of the first tasks of a scientific study of social inequality is to specify and define what aspects and dimensions we are examining. As Sen (1992) points out, all social ethics make some form of equality worth pursuing. The desired equality may not necessarily be in outcomes but in opportunities or basic rights. In this book, we are interested in social inequality as it relates to welfare and the ways in which changes in institutional arrangements and public interventions may have an impact on the level and distribution of welfare and potentially erode redistributive processes.

We adopt a broader perspective on welfare and inequality than merely that of studying gross domestic product (GDP) per capita or the distribution of income. This book is largely about how the activities and programmes of the welfare state affect patterns of social inequality. While the capacity for redistributing income is a key characteristic of welfare states, other important characteristics include the ability to provide free or affordable services (for example, related to health and care) of high quality to all who need such services and to protect individuals against illness, incapacity and premature death.

Aim of the book

When investigating the role of welfare states in changing social inequalities, we need precise understandings of both the goals and the designs of welfare states and of the achieved patterns of welfare. Such patterns – what researchers often term 'outcomes' – are both determined by the efforts of welfare states and influenced by other societal players such as employers, voluntary organisations and families, and in many instances by individuals themselves. In some cases families, voluntary organisations and employers complement one another, as well as complementing the welfare provided by government. In other cases these groups serve as alternative ways of meeting the same kind of need.

The role of Nordic welfare states has not only been to ameliorate problems after they have occurred but also to prevent such problems from happening in the first place. International scholarship has increasingly framed such prevention in terms of 'social investment' (see, for example, Giddens, 1998; Jenson, 2001; Esping-Andersen et al, 2002; Morel et al, 2011). The aim is to prevent societal structures from making it difficult for individuals and groups to realise their full human potential. Many structural factors are greatly significant for the individual's life chances by shaping the conditions for his or her choices and adjustments. Basic conditions include *when* one was born, *where* one was born and *who* one's parents are, conditions over which no person has any influence. The Nordic welfare model thus seeks both to modify current patterns of income inequality and well-being and to reduce social inequalities in individuals' chances of finding a job, forming a family and excelling in society. This goal entails a much bigger role for the nation state in securing the welfare of its residents than we usually see in other countries. Whether the Nordic welfare model is more successful at curbing social inequalities than other welfare models in the face of changing structural or external factors is a key issue for empirical investigation.

The purpose of the book is therefore to answer the big question: *Are the Nordic countries stemming the international tide of inequality better, worse or perhaps just differently than other countries?*

Given the comparatively strong and persistent values attached to equality and equalisation in the Nordic countries, an obvious task for research is the investigation of the extent to which the circumstances of Nordic countries are actually characterised by equality, regardless of whether these empirical patterns are framed as 'initial conditions' before redistribution efforts or as 'outcomes' – achievements or shortcomings – of such efforts. A related issue is whether the different Nordic countries have the same capacity for redistribution, despite the somewhat dissimilar institutional designs of their welfare provisions.

Studying changes in social inequality

Do we see new forms of inequality?

While the Nordic countries may have returned to earlier and even higher levels of inequalities in some areas, we are also more likely to find new mechanisms behind inequality, and possibly new forms of inequality related to, for example:

- greater migration-driven ethnic diversity;
- more changeable patterns of partnering, parenting and cohabitation;
- growing contrasts between the purchase power of dual and single-earner households;
- new panoramas of health and social adjustments in the Nordic populations;
- redefined division of responsibilities for risk protection and service provisions between public and private actors.

Several chapters in this book deal with such new forms of, and mechanisms underlying, the emerging patterns of social inequality.

Are we now framing inequality in new ways?

Partly related to changes in forms and mechanisms, we also see that the framing or vocabulary of social inequality is now significantly different from that of two or three decades ago. For example, both policy makers and researchers have adopted the discourses of exclusion, misrecognition, segregation, discrimination and inaccessibility – terms that were hardly known or used much more rarely three decades ago. As a result of this shift, when people today speak of increasing inequalities they may have in mind something different from or more complex than traditional class inequalities.

The Nordic countries are currently struggling to absorb and accommodate equality conceived as 'equal worth' and 'parity of participation' (Fraser, 1995, 2008; Hobson, 2003), rather than giving in to the impulse to treat equality only as a question of 'sameness' or 'homogeneity' (Gullestad, 1996, 2001). Notions or myths of homogeneity have historically served as conditions for Nordic willingness to share risks and redistribute resources through collective and solidaristic arrangements. Some scholars believe that increased difference and heterogeneity are undermining the condition of homogeneity, and thereby directly or indirectly weakening earlier mechanisms for equalising circumstances and living conditions (see, for example, Alesina and Glaeser, 2004; Putnam, 2007). In Chapter Two, Henning Finseraas in particular takes up and responds to this prominent strand of current international research.

The Nordic welfare model and inequality

Regardless of whether people believe that inequality is good or bad for society, they usually agree that, globally, the Nordic countries have made the greatest efforts to curb inequalities. Historically, the development of the Nordic welfare model differed among the Nordic countries, with Denmark and Sweden being early movers and Finland the laggard (for more, see Kangas and Palme, 2005; Christiansen et al, 2006). Nonetheless, although constitutive principles such as universal coverage and collective financing were introduced early in social insurance schemes, the Nordic welfare model became distinct from other country models only when public sector services were introduced and expanded from the 1960s onwards. The Nordic scope of the more or less universal access to a wide range of public sector services is unparalleled in the world. Equal access to benefits has also contributed to a large degree of equality in outcomes. The ability to balance equality and efficiency has attracted attention outside the Nordic countries since the 1960s.

A passion for equality?

Equality and equalisation of people's circumstances have been values or ideals enjoying wide popular and electoral support in the Nordic countries, to the point where some observers have talked about a 'passion for equality' (see, for example, Graubard, 1986; Marklund, 1988). Such values are reflected in the objectives and premises for public policies to provide universal income protection and access to high-quality services and to a considerable extent, even for the system of collective bargaining about wages and occupational benefits. It is not entirely clear whether the ideal of equality is shaped by institutions and actors, or whether the institutions and elite actors are shaping the values and norms.

According to Walter Korpi and Joakim Palme (1998), a paradox of redistribution exists. They argue that in a universal welfare state redistribution includes the middle classes, thereby gaining their support for broader redistributive policies that benefit not only the middle class demand for generous social insurance and high quality services but also the low-income groups who receive more and better benefits than they otherwise would have. In contrast, targeted redistribution in selective welfare states that give benefits only to the lowest income group tends to result in lower benefits for these groups. Bo Rothstein (1998) argues along the same lines when he states that over time, the initial choices of the establishment of universal programmes influence the values of citizens. These citizens then become more solidaristic and ask for more redistributive institutions. Whether ideals or institutions came first is a question resembling that of the chicken-or-the-egg. Whatever the cause, the existence of these institutional arrangements has likely served to maintain or reproduce the value of equality or the preference for relatively small differences in the social and economic circumstances among inhabitants of the Nordic countries.

A passion for work?

The Nordic populations also share a passion for work. It is both a goal and a means. Participation in work is broadly seen as a goal in itself. Similarly, lack of work is broadly conceived as a problem for both the jobless person and society at large. Thus, having a job is understood as being the key to achieving autonomy and emancipation. For example, since the 1960s Nordic women have entered the labour market in increasing numbers, culminating with the conversion of many part-time jobs to full-time jobs in the 1990s and 2000s (Leira, 1992; Lewis, 1992, 2006; Lister, 2009). The aim of gender equality through women's participation in the labour market reads as a 'one long farewell' to women's role as housewives and economic dependents (Ann Orloff, forthcoming).

Work is also crucial for the sustainability of the Nordic welfare model. Simply put, because the model is extensive it is also costly, thereby demanding that as many people as possible engage in paid work and pay taxes and social security contributions that finance the model. People are either in work (and earning an income through which they can provide for themselves) or they are out of work (and in almost all cases receiving social security or social assistance benefits). So, the more people who work, the more people finance the model, the fewer receive benefits.

Reflecting the well-known trade-off between equality and efficiency, many outside the Nordic countries believe that the Nordic welfare model is a paradise for the work-shy. Moreover, some welfare state scholars may have been misled by the concept of decommodification, one of the guiding principles of the famous typology of welfare states by Gøsta Esping-Andersen (1990), believing that the Nordic countries have sought to make people independent of the labour market. Indeed, these scholars portray the Nordic welfare states as being high on 'decommodification' (a measure of the degree to which citizens were independent of the cash nexus, the labour market, through accessible and generous benefits). However, nothing could be further from the truth: a number of measures aim at full employment. In addition to education, active labour market policies, childcare, taxation, social assistance, healthcare and various forms of social care all have the aim of enabling participation in the labour force, and more generally, in society at large.

The Nordic governments expect most people receiving non-employment benefits to attempt to find work. As part of planning their re-entry into the labour market, most benefit claimants interact with agencies such as employment exchanges, social workers and doctors. As various chapters in this book document, the Nordic countries provide not only relatively accessible and generous benefits, but also strong obligations for benefit recipients to accept activation offers, work offers, or both (Kvist, 2002; Johansson and Hvinden, 2007b). When claimants do not comply with such requirements, they often face harsh sanctions such as the temporary or permanent reduction of benefits, if not their complete withdrawal.

Many benefits reward employment. Social insurance schemes in the Nordic countries reward individual employment in much the same way as elsewhere in Europe. Generally, the longer that one has worked and the more that one has earned, the bigger contributions one has made, then the larger benefits one is likely to receive if one becomes ill, work-disabled, unemployed or old. Guaranteed minimum benefits ensure the adequacy of benefits, and benefit ceilings curb the generosity of benefits for middle and high earners. If the Nordic countries had Robin Hood-style systems, one would expect high guaranteed minimum benefits and low benefit ceilings. True, Nordic guaranteed minimum income benefits are often larger for social insurance than elsewhere in Europe (but no longer so for social assistance; see Kuivalainen and Nelson, Chapter Four). But benefit ceilings in the Nordic countries are set so high that middle-income earners receive benefits as high as they would in Continental European countries. Finland, for example, has no benefit ceiling for most social insurance schemes, making it 'more Continental' than Germany in this regard. One interpretation is that the loyalty of the crucial middle classes comes at a price, as stipulated by the 'paradox of redistribution' thesis.

These supportive, coercive and rewarding measures all aim at motivating individuals and helping them find work. Policies for boosting employment have the double aim of enabling people to support themselves in the labour market and of reducing social expenditure. In short, the Nordic welfare model is extremely oriented towards work and employment. Changing social inequality is therefore primarily a matter of changing accessibility to the labour market and enabling all social groups to participate irrespective of their gender, age, education or skills, ethnicity, or place of residence.

How can social inequality be changed?

Taking from the rich and giving to the poor, known as vertical redistribution, has, since the days of Robin Hood, constituted a central way of changing social inequality. The chief instrument of the welfare state is direct cash redistributional policies, that is, taxes and cash benefits. To protect everyone against destitution, a social safety net exists in the form of social assistance and other minimum income schemes in all European countries. From the Nordic viewpoint, however, because other policies (education, active labour market policies and social insurance) are supposed to help people maximise their chances of becoming self-providers, means-tested social assistance should be relatively generous and go to small groups as well. In Chapter Four, Susan Kuivalainen and Kenneth Nelson investigate whether developments over the past 30 years leave this picture intact or whether we need to reconsider our understanding of 'last resort' social assistance in the Nordic countries.

Distribution over the life course, known as horizontal redistribution, is another key function of the welfare state (see e.g. Salverda et al, 2011). Children and young people, or their families, receive benefits such as child family allowances, subsidised childcare and education. Adults receive benefits such as pensions, healthcare and social care. Distribution over the life course depicts how people of working age both *pay back*, through tax and social security contributions, what they have received, and *pay towards* their retirement. The Nordic welfare model has moved beyond the traditional demogrants such as child family allowances and old age pensions, which appear in all types of welfare states associated with encompassing services. Indeed, it is the important role of social service that makes the Nordic welfare model unique. In Chapter Five Meagher and Szebehely examine the development of day care services for children.

Insurance is an important instrument of distribution, with a variety of social insurance programmes paying out benefits (for example, income transfers) to people who become unemployed, ill or work-disabled. As with other welfare models, the Nordic countries have extensive social security schemes for wage earners. What makes the Nordic countries stand out here is not so much the social security benefits (which are not always particularly accessible or generous), but rather the way in which these benefits come bundled with active labour market policies, encompassing childcare, free healthcare, rehabilitative measures and other benefits that help transitions back into work.

Indeed, the most distinct Nordic instrument for reducing social inequalities is not cash benefits such as social assistance and social insurance, but a vast amount of services in the three core areas of the welfare social services: society, education and health. Most obviously, most Western societies have healthcare arrangements so that people can usually afford medical treatment regardless of the size of their wallet. But benefits-in-kind also refer to the care sector more generally. As highlighted by classic texts on the development of welfare states, the social services constitute a cornerstone for reducing social inequalities by giving equal access to healthcare, elderly care, education and hence guaranteeing equal opportunities in life (Tawney, 1964; Titmuss, 1974).

Positive and negative impacts of Nordic equality

A substantial strand of scholarship has argued that fairly equal patterns in the circumstances of the inhabitants of the Nordic countries have contributed to several positive traits in these countries. These include solidarity with other than one's own (extended) family, high inter-personal and inter-group trust, collaboration, willingness to enter pacts with groups with other interests, social capital, economic effectiveness, engagement in voluntary activities and taking responsibility for society and the common good (see, for example, Wilkinson and Pickett, 2009; for counter-arguments, see Snowdown, 2010). Some researchers maintain that Nordic social equality is part of a self-reinforcing and self-sustaining process involving complementarities and positive feedbacks, that is, an 'equality multiplier' (Barth and Moene, 2010; Austen-Smith et al, 2008).

By contrast, other observers have argued that Nordic equality is (also) associated with less desirable and unintended consequences. These include an undermining of the incentive to work (especially at the lower end of the income distribution); a tendency to marginalise or exclude the less qualified, fit or productive; and a lack of dynamism and innovation, a lack created by excessive public responsibility for people's well-being, interference with people's private arrangements and heavy tax burdens (see, for example, Andersen et al, 2007). Yet others argue that the high responsibility of the state might also undermine other formal and informal social contacts, networks and care. These scholars see too little freedom of choice and self-responsibility in the Nordic countries.

Welfare regimes and inequality

No matter how hard scholars and observers disagree about equality being good or bad for economic growth and other issues, they all agree that the Nordic welfare model is the showcase for reducing inequality. When contrasted with the Anglo-Saxon or Continental European welfare models, the Nordic model has indeed stood out for curbing inequalities (Esping-Andersen, 1990; Esping-Andersen and Myles, 2011). But what are the differences in these three welfare models?

The Anglo-Saxon welfare model emphasises private initiative. The state secures welfare when markets and families fail. Private welfare arrangements abound in this model, especially when compared to those in the two other models. The state promotes private welfare schemes, not least through favourable tax treatment. The lion's share of state welfare provisions is targeted at the needy, primarily through means-tested minimum income schemes for those outside the labour market and with tax credits for low-income workers, with particularly advantageous arrangements for families.

The Continental European welfare model illustrates how the state does not necessarily redistribute but rather preserves and reflects inequalities in the labour market. When initially introducing social insurance in the 1880s, German Chancellor Bismarck did not want to reduce inequalities but instead wanted to prevent revolution by obtaining the loyalty of the working classes. Following in this tradition, the Continental European social insurance arrangements have been reproducing the existing stratification in the labour market. People have to earn access to benefits by paying social insurance contributions; the size of the benefits has often been set as a share of former earnings, and the duration of some benefits (such as unemployment insurance) has been related to the length of the previous work record. Labour market inequalities then translate into other social inequalities when people receive welfare benefits. Room for private welfare schemes has been crowded out by the relatively generous statutory schemes for middle-income earners. Public social services have been more or less scarce, because providing social care, for example, has been the responsibility of either families or the voluntary sector. Child family allowances have been comparatively generous, helping families meet their needs without mothers needing to work and hence children needing to go to day care centres while mothers work.

Historically, and in contrast to the other two models, the Nordic welfare model has emphasised reducing social inequalities. Attempting to narrow the gap in social inequality has involved more than taking from the rich and giving to the most poor or facilitating social insurance and savings mechanisms for those with jobs. Changing social inequality has meant changing the roots of inequality, whether these roots are based in the market, civil society or families. State interventions have received more support and acceptance in countries with the Nordic model than in those with the other two welfare models. In the name of equality, generous state welfare provision and regulation have crowded out market provision and are available not only for the poor but also for the middle classes.

Pressures on the Nordic welfare model and inequality

Many argue that the welfare state has always been in crisis or under pressures that have changed over time (Esping-Andersen, 1999; Jæger and Kvist, 2003). Historically, the most common pressure has been connected to the 'big trade-off between equality and efficiency' (Okun, 1975). Welfare states attempt to create some form of equality by collecting taxes; spending money leads to inefficiencies. Relatively sound public finances and ratings by global credit agencies at the top positions in various competitiveness rankings suggest that the Nordic countries have managed to avoid this trade-off. In addition, many of the current pressures relate to factors outside the welfare state and may in effect call for more rather than less of a welfare state of the Nordic equality type. For example, extensive and inexpensive childcare can be viewed as serving two goals: first, it reduces social inequalities by enabling traditional carers (mostly women) to combine work and family life, thereby boosting the labour supply, which is crucial with ageing populations. Second, such childcare constitutes a social investment in children, who will eventually become better workers and taxpayers.

Overall, the pressures on the Nordic welfare model and inequality are internal and external. Internal pressures stem from demographic changes such as the growth of ageing populations and minority group populations. External pressures primarily stem from economic factors such as globalisation and the financial crisis. Yet other pressures result from social or political changes.

Ageing population

The Nordic populations are undergoing profound demographic changes, as are almost all Western industrialised countries. Large cohorts are retiring as smaller cohorts are entering the labour market. Not only are the elderly living longer, but the share of elderly is also increasing, a situation known as the 'double-ageing' challenge.

When fewer people have to take care of more older people, questions related to equality and welfare arise. Because the Nordic welfare model has universal and largely tax-financed national old age pensions, as well as social and health services for the elderly, pressure for reform builds, to ensure the model's economic sustainability and to find enough staff to provide services. The Nordic countries have already reformed old age pensions, trying to raise retirement ages and reduce the generosity of pensions, with obvious distributional impacts. Moreover, the ageing of the population intensifies the competition for labour, and the public sector will find it increasingly difficult to attract and retain sufficient numbers of service workers (ranging from social and health assistants, nurses and child carers to highly skilled doctors). As both economic and staff issues jeopardise the prospects of the Nordic welfare model, they also affect social inequality, which the model has done so much to reduce. Thus ageing populations may create a crowding out effect on the comprehensiveness of the Nordic model, both in benefits for the elderly and in the form of fewer resources available for other welfare state policies.

Multicultural societies

Another demographic development over the last 30 years has been the development of multicultural societies. Driven by immigration, increased ethnic diversity involves more multifaceted sets of values and preferences, for example in gender and family issues, in the Nordic countries. Partly because of these changes and partly because of patterns of job qualifications and language skills, as potential employers perceive them, overall employment rates are lower for several of the newer ethnic groups in the Nordic countries (see Chapter Nine, this volume). Together with the way in which the Nordic countries have designed their income maintenance systems, lower employment rates contribute to a higher risk of poverty in these newer ethnic groups.

Immigration and the lower employment rates of immigrants and their descendants may also prove an economic pressure on the Nordic welfare model. Such pressures occur if immigrants and their descendants withdraw more money from the welfare state in the form of social protection, health services and other benefits than they contribute through taxes and social security contributions. Chapter Nine discusses the relationships between immigration-driven ethnic diversity and the economics of the welfare state.

Finally, increases in multiculturalism may create pressures for the Nordic welfare model and social inequality by jeopardising national support for it. If majority citizens become less willing to pay taxes because they believe their tax money is going to people unlike themselves, immigration and multiculturalism may thus constitute a pressure on the model even without real economic pressures being exerted on it (see Chapter Two, this volume).

New policies

Ongoing restructuring of public welfare provisions, motivated by concerns about demographic ageing and long-term sustainability (especially of the income maintenance systems and the perceived need to improve incentives to labour market participation) may also have adverse distributional consequences. People belonging to groups that employers are less likely to see as attractive job recruits or who may be victims of discrimination – for example, low-skilled people – members of minority ethnic groups, or people with disabilities – are at risk of being negatively affected by such restructuring of welfare provisions. In such cases, supply-related measures such as improved financial incentives or the 'upskilling' of individuals without work will prove insufficient. Although stronger demand-oriented measures such as positive duties for employers and other forms of affirmative action may help, such measures may challenge Nordic agreements between employers, trade unions and governments and therefore may attract resistance for constituting undue interference with employer prerogatives and a good collaborative climate between the social partners (Hvinden, 2010).

Finally, some scholars argue that the Nordic welfare model is an old system in a new world and that its strong emphasis on universalism and equalisation is outdated. Universalistic one-size-fits-all solutions, they argue, should give way to more differentiated solutions based on group needs or even on personalised provisions planned in close dialogue with the individual in question. Freedom of choice has become more important, at least when one goes beyond a guaranteed minimum of provision and quality of standard in still more areas of the welfare state (Kvist and Greve, 2011). These criticisms come in several forms: for some, a demand that the entire model change; for others, necessary adaptations for ensuring the survival of the model's most fundamental basis (for discussions, see Gier and van den Berg, 2005; Johansson and Hvinden, 2007a; Greve, 2007; Hanssen and Helgesen, 2011). What the critics argue in common is that the Nordic countries should promote freedom of choice in their policies and a weakening of the passion for equality or at least for universal solutions. So the question remains: have the Nordic countries become more similar to other wealthy countries? For more on changing attitudes, see Chapter Three, and for more on policy responses, see Chapter Eight.

Structure of the book

This book stands in a series of applied empirical social research on the Nordic welfare model. The first two books in this tradition highlighted the historical development of the Scandinavian welfare model and the tradition of Level of Living Surveys (Erikson et al, 1987; Hansen et al, 1993). The next two books took stock of the Nordic welfare model, especially how it fared in the financially difficult 1990s, in Finland and Sweden in particular (Kautto et al, 1999, 2001). The conclusion of the latter book was that, although the distinct policy traits of the Nordic welfare model seemed intact, many scholars contributing to these books anticipated adverse changes over time, after different social, economic and policy programme changes were implemented and had resulted in outcomes such as higher poverty and increasing inequality.

As a full decade has passed since the 2001 publication of the last book, we are confident that we can now tap into such effects outcomes from the changes in the late 1990s and that we can assess whether they are marginal or fundamental in scope and nature. To examine whether changes are fundamental or marginal, the analysis in the following chapters are – as far as the data permit – covering a period of about three decades.

So are we witnessing the end of equality and the Nordic welfare model? Creating an anthology on changing social inequality entails investigating what is happening over a broad spectrum of themes and policies. To compare developments in only one area involves the risk of never knowing whether that area was representative of the overall development or not. In social science jargon, the 'external validity' of the findings would be low. We thus aim at increasing the external validity of the findings by investigating a number of crucial aspects and comparing their findings in a concluding analysis.

Can we change social inequalities? Another reason for analysing a wide range of the factors and policies in the Nordic welfare model is that reducing social inequality depends on a series of different efforts. To do justice to this broad notion of social inequalities, one must include studies on many of the dimensions that serve as conditions for the model. Only by assessing these efforts in a wider context can one see whether the capacity of the Nordic states for reducing social inequalities is changing.

Changing social inequalities is at the heart of the Nordic welfare model in the broad sense set out earlier. If we find increased demographic, social and economic pressures, and decreased support, as well as more inegalitarian policies put in place, the Nordic welfare model as we know it, with its strong emphasis on reducing social inequalities, is history. Put less bluntly, we would have to conclude that the Nordic welfare model at the very least is undergoing a transformation (see also Kvist and Greve, 2011).

Each of the chapters in this book contains analyses focusing on one or several aspects of social inequality. To the extent that the data allow, the analyses are cross-national in three ways, so as to better inform our assessment of how the Nordic countries are doing vis-à-vis other countries in changing social inequality. First, the design is comparative because the chapters cover various situations in different countries at the same time, providing knowledge about relative differences across countries. Second, the design is comparative because the analyses include changes *within* countries over time, providing knowledge of the degree of change. Third, the design is comparative because the authors study developments *over time* across countries, enabling us to determine whether we are witnessing the same trends in countries and, if so, whether these trends lead to convergence or to a movement in the same direction but with persistent diversity (Kautto and Kvist, 2002). In the concluding chapter we examine the major findings along these same three dimensions. We hope that these design features will help to produce an overall analysis that is informatively greater than the sum of its parts.

Nonetheless, we allow for large variations between the chapters in the methods and data employed, as the authors have chosen the ones they thought best for approaching a specific issue or factor of changing social inequality. As editors, we thought it important to have complementary disciplines and approaches represented by the authors in investigating the same two questions: how do the Nordic countries fare with regard to equality in comparison with non-Nordic countries? What changes have we seen?

Chapters

Public support for the welfare state model of the Nordic countries is, in the long run, a necessary prerequisite for its survival. The increased ethnic heterogeneity in Europe in general and possibly in the Nordic countries in particular raises important questions and challenges for social inequalities, as well as for the support of the Nordics welfare states' attempts at reducing such inequalities. Moreover, if support for the welfare state erodes, so does the possibility of maintaining a universalistic welfare state model.

In Chapter Two, Henning Finseraas focuses on intense international discussions of the possibilities for welfare state redistribution in the context of more ethnically diverse societies. In particular, he tests two mechanisms of why and how ethnic diversity may undermine citizen support for welfare state programmes. The first mechanism, the 'anti-solidarity' hypothesis, starts from the suggestion that a major reason why the US has not developed a European-style welfare state is its greater ethnic diversity. Simply stated, this hypothesis says that voters become less supportive of the welfare state if they harbour some degree of animosity towards minorities. The second mechanism is the 'distraction' hypothesis. It starts from the assumption that while voters basically have a Left or a Right view on redistribution issues, they now – at an increasingly rate – also have a Left or a Right view on immigrants and immigration policies.

In other words, an increasing number of citizens with cross-cutting preferences might, in turn, 'distract' voters from voting according to their Left or Right redistribution preferences. Finseraas uses several waves of the European Social Surveys to empirically see to what extent we can find support for these mechanisms in Europe. Although Finseraas' analyses are done for Europe, the results are highly relevant for the future of the Nordic welfare state.

Public support for the welfare state is also the subject in Chapter Three by Mads Meier Jæger. Jæger, however, focuses on what he calls the configurational and qualitative aspects of welfare attitudes. He argues that the conventional portrait of the Nordic citizens as being passionate about both equality and their support for the welfare state is much too simplistic. To understand people's welfare state attitudes, Jæger says we must instead look at specific dimensions, especially at which type of welfare state the electorate want to support. People are not merely for or against redistribution; they may also categorise who should receive support in terms of the 'deserving' or 'undeserving'. Jæger distinguishes between three types of citizens: supporters of an unconditional welfare state, supporters of a conditional welfare state model and more general welfare sceptics. His hypothesis is that citizens of the Nordic countries tend to favour an unconditional welfare state model, whereas citizens within other welfare regime countries are more likely to favour a conditional model. He uses data from the International Social Survey Programme (ISSP) at four times, looking both at the cross-national picture and at changes over time within countries.

In Chapter Four Susan Kuivalainen and Kenneth Nelson compare trends in the means-tested minimum income arrangements in four Nordic countries (Denmark, Finland, Norway and Sweden) with those in three other European countries (Germany, the Netherlands and the UK) over two decades. The comparison enables the authors to examine whether the Nordic arrangements for means-tested support have retained their distinct character. Earlier research suggests that while means-tested income support amounts to a small proportion of the overall income protection provided in the Nordic countries, such support is fairly generous and able to alleviate poverty for those who receive it. Arguing that several changes point towards a different role for means-tested support in the Nordic countries, the authors present findings that clarify this issue. They also ask how the institutional framework for means-tested income support has developed in the seven countries under study. Finally, they examine how the patterns of outcomes have changed, that is, whether benefits have become more or less generous and whether the protection against poverty offered by these benefits has improved. Using original data of high quality and with a long time-series, Kuivalainen and Nelson provide precise and novel knowledge about the trends in outcomes, offering a surprising picture of the role played by means-tested support in reducing or reproducing social inequality over a 20-year period.

One important mechanism in increasing social inequality could be the reduced availability of free or affordable high quality services. A distinct trait of the Nordic welfare state has been its key role as a provider of a range of services related to health, education and care, and thereby as a major employer for women in particular. The availability of affordable and publicly provided services of high quality has relieved families, especially their female members (given the traditional gendered division of labour), of unpaid work as carers for children, people with disabilities and older people. This defamilisation of care has enabled more women to take up paid work and has thus promoted greater gender equality. While families (along with not-for-profit and for-profit actors) remain important providers of care (or care services), the trend in the Nordic countries and many other countries has for a long time been towards a more prominent role for tax-funded public provision of such services. The reason for expanding tax-funded public services is both to stimulate female labour market participation and to ensure universal access to high-quality services irrespective of class, gender, age, ethnicity, faith or geographical area of living.

In Chapter Five, Gabrielle Meagher and Marta Szebehely analyse the development of childcare models in the Nordic countries in a comparative perspective. They focus on two public childcare-related measures of particular significance for determining the overall equality of outcomes: childcare services and financial benefits (especially care allowances offered in lieu of a publicly funded childcare place). The authors ask what effects different childcare models – and changes therein – have for gender and class equality and for equality between ethnic groups. They review developments in childcare policies in four Nordic countries (Denmark, Finland, Norway and Sweden) over the past three decades, and use Nordic and European quantitative data to analyse equality outcomes, drawing comparisons with seven other European countries (France, Germany, Greece, Italy, the Netherlands, Poland and the UK). Finally, they contrast the likely equality impacts of reliance on financial benefits such as childcare allowances and the marketisation of services, as opposed to the public provision of such services.

In Chapter Six M. Azhar Hussain, Olli Kangas and Jon Kvist scrutinise the relationship between the labour market, employment, unemployment protection and poverty rates in different welfare states. They analyse whether regime-based difference exists in the consequences of these interactions. The question is whether the primary characteristics of the Nordic welfare state remain distinct or whether the European nations have become more similar in terms of employment patterns, the generosity of unemployment insurance and the incidence of poverty among people in different labour market positions. Their analyses are based on the European Community Household Panel (ECHP) survey and the EU Statistics on Income and Living Conditions (EU-SILC).

Their analysis demonstrates that the findings across countries are strongly affected by the subgroups on which scholars choose to focus, and that seemingly similar subgroups, such as the long-term unemployed, are indeed different. For example, for the issue of generosity they emphasise that scholarly conclusions may depend on whether researchers focus on low-paid, average-paid or well-off employees. In terms of employment patterns and poverty, the long-term unemployed may be differently selected among welfare regimes.

Health status and health risks are key features for people's lives and welfare. Public health issues were at the forefront of many of the early social policy reforms in the Nordic countries (see Lundberg et al, 2008). Thus the importance of investigating to what extent the welfare state in general and the Nordic ones in particular can influence such conditions is clear. Health inequalities constitute a much more difficult task for the welfare state to tackle than, for example, income inequalities, as income can be redistributed from one person to another while health cannot.

In Chapter Seven Clare Bambra discusses the relation between the Nordic welfare state and health inequalities. Given that research generally has found that population health is enhanced by universal and relatively generous welfare states of the Nordic kind, she focuses on the question of whether the Nordic welfare states also appear to reduce health inequalities. Bambra conducts an overview of the comparative studies on health inequalities and then thoroughly discusses the different mechanisms between policies and health. She tackles the question of how it is possible that marked health inequalities continue to exist in the Nordic countries.

Concern about growing income inequality in the Western world is one starting point for this book. Earlier research has emphasised the Nordic success in terms of alleviating poverty and creating a relatively low degree of income inequality. This success has often been regarded as a central feature of the Nordic model. Johan Fritzell, Olof Bäckman and Veli-Matti Ritakallio scrutinise these outcomes in Chapter Eight, raising the question of whether the Nordic countries remain a family of their own in these respects. They study trends and overall cross-national differences, and make both subgroup analyses and a poverty persistence analysis using national sources, the Luxembourg Income Study (LIS) and data from the EU-SILC. They begin by studying the trends within the Nordic countries over the last two decades. They also discuss the results of recent analyses of income inequality in Western societies. In their poverty analyses they focus on the distinction between old and new social risks. While for years the Nordic welfare states have been successful at alleviating poverty in old social risk categories such as children and older people, the question is whether they are equally successful at handling 'new' social risk categories such as young adults and immigrants. This chapter thus also concerns an issue raised in earlier chapters – that of ethnic heterogeneity.

In Chapter Nine Christer Gerdes and Eskil Wadensjö examine the relationship between immigration and the economic sustainability of the Nordic welfare model. After describing the different waves of immigration into the Nordic countries, they set out various ways in which the linkage between immigration and economic sustainability have been discussed and examined. Finally, they discuss whether economic reasons exist for government interventions and, if so, what policy responses may be appropriate.

Finally, the question of whether the Nordic countries have stemmed the international tide of inequality better, worse or merely differently from other Western countries is the question to which we turn in the concluding chapter. Applying the results of the analyses in the various chapters, we compare trends across different aspects of inequality and the Nordic welfare model. This comparison enables us to identify whether countries belong to the same groups or models and to examine whether differences, if any, have become larger or smaller over the last three decades. In particular we pay attention to whether the preconditions in forms of norms, values and economic sustainability enable the preservation or development of the Nordic welfare model's focus on changing social inequalities.

References

Alesina, A. and Glaeser, E. (2004) *Fighting poverty in the US and Europe: A world of difference*, Oxford: Oxford University Press.

Allardt, E. (1975) Att *ha, att älska, att vara* [*Having, loving, being*], Lund: Argos.

Allardt, E. (1993) 'Having, loving, being: an alternative to the Swedish model of welfare research', in M. Nussbaum and A. Sen (eds) *The quality of life*, Oxford: Oxford University Press, pp 88-95.

Andersen, T.M., Holmström, B., Honkapohja, S., Korkman, S., Söderström, H.T. and Vartiainen, J. (2007) *The Nordic model: Embracing globalization and sharing risks*, Helsinki: The Research Institute of the Finnish Economy (ETLA) and Taloustieto Oy.

Atkinson, A.B. (2008) *The changing distribution of earnings in OECD countries*, Oxford: Oxford University Press.

Atkinson, A.B. and Morelli, S. (2010) 'Inequality and banking crises: a first look', Paper presented at the Global Labour Forum, International Labour Organization, Turin, Italy.

Atkinson, A.B., Cantillon, B., Marlier, E. and Nolan, B. (2002) *Social indicators: The EU and social inclusion*, Oxford: Oxford University Press.

Austen-Smith, D., Frieden, J.A., Golden, M.A., Moene, K.O. and Przeworski, A. (eds) (2008) *Selected works of Michael Wallerstein: The political economy of inequality, unions, and social democracy*, Cambridge: Cambridge University Press.

Barth, E. and Moene, K.O. (2010) *The equality multiplier*, Working Paper, March, ESOP (Centre for the Study of Equality, Social Organization, and Performance), Oslo, Norway: Department of Economics, University of Oslo (www.esop.uio.no/research/working-papers/the_equality_multiplier.xml).

Christiansen, N.F., Edling, N., Haave, P. and Petersen, K. (2006) *The Nordic model of welfare: A historical re-appraisal*, Copenhagen: Museum Tusculanum Press.

Erikson R., Hansen, E.J., Ringen, S. and Uusitalo, H. (eds) (1987) *The Scandinavian model: Welfare states and welfare research*, Armonk, New York: M.E. Sharpe.

Esping-Andersen, G. (1990) *Three worlds of welfare capitalism*, Cambridge: Polity Press.

Esping-Andersen, G. (1999) *Social foundations of postindustrial economies*, Oxford: Oxford University Press.

Esping-Andersen, G. and Myles, J. (2011) 'Economic inequality and the welfare state', in W. Salverda, W.B. Nolan and T. Smeeding (eds) *The Oxford handbook of economic inequality*, Oxford: Oxford University Press, pp 639-64.

Esping-Andersen, G., Gallie, D., Hemerijck, A. and Myles, J. (2002) *Why we need a new welfare state*, Oxford: Oxford University Press.

Europe 2020 (2010) 'Europe 2020: A strategy for smart, sustainable and inclusive growth', Communication from the Commission, Brussels, 3.3.2010 COM(2010) 2020 final.

Fritzell, J. and Lundberg, O. (2005) 'Fighting inequalities in health and income – one important road to welfare and social development', in O. Kangas and J. Palme (eds) *Social policy and economic development in the Nordic countries*, UNRISD Series, New York and Basingstoke: Palgrave, pp 164-85.

Fraser, N. (1995) 'From redistribution to recognition? Dilemmas of justice in a "post-Socialist" Age', *New Left Review*, vol 212, pp 69-98.

Fraser, N. (2008) *Scales of justice: Reimaging political space in a globalizing world*, Cambridge: Polity Press.

Giddens, A. (1998) *The third way. The renewal of social democracy*, Cambridge: Polity Press.

Gier, E. de and van den Berg, A. (2005) *Managing social risks through transitional labour markets: Towards an enriched European Employment Strategy*, Apeldoorn-Antwerpen: Het Spinhuis Publishers.

Graubard, S.M. (1986) *Norden – The passion for equality?*, Oslo: Norwegian University Press.

Greve, B. (2007) 'What characterise the Nordic welfare state model?', *Journal of Social Sciences*, vol 3, no 2, pp 43-51.

Gullestad, M. (1996) *Everyday life philosophers*, Oslo: Norwegian University Press.

Gullestad, M. (2001) 'Imagined sameness: shifting notions of "us" and "them" in Norway', in L. Ytrehus (ed) *Images of otherness*, Kristiansand: Høyskoleforlaget, pp 32-53.

Hansen, E.J., Ringen, S., Uusitalo, H. and Erikson, R. (eds) (1993) *Welfare trends in the Scandinavian countries*, Armonk, New York: M.E. Sharpe.

Hanssen, G.S. and Helgesen, M.K. (2011) 'Multi-level governance in Norway: universalism in elderly and mental health care services', *International Journal of Sociology and Social Policy*, vol 31, no 3-4, pp 169-72.

Hobson, B. (ed) (2003) *Recognition struggles and social movements: Contested identities, agency and power*, Cambridge: Cambridge University Press.

Hvinden, B. (2010) 'The Nordic welfare model and the challenge of globalisation', in M. Böss (ed) *The nation state in transformation: Economic globalisation, institutional mediation and political values*, Århus: Aarhus University Press, pp 292-314.

ILO (International Labour Organization) (2008) *World of work Report 2008: Income inequalities in the age of financial globalization*, Geneva: ILO.

Jenson, J. (2001) 'Re-thinking equality and equity: Canadian children and the Social Union', in E. Broadbent (ed) *Democratic equality. What went wrong?*, Toronto: University of Toronto Press, pp 111-29.

Johansson, S. (1970) *Om levnadsnivåundersökningen* [*On the Level of Living Survey*], Stockholm: Allmänna förlaget.

Johansson, S. (1979) *Towards a theory of social reporting*, Stockholm: Swedish Institute for Social Research.

Johansson, H. and Hvinden, B. (2007a) 'Opening citizenship: why do we see a new understanding of social citizenship?', in B. Hvinden and H. Johansson (eds) *Citizenship in Nordic welfare states: Dynamics of choice, duties and participation in a changing Europe*, London: Routledge, pp 3-18.

Johansson, H. and Hvinden, B. (2007b) 'Nordic activation reforms in a European context: a distinct universalistic model?', in B. Hvinden and H. Johansson (eds), *Citizenship in Nordic welfare states: Dynamics of choice, duties and participation in a changing Europe*, London: Routledge, pp 53-66.

Jæger, M.M. and Kvist, J. (2003) 'Pressures on state welfare in post-industrial societies: is more or less better?', *Social Policy & Administration*, vol 37, no 6, pp 555-72.

Kangas, O. and Palme, J. (eds) (2005) *Social Policy and Economic Developments in the Nordic Countries*, Houndsmills: Palgrave MacMillan.

Kautto, M. and Kvist, J. (2002) 'Parallel trends, persistent diversity: Nordic welfare states in the European and global context', *Global Social Policy*, vol 2, no 2, pp 189-208.

Kautto, M., Fritzell, J., Hvinden, B., Kvist. J. and Uusitalo, H. (eds) (2001) *Nordic welfare states in the European context*, London: Routledge.

Kautto, M., Heikkilä, M., Hvinden. B., Marklund, S. and Ploug, N. (eds) (1999) *Nordic social policy: Changing welfare states*, London: Routledge.

Kenworthy, L. (2011) *Progress for the Poor*, Oxford: Oxford University Press.

Korpi, W. and Palme, J. (1998) 'The paradox of redistribution and the strategy of equality: welfare state institutions, inequality and poverty in the Western countries', *American Sociological Review*, vol 63, no 5, pp 661-87.

Kvist, J. (2002) 'Changing rights and obligations in unemployment insurance', in R. Sigg and C. Behrendt (eds) *Social security in the global village*, International Social Security Series No 8, New Brunswick, NJ: Transaction Publishers, pp 227-45.

Kvist, J. and Greve, B. (2011) 'Has the Nordic welfare model been transformed?', *Social Policy & Administration*, vol 45, no 2, pp 146-60.

Leira, A. (1992) *Welfare states and working mothers*, Cambridge: Cambridge University Press.

Lewis, J. (1992) 'Gender and the development of welfare regimes', *Journal of European Social Policy*, vol 2, no 3, pp 159-73.

Lewis, J. (2006) 'Work/family reconciliation, equal opportunities and social policies', *Journal of European Public Policy*, vol 13, no 3, pp 420-37.

Lister, R. (2009) 'A Nordic nirvana? Gender, citizenship and social justice in the Nordic welfare states', *Social Politics: International Studies in Gender, State and Society*, vol 16, no 2, pp 242-78.

Lundberg, O., Åberg Yngwe, M., Kölegård Stjärne, M., Björk, L. and Fritzell, J. (2008) *The Nordic Experience: Welfare States and Public Health*, Health Equity Studies No 12, Centre for Health Equity Studies (CHESS), Stockholm University & Karolinska Institutet.

Marklund, S. (1988) *Paradise lost? The Nordic welfare state and the recession 1975-1985*, Lund: Arkiv förlag.

Morel, N., Palier, B. and Palme, J. (2011) *Towards a social investment welfare state?*, Cambridge: Polity Press.

OECD (Organisation for Economic Co-operation and Development) (2008) *Growing unequal? Income distribution and poverty in OECD countries*, Paris: OECD.

Okun, A.M. (1975) *Equality and efficiency: The big tradeoff*, Washington DC: Brookings Institution Press.

Orloff, A. *Farewell to Maternalism? State Policies, Feminist Politics and Mothers' Employment*, forthcoming

Putnam, R. (2007) '*E Pluribus Unum*: diversity and community in the twenty-first century. The 2006 Johan Skytte Prize Lecture', *Scandinavian Political Studies*, vol 30, no 2, pp 137-74.

Reich, R.B. (2010) *Aftershock: The next economy and America's future*, New York: Random House.

Rothstein, B. (1998) *Just institutions matter. The moral and political logic of the universal welfare state*, Cambridge: Cambridge University Press.

Salverda, W. Nolan, B. and Smeeding, T.M. (eds) (2011) *The Oxford handbook of economic inequality*, Oxford: Oxford University Press.

Sen, A. (1985) 'Well-being, agency and freedom, the Dewey lectures 1984', *Journal of Philosophy*, vol 82, no 4, pp 169-221.

Sen, A. (1992) *Inequality reexamined*, Cambridge, MA: Harvard University Press.

Snowdown, C. (2010) *The spirit level delusion: Fact-checking the Left's new theory of everything*, Ripon: Little Dice.

Stiglitz, J.E., Sen, A. and Fitoussi, J.-P. (2010) *Mismeasuring our lives: Why GDP doesn't add up*, New York: The Free Press.

Tawney, R.H. (1964) *Equality*, London: Allen & Unwin.

Titmuss, R.M. (1958) *Essays on the welfare state*, London: Allen & Unwin.

Titmuss, R.M. (1974) *Social policy*, London: George Allen & Unwin.

Wilkinson, R. and Pickett, K. (2009) *The spirit level: Why more equal societies almost always do better*, London: Allen Lane.

TWO

Anti-immigration attitudes, support for redistribution and party choice in Europe

Henning Finseraas[1]

Introduction

The increasing level of ethnic heterogeneity[2] in Europe has spurred a debate about the relationship between ethnic diversity and income redistribution by the state. The current debate is much inspired by Alesina and Glaeser's (2004) sceptical view of the possibility of reconciling ethnic diversity and generous welfare arrangements.[3]

The debate about the relationship between ethnic diversity and the welfare state is of particular interest for the Nordic countries, which developed their comparatively generous welfare states in a context of ethnic homogeneity. Over the last three decades, however, non-Western immigration has made the Nordic countries less homogeneous. In Denmark and Norway, issues of integration of immigrants have been high on the public and political agendas for some time, and both countries have relatively large anti-immigration parties in their parliaments. In Sweden, the immigration issue was hotly contested in the 2010 election, and the Sweden Democrats, an anti-immigration party, won 20 seats in the Swedish parliament. Anti-immigration parties are, or have very recently been, represented in the Finnish and Icelandic parliaments as well. Therefore, the issues that this chapter discusses are highly important for all the Nordic countries.

This chapter focuses on two mechanisms through which ethnic heterogeneity can have an impact on the degree of redistribution. First, ethnic heterogeneity might decrease voters' support for redistribution and thus shift the political centre of gravity on the redistributive dimension in a Rightist direction. Alesina and Glaeser (2004) argue that voter animosity towards minorities is an important reason why the US has a much smaller welfare state than most European countries: racist attitudes directly reduce the preferred level of redistribution because redistribution disproportionably benefits immigrants, or is perceived as doing so. Using the language of Roemer et al (2007), I label this potential mechanism the 'anti-solidarity' hypothesis, for which there exists weak support, at best, in studies of European cross-sectional survey data (Finseraas, 2008; Senik et al, 2009; but see Eger, 2010). This chapter expands on these studies by exploring the relationship between change in xenophobia and change in support for redistribution at the aggregate level between 2002 and 2008. Examining whether these variables move together over time is obviously a better test of the 'anti-solidarity' hypothesis than examining the association at one point in time, especially since there are some indications that changes in the size of the immigrant population is negatively correlated with changes in social spending (Soroka et al, 2006).

Second, ethnic heterogeneity might increase the saliency of political issues that function as 'wedge issues' splitting the pro-redistributive voters at the ballot box. This scenario can potentially undermine support for redistributive parties, make it less attractive to run on a pro-redistributive political platform, or both if the group of voters with a Leftist view on redistribution and a Rightist view on immigration policy is large and growing, or if this group of voters increasingly votes according to its immigration policy preference rather than its preference for redistribution. If this group of voters increases in size or increasingly follow their immigration policy preference at the polls, the saliency of the immigration issue can reduce the level of redistribution even if voter xenophobia does not influence the demand for redistribution. I label this potential mechanism the 'distraction' hypothesis, because policy issues related to immigration are fairly recent political issues that distract some voters from voting according to the traditional Left–Right issue of redistribution. Roemer et al (2007) have found support for a somewhat similar logic in data from the US, the UK, France and Denmark (see also Vernby and Finseraas, 2010).

Compared to previous research I increase the number of countries in the analysis and examine a larger number of variables that can potentially explain the voting behaviour of anti-immigration voters. I identify voters with a Leftist redistribution preference and a Rightist immigration preference, and explore the voting behaviour of these voters in 17 European countries. I then ask in what contexts these voters cast their vote for a Leftist party, that is, vote according to their redistributive preference rather than their immigration policy preference.

The rest of the chapter is structured as follows. The following section gives a short overview of the literature. The next two sections examine the anti-solidarity hypothesis and the distraction hypothesis, respectively. The last section concludes.

Xenophobia and redistribution

In an effort to explain why the US has a less generous welfare state than the West European countries, US economists Alesina and Glaeser (Alesina et al, 2001; Alesina and Glaeser, 2004) explore the role of pre-government wage inequality, income volatility, beliefs about social mobility, political institutions, and what they call 'racial' heterogeneity.[4] They conclude that political institutions and 'racial' heterogeneity are the most important factors for explaining the US–European divide.

Given these findings, they suggest that the increasing 'racial' heterogeneity in Europe is likely to undermine the redistributive dimension of the European welfare states (Alesina and Glaeser, 2004, p 219). Drawing on conflict theory, which posits that people are more likely to look favourably on members of their own group (see Putnam, 2007, for an extensive review of the literature), they emphasise how 'racial' issues have always been political wedge issues in the US, and how views on redistribution from rich to poor are strongly shaped by views about minorities (see also Gilens, 1995). They therefore suggest that the demand for redistribution is smaller in the US than in most European countries because majority group voters do not want to redistribute income to minority group poor, who they perceive as undeserving recipients of government support. Alesina and Glaeser believe that a majority–minority gap in redistributive preferences is more likely to occur in ethnically diverse countries, because the potential gain to opportunistic politicians from 'playing the race card' is higher, that is, the saliency of majority–minority issues is on average higher. Following Roemer et al (2007), I label an effect of xenophobia on redistribution as an 'anti-solidarity effect'.

Some of Alesina and Glaeser's basic assumptions as to why increasing ethnic heterogeneity is likely to matter for European demand for redistribution are not unrealistic: immigrants are disproportionably represented among receivers of at least some social benefits in at least some countries (Brüker et al, 2002), are less integrated in the labour market (Causa and Jean, 2006), and Europeans tend to view immigrants as less deserving recipients of government support than other groups with a high risk of poverty (van Oorschot, 2006).

There are of course reasons to be sceptical of the idea that the US experience is instructive for Europe. As Pontusson (2006) points out, the US has a very different immigration history, including slavery, and several European countries have developed generous welfare arrangements despite religious diversity, suggesting that Europeans can cope with diversity. Moreover, immigration to Europe is occurring in a context in which well-developed welfare states are already in place, and 'playing the race card' to prevent the development of a generous welfare state might be easier than turning voters against the status quo. Very little empirical research using European data exists on the relationship between animosity towards immigrants and demand for redistribution. Finseraas (2009) finds no relationship between ethnic heterogeneity and the level of demand for redistribution, which can be understood in light of a complex relationship between attitudes toward immigrants/immigration and preferences for redistribution (Finseraas, 2008). More specifically, voters opposing the equal granting of rights to immigrants are less likely to support redistribution, while voters expressing a concern that immigration is a threat to wages and employment are more likely to support redistribution (see also Crepaz, 2007). Nonetheless, both relationships are weak. Senik et al (2009) identify a negative relationship between the perceived number of immigrants in society and native-born citizens' support for the welfare state; however, the size of this effect is weakest for preference for redistribution and the average effect masks strong cross-national variation. Crepaz (2006), using three waves of the World Values Survey, analyses aggregate changes in welfare state support. He finds no relationship between the size of the foreign population, or countries' implementation of multicultural policies, and change in welfare state support. Finally, a debate also exists as to what degree ethnic fractionalisation influences the level of social trust (Putnam, 2007; Hooghe et al, 2009). While social trust might influence the support for active government policies, the hypothesis of a negative relationship between fractionalisation and level of social trust has received scant empirical support (Soroka et al, 2004; Crepaz, 2006).

This chapter examines both sides of the anti-solidarity argument. First, I briefly examine whether anti-immigrant sentiment is more widespread, and increasing, in ethnically diverse countries. Second, I examine the relationship between anti-immigrant sentiment and support for redistribution. While the previous literature has focused on the cross-sectional relationships, I investigate the more relevant issue of whether an increase in anti-immigrant sentiments is associated with a decrease in support for redistribution.

In a series of publications, John E. Roemer and co-authors emphasised a mechanism by which xenophobia influences the degree of redistribution indirectly via the political system, rather than directly through voter preferences for redistribution (Roemer and van der Straeten, 2005, 2006; Roemer et al, 2007). In this formal model of redistribution, voters have preferences over both redistribution and immigration policy. Traditionally, the Leftist party jointly supports redistribution and multicultural policies, while the Rightist party jointly opposes redistribution and multicultural policies. In so far as a non-negligible share of voters are thus forced to choose between voting according to their redistributive preference or their immigration preference, the degree of redistribution might be reduced despite a high demand for redistribution, because those who support redistribution vote according to their immigration policy preference. In so far as this effect causes a reduction in the vote share of Leftist parties, we should expect less redistribution because Leftist parties implement more generous welfare arrangements than Rightist parties (Korpi and Palme, 2003; Allan and Scruggs, 2004). Roemer et al propose that in the long run a high saliency of the immigration issue might force the Left to shift its political platform on redistribution to the Right, while the Right might be able to maintain its Rightist position on redistribution without losing votes. They call this effect of xenophobia a 'policy bundle' effect (Roemer et al, 2007). More generally, one might call this effect a 'distraction' effect because voters are 'distracted' from voting according to their preference for redistribution (De La O and Rodden, 2008).

Roemer et al use data from Denmark, France, the UK and the US to present results consistent with their theory. Huber and Stanig (2007) find that poor voters are more likely to vote for a Rightist party in ethnically heterogeneous countries. Vernby and Finseraas (2010) find that party polarisation over multicultural issues reduces Left voting in several countries, mainly due to policy bundling, not feelings of anti-solidarity. In addition, some related research explores the importance of non-economic preferences for voting, although these papers do not focus on xenophobia: De La O and Rodden (2008) find that the rich are as likely to vote against their economic interest as the poor, and Gelman et al (2008, p 106) argue that 'in much of Europe (...) politics feels more like a culture war than a class war' because non-economic issues are so important for vote choice in many countries.

In this chapter I examine the potential of the immigration issue to function as a wedge issue by examining the size of the electorate with cross-cutting preferences on the two dimensions, and the change of that size between 2002 and 2006. Next, I examine the voting behaviour of this group of voters with cross-cutting preferences, compared to voters with 'pure' preferences, and explore in what contexts they are particularly likely to vote against their preference on redistribution, that is, defect from the Left.

Anti-solidarity hypothesis

I use data from the four rounds of the European Social Survey (ESS) to assess the anti-solidarity hypothesis, that is, that racial heterogeneity is associated with higher levels of animosity towards immigrants, an attitude that undermines support for redistribution. The most important contribution to the literature is that I rely on longitudinal data to explore whether an increase in negative sentiments toward immigrants is associated with a decrease in the support for redistribution.

The first round of the ESS took place in 2002/03, the second, in 2004/05, the third, in 2006/07 and the latest, in 2008/09. I exclude the post-communist countries because they are not included in this volume in general; moreover, the immigration–welfare state debate primarily concerns European countries with well-developed welfare states. Thus the analysis is based on data from 17 countries: Austria (AT), Belgium (BE), Denmark (DK), Finland (FI), France (FR), Germany (DE), Greece (GR), Ireland (IE), Italy (IT), Luxembourg (LU), the Netherlands (NL), Norway (NO), Portugal (PT), Spain (ES), Sweden (SE), Switzerland (CH), and Great Britain (GB). Unfortunately, not all countries participated in every round, leaving me with a total of 61 country-year observations.

Support for redistribution is measured through the following survey item: 'Please say to what extent you agree or disagree with the following statement: "The government should take measures to reduce differences in income levels"'. There are five possible answer categories, from 'agree strongly' to 'disagree strongly'. This survey item is widely used in the literature on support for redistribution (see, for example, Cusack et al, 2006; Jæger, 2006; Rehm, 2009). Every survey item has its pros and cons. On the positive side, the question specifically refers to government action to reduce inequality; on the negative side, it does not remind respondents that more redistribution has a cost.

To simplify the analysis, I recode support for redistribution into a dummy variable where 1 equals 'agree' and 'agree strongly' and 0 equals all other categories. The data reveal that the European demand for redistribution is almost overwhelming: the mean share answering 'agree' or 'agree strongly' for the 61 country-year observations are 69 per cent. Ninety-three per cent (!) of Greek respondents in round two demand more redistribution, while the lowest demand is among Danish respondents (round two) with 'only' 38 per cent support for more redistribution. Indeed, Denmark is the only country where the majority of respondents do not favour more redistribution. As for changes over time, Norway has experienced the strongest decline in support for redistribution, as support dropped from 71 per cent in round one to 60 per cent in round four. Germany has witnessed the strongest increase, from 58 to 68 per cent.

To measure animosity towards immigrants, I rely on three variables. The first captures a general level of animosity: 'Is [country] made a worse or a better place to live by people coming to live here from other countries?'. Respondents are asked to state their position on this issue on a scale from 0 ('worse place to live') to 10 ('better place to live'). Again, I simplify the analysis by recoding the variable into a dummy, although I readily admit that the choice of cut-off point is more difficult to defend for this question than for the redistribution question. I choose a very restrictive cut-off point: only the three lowest scores are coded as 1, while all other answers are set to 0. An initial analysis reveals that results are not sensitive to this rather arbitrary choice of cut-off point.

The second variable captures a concern for the effect of immigration on the country's economy: 'Would you say it is generally bad or good for [country]'s economy that people come to live here from other countries?'. Again, respondents choose their position on a scale from 0 ('bad for the economy') to 10 ('good for the economy'), and I recode it as I did for the previous question.

The descriptives for these two variables are very similar, with a mean score of 14 per cent for 'immigrants make [country] worse' and 15 per cent for 'immigration makes the economy worse'. The lowest share (5 per cent) for 'make [country] worse' occurs in Sweden (rounds one and four), while the lowest share (5 per cent) for 'make the economy worse' occurs in Switzerland (round four). Greece stands out on the other end of the scale with 40 per cent (rounds two and four) saying that immigration 'makes the country worse' and 40 per cent (round four) that immigrants 'make the economy worse'. As to changes over time, no uniform trend appears across Europe. The strongest decline in 'make [country] worse' is in Belgium (down by seven percentage points), while the strongest decline in 'bad for the economy' is in Ireland (down by eight percentage points). Italy has witnessed the strongest increase on both questions (up by 12 and 11 percentage points respectively).

The third variable is an immigration policy variable: 'To what extent do you think [country] should allow people of a different race or ethnic group from most [country] people to come and live here?'. Respondents choose between 'many', 'some', 'few' or 'none'. I collapse the 'few' and 'none' categories into a dummy variable capturing support for a restrictive immigration policy. The mean score on this variable is 47 per cent, with a minimum score of 13 per cent (Sweden, round four) and a maximum score of 84 per cent (Greece, round four). Again, no uniform trend appears across countries. The strongest increase is in Spain (12 percentage points), while the strongest decline is in Finland (9 percentage points).

The basic premise of the anti-solidarity effect is that 'racial' fractionalisation – defined as the probability that two randomly drawn people have different 'racial' backgrounds (as defined by the US Census) (Alesina et al, 2001; Alesina and Glaeser, 2004) – in general increases out-group suspicions. Indeed, the correlation between 'racial' fractionalisation and support for the claim that immigrants 'make [country] worse' is positive and significant at the 5 per cent level (t=2.10, p=0.05), and the correlation between 'racial' fractionalisation and support for the claim that immigrants 'make the economy worse' is positive and significant at the 10 per cent level (t=1.89, p=0.08). However, the correlations are driven by the high level of anti-immigrant sentiment in Greece. No relationship exists between 'racial' fractionalisation and support for a restrictive immigration policy.

Wanting to closely follow Alesina and Glaeser, I rely on the 'racial' fractionalisation data. However, the validity of the 'racial' fractionalisation index can be questioned. For example, according to the index Norway is considerably more heterogeneous than Denmark and Austria, and Norway's fractionalisation score is at the European average. This score is difficult to reconcile with OECD (Organisation for Economic Co-operation and Development) calculations of the size of the foreign-born population in the OECD countries (OECD, 2006); indeed, Alesina and Glaeser (2004, p 171) themselves characterise Norway as 'truly homogeneous'. If I instead rely on Alesina et al's (2003) ethnic fractionalisation index, which they sometimes use as an alternative to the 'racial' fractionalisation index, no relationship appears between fractionalisation and support for any of the anti-immigrant statements.

As yearly fractionalisation data does not exist, I cannot examine the relationship between change in negative sentiments and change in fractionalisation. Nonetheless, there is no evidence that changes in negative sentiments from the first round to the last round are associated with the initial level of 'racial' or ethnic fractionalisation.

Table 2.1 presents a series of regressions that evaluate the relationship between anti-immigrant sentiments and support for redistribution. Column 1 presents the results from a regression of support for redistribution in round one and the level of inequality (based on disposable income at the household level) (OECD, 2008a) and 'racial' fractionalisation. As expected, support for redistribution is higher in more unequal countries. There is no significant effect of 'racial' fractionalisation. The same holds true with the ethnic fractionalisation index. Columns 2-4 presents the results from a two-way fixed effects regression, that is, including a full set of country and year (ESS-round) dummies to evaluate whether an increase in anti-immigrant sentiment is related to change in support for redistribution. As evident, none of the anti-immigrant coefficients are negative or significant. Finally, Column 5 shows the regression of the level of inequality and 'racial' fractionalisation on change in redistribution support between the first and the last observation for each country. None of the coefficients are significant.

The results here do not square well with the idea that demand for redistribution in Europe will decrease because 'racial' fractionalisation increases negative sentiment toward 'undeserving' immigrants. While longer time-series (or, even better, individual-level panel data) would clearly yield a better test of the anti-

Table 2.1: Linear regression: the dependent variable is support for equalisation of income differences

	Redistribute	Redistribute	Redistribute	Redistribute	DRedistribute
'Racial' fractionalisation	0.03 (0.85)				−0.08 (0.44)
Income inequality	0.02** (0.006)				−0.001 (0.003)
Immigration is bad for the economy		0.07 (0.17)			
Immigration makes the country worse			0.26 (0.19)		
Country should not allow immigration				0.05 (0.12)	
Constant	0.21 (0.17)				−0.05 (0.09)
Observations	17	61	61	61	17
Number of countries	17	17	17	17	17
Country fixed effects		Yes	Yes	Yes	
Wave fixed effects		Yes	Yes	Yes	
R-squared	0.40	0.10	0.13	0.10	0.02

Note: Standard errors in parentheses.
* significant at 10%; ** significant at 5%; *** significant at 1%.

solidarity hypothesis, the data analysed here is the best comparative data currently available.

Distraction hypothesis

As discussed earlier, voter xenophobia can reduce the amount of redistribution even in the absence of an anti-solidarity effect that lowers the demand for redistribution. According to this mechanism, income redistribution can be reduced if the group of voters with cross-cutting preferences – that is, voters who support redistribution but oppose liberal immigration policies – is large and growing, and if this group votes according to its immigration policy preference rather than its preference for redistribution. If so, Leftist parties lose support. Given the assumption that the Left, if elected, will implement policies that redistribute more income than the Right, a weakening of Leftist parties implies less redistribution of income. Leftist parties have historically promoted redistribution from rich to poor to a stronger degree than non-Leftist parties, and although some argue that partisanship has ceased to play an important role for welfare state policies (see, for example, Pierson, 1996), the most comprehensive empirical studies suggest that who governs still matters (Korpi and Palme, 2003; Allan and Scruggs, 2004).

The remainder of this chapter explores the voting choice of voters with cross-cutting preferences: do these voters vote according to their redistributive preference or their immigration policy preference? Or, more specifically, in what contexts are these voters less likely to follow their preference for redistribution at the ballot box?

I identify voters with cross-cutting preferences by constructing a dummy variable where those who want more redistribution and a more restrictive immigration policy are coded 1, while voters with any other combination of these preferences are coded 0. Obviously, the size of this group in each country varies both with the level of redistribution support and the level of opposition to liberal immigration policy in that country. The size of this group in the 17 countries appears in Table 2.2. Voters with cross-cutting preferences constitute 74 per cent of the Greek electorate but only 10 per cent of the Swedish electorate. While the group is generally larger in unequal countries, Finland clearly stands out as different, with a relatively large group of voters with cross-cutting preferences. Overall, no clear general trend appears for the size of this group over time, and most changes over time are small. Switzerland and Spain have experienced a growth in the size of this group, while in Norway it has gradually declined, and a clear drop in the size of this group from 2006 to 2008 is evident in the Netherlands.

An analysis of the background characteristics of voters with cross-cutting preferences (not shown) reveals that students, young voters, religious voters, high-income voters, highly educated voters and men are less likely to have cross-cutting preferences. Retired people are more likely to have cross-cutting preferences.

The dependent variable in the rest of the chapter is whether the respondent voted for a Leftist party in the previous general election. Assuming that Leftist parties are the main political force behind income redistribution in a multiparty

Table 2.2: Percentage of the voters that jointly support redistribution and a restrictive immigration policy

	2002	2004	2006	2008
Austria	38	31	37	–
Belgium	31	31	29	28
Denmark	18	17	15	16
Finland	47	41	44	41
France	37	39	39	35
Germany	26	29	31	27
Greece	74	73	–	–
Ireland	26	26	22	–
Italy	27	32	–	–
Luxembourg	32	30	–	–
Netherlands	24	25	28	20
Norway	30	26	25	22
Portugal	51	54	51	55
Spain	33	33	42	45
Sweden	10	10	9	7
Switzerland	19	23	27	25
UK	31	28	29	29

system (as I do, by examining support for Leftists parties) is somewhat controversial, as several (Christian Democratic) parties in Continental Europe have been important in the development of the welfare state (Manow, 2009). However, egalitarianism is typically associated with the Social Democratic (Scandinavian) welfare states, while the conservative welfare state associated with the Christian Democratic parties have a lower level of vertical income redistribution (Esping-Andersen, 1990). I recode the party choice variable in the ESS surveys into a dummy where those who voted for a Leftist party are coded 1 and those who voted for a non-Leftist party or who cast a blank vote are coded 0. Non-voters are coded as missing. A list of parties classified as Leftist is included in the Appendix at the end of this chapter.

Figure 2.1 shows the percentage difference in Left voting between voters with cross-cutting preferences and 'Pure Leftists', that is, voters who support redistribution and a liberal immigration policy, in the available country years. The surveys are sorted by year of survey and size of the percentage difference between these two voter groups. The group with cross-cutting preferences is significantly less likely to vote Left in a majority of the country-years. The difference is clearly largest in Switzerland, while it is insignificant in Sweden, Portugal, Luxembourg, Ireland, two of the Greek rounds and two of the rounds from the UK. Moreover, no general trend is evident from the first to the third survey.

The aim of the final part of this chapter is to explain cross-national variation in this difference, that is, why voters with this combination of preferences are particularly more unlikely to vote Left in some countries than in others.

Table 2.3 shows results from a series of multilevel random-coefficient logit regressions (Gelman and Hill, 2007), with Left voting as the dependent variable and the dummy for cross-cutting preferences and interactions with this dummy as the independent variables of main interest.[5] Because I want to understand how voters with cross-cutting preferences behave as compared to the pure Leftists (the benchmark), I also include a dummy for those opposing redistribution and interactions with this dummy in the regressions. The intercept, the coefficient for cross-cutting preferences, and the coefficient for opposing redistribution are allowed to vary across countries. A vector of relevant control variables is included in most specifications.[6] I include only one survey for each country (the first round of the ESS), mainly because most of the country-level data is not annually available. All the continuous variables are centred on their mean score for making interpretation of the reported coefficients easier.

The simple model in column 1 shows, unsurprisingly, that those opposing redistribution and those with cross-cutting preferences are less likely to vote Left than those with pure Left preferences. The effect is politically important as, on average across surveys, a voter with cross-cutting preferences is 14 percentage points less likely to vote Left than one with pure Left preferences. However, as Figure 2.1 also shows, the average effect of having cross-cutting preferences conceals a large degree of cross-national variation. Thus to what degree the group with cross-cutting preferences vote according to their economic preference (that

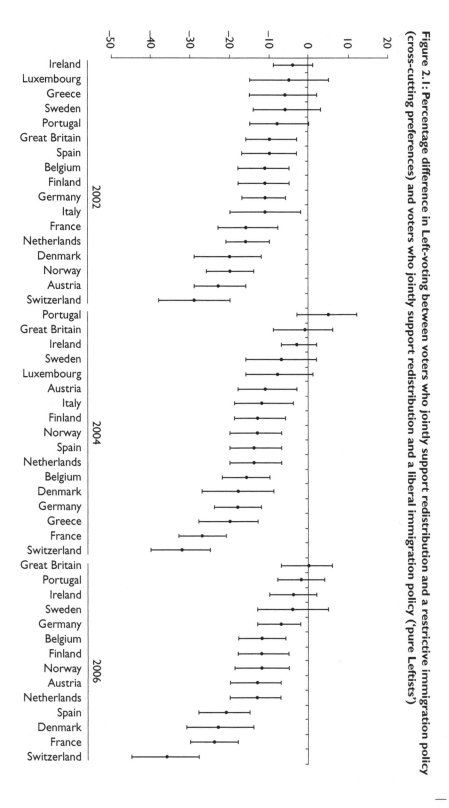

Figure 2.1: Percentage difference in Left-voting between voters who jointly support redistribution and a restrictive immigration policy (cross-cutting preferences) and voters who jointly support redistribution and a liberal immigration policy ('pure Leftists')

Table 2.3: Multilevel logistic regression: dependent variable is whether the respondent voted for a Left party

	(1)	(2)	(3)	(4)	(5)	(6)
Cross-cutting preference	−0.57*** (0.06)	−0.58*** (0.06)	−0.59*** (0.06)	−0.59*** (0.07)	−0.59*** (0.06)	−0.59*** (0.06)
Cross-c pref*Red. distance		−0.01 (0.02)				
Cross-c pref*Im. Distance		−0.05*** (0.02)				
Cross-c pref*Im. Saliency			−0.12** (0.05)			
Cross-c pref*'Race' frac.				0.20 (2.28)		
Cross-c pref*Inequality					0.03** (0.01)	
Cross-c pref*Unemp. Ratio						−0.24** (0.10)
Oppose redistribution	−1.07*** (0.09)	−1.09*** (0.08)	−1.08*** (0.09)	−1.09*** (0.10)	−1.07*** (0.08)	−1.07*** (0.07)
Oppose redist*Red. distance		−0.05** (0.02)				
Oppose redist*Im. Distance		−0.02 (0.02)				
Oppose redist*Im. Saliency			−0.06 (0.08)			
Oppose redist*'Race' frac.				−3.10 (1.47)		
Oppose redist*Inequality					0.05*** (0.02)	
Oppose redist*Unemp. ratio						−0.44*** (0.06)
Redistribution distance		−0.02 (0.04)				
Immigration distance		−0.01 (0.04)				
Immigration saliency			0.15 (0.10)			
'Racial' fractionalisation				2.86 (4.08)		
Inequality					0.02 (0.03)	
Unemployment ratio						−0.13 (0.21)
Income		−0.04*** (0.01)	−0.04*** (0.01)	−0.04*** (0.01)	−0.04*** (0.01)	−0.04*** (0.01)
Churchgoer		−0.87*** (0.04)	−0.87*** (0.04)	−0.87*** (0.04)	−0.87*** (0.04)	−0.87*** (0.04)
Male		−0.12*** (0.03)	−0.12*** (0.03)	−0.12*** (0.03)	−0.12*** (0.03)	−0.12*** (0.03)

(continued)

Table 2.3: Multilevel logistic regression: dependent variable is whether the respondent voted for a Left party (continued)

	(1)	(2)	(3)	(4)	(5)	(6)
Education		–0.01**	–0.01**	–0.01***	–0.01***	–0.01**
		(0.005)	(0.005)	(0.005)	(0.005)	(0.005)
Young		–0.03	–0.03	–0.03	–0.04	–0.04
		(0.04)	(0.04)	(0.04)	(0.04)	(0.04)
Old		–0.21***	–0.21***	–0.21***	–0.21***	–0.21***
		(0.04)	(0.04)	(0.04)	(0.04)	(0.04)
Constant	0.30**	0.72***	0.70***	0.72***	0.71***	0.71***
	(0.12)	(0.12)	(0.12)	(0.12)	(0.12)	(0.12)
Log likelihood	–12,802	–10,577	–10,581	–10,584	–10,579	–10,579
Number of observations	19,959	16,903	16,903	16,903	16,903	16,903
Number of countries	17	17	17	17	17	17
Standard deviation: effect of cross-cutting preference	0.19	0.15	0.14	0.21	0.15	0.17
Standard deviation: effect of no redistribution	0.32	0.27	0.34	0.27	0.27	0.24
Standard deviation: constant	0.50	0.48	0.45	0.48	0.48	0.48

Note: Standard errors in parentheses.
* significant at 10%; ** significant at 5%; *** significant at 1%.

is, vote Left), despite their views on immigration policy, varies substantially across countries.

Perhaps the most obvious explanation for the cross-country variance in the level of 'distraction' is to what degree the political parties force voters to choose between their opposing preferences. Theoretically, a voter with cross-cutting preferences will be less likely to vote Left if the distance between the Left parties and the most immigration-hostile party on the redistributive dimension is small, simply because the expected utility loss from voting against his or her redistributive preference is smaller. Similarly, that same voter will be more likely to vote Left if the distance between the Left parties and the most immigration-hostile party on the immigration issue is small. Theoretically, if there exists a party with a Leftist position on redistribution and a Rightist position on immigration, the distraction effect on redistributive policy outcomes can disappear altogether. Empirically, however, this combination is rare (see the following discussion and van der Brug and van Spanje, 2009).

Benoit and Laver (2006) conducted a survey of political experts in 47 countries, asking them to state the positions of the political parties in their respective country on a range of different political issues, including on immigration/integration and a dimension they call 'taxes versus spending'. I use this data to identify the most moderate Left party on the taxes versus spending dimension and the most immigration-hostile party on the immigration dimension. I then calculate the absolute difference between the positions of these two parties on the two dimensions. These variables thus indicate how much utility a cross-pressured voter loses on the redistributive dimension if he or she follows his or her preference on the immigration issue when casting a vote (that is, votes for the radical Right), and how much utility he or she loses on the immigration dimension if following his or her redistributive preference (that is, votes for the Left). The scores are zero if the immigration-hostile party and the moderate Left party have the same positions. A positive score on the two variables suggests that the immigration-hostile party has a more conservative position. The results tell us whether voters with cross-cutting preferences care more about the 'new' issue of immigration or the 'old' issue of redistribution when deciding for whom to vote.

Column 2 includes the measures of party distance on the two dimensions and interactions with the voter groups. The coefficients should be interpreted in the following way: the coefficients for redistribution distance and immigration distance tell us how the propensity of Left voting among the pure Leftists depends on redistributive distance and immigration distance, respectively. We need to interpret these coefficients in this way because there are three groups of voters, and the model includes interaction terms with two of these groups – those with cross-cutting preferences and those who oppose redistribution. Therefore, pure Leftists (pro-redistribution and pro-immigration) are the reference group.

Significant coefficients for redistribution distance and immigration distance suggest that pure Leftists are more or less likely to vote Left depending on the scores on these variables. The coefficients for the interaction terms tell us whether redistribution distance and immigration distance influence the propensity of Left voting differently for voters with cross-cutting preferences and those who oppose redistribution (compared to the pure Leftists), respectively. Significant coefficients suggest that the propensity of Left voting in these voter groups are more sensitive to redistribution distance and immigration distance compared to the pure Leftists. If coefficients are negative (positive), the gap between the group of voters with pure Left preferences and the two other groups are larger (smaller), that is, the group of Left voters are more homogeneous (heterogeneous) in their preferences.

The results in column 2 reveal that voters with cross-cutting preferences are less likely to vote Left if the distance between the moderate Left party and the immigration hostile party is large on the immigration policy dimension (because the coefficient Cross-c pref*Im. distance is negative and significant). The substantial effect is small, however, as the probability of left voting decreases by approximately one percentage point. The distance on the redistributive dimension does not matter (Cross-c pref*Red. distance is insignificant). In other words, the results suggest that, as a short-term strategy (given relatively fixed voter preferences in the short term) for capturing these voters, the Left has to change its position on the immigration dimension rather than moving leftwards on the redistributive dimension. While the Left can abandon this group of voters and instead aim to attract other voter groups to compensate for the loss, the historical closeness between the Left and voters with the socioeconomic background of the pro-redistributive-anti-immigration voters suggests that the major Left party is more likely to change its position on the immigration dimension. Indeed, we have seen this trend over the last decade, particularly in Denmark and Norway. At the same time, the populist Right parties, at least in Scandinavia, have moved leftwards on the redistributive dimension. Together these results suggest that political parties are adjusting to the mismatch between voters and parties (van der Brug and van Spanje, 2009) on these two dimensions. Multiculturalists on the Left concerned with, and opposed to, this development should note that the strong negative coefficient for those having cross-cutting preferences suggests that the Left will benefit more from reducing the level of anti-immigrant sentiment among the voters (see also Vernby and Finseraas, 2010). However, how to do so, and whether moving rightwards on the immigration dimension will help to achieve this result, remains an open question. Moreover, as previously noted, the Left's total loss of voters as a result of its liberal position on the immigration dimension appears fairly small.

As expected, the coefficient for Oppose redist*Red. distance is negative and statistically significant, that is, voters opposing redistribution are sensitive to the positions on the redistributive dimension[7] while insensitive to the distance on the immigration dimension (the coefficient Oppose redist*Im. distance is insignificant). Finally, pure Leftists are insignificant for both distances, because the coefficients for redistributive distance and immigration distance are insignificant. Apparently, these voters will 'always' vote for the Left.

Beyond party polarisation, the saliency of the immigration issue in the political competition might also be important. Benoit and Laver's (2006) survey included a question asking the political experts to state the relative importance of the different issues in the political campaigns. Thus I explore whether the saliency of the immigration issue influences the voting decision of the three groups of voters. The results appear in column 3. The coefficients can be interpreted in a similar manner as those reported in column 2. While the coefficient for the immigration saliency variable is positive, suggesting that pure Leftists are more likely to vote Left if immigration saliency is high, the coefficient is not significant at conventional levels. The interaction with cross-cutting preferences is negative and clearly statistically significant, suggesting that voters with cross-cutting preferences clearly react differently to saliency than the pure Leftists. Although the difference between these two groups' probability of voting Left increases by three percentage points if saliency increases by one unit, the predicted probability of voting Left for the group with cross-cutting preferences is not affected.

The causal argument in Alesina and Glaeser (2004) is that 'racial' fractionalisation generally increases the saliency of the immigration issue. However, the relationship between these two variables is weak, because some of the countries in which the immigration issue is very salient have a low fractionalisation score (particularly Denmark). It is therefore no surprise that the results in column 3 show the level of fractionalisation as not important for any of the groups. Conclusions remain the same with use of the ethnic fractionalisation index.

Column 4 shows whether the level of income inequality reduces the level of 'distraction'. The results show that although voters with cross-cutting preferences are more likely to vote according to their redistributive preference when the level of inequality is high, the substantial effect is small (one percentage point). However, the results also show that voters who oppose redistribution are more likely to vote Left when the level of inequality is high. This finding is difficult to understand theoretically, and it questions whether a causal effect of inequality exists for the probability of Left voting. Finally, pure Leftists are unaffected by the level of inequality.

Immigrants' degree of labour market participation is substantially lower than that of the native-born in all 17 countries. Causa and Jean (2006) find that the size of the gap depends on labour market policies: generous unemployment benefits and a high tax wedge on labour is detrimental to immigrants' labour market participation rates relative to that of the native-born. Because low labour market participation of immigrants suggests that more generous unemployment benefits will benefit them, it appears plausible that a relatively weak performance of immigrants on the labour market makes those with cross-cutting preferences less likely to vote according to their redistributive preference. To obtain a ratio of unemployment among foreign-born relative to native-born, I rely on OECD data on the unemployment rate among native-born and among foreign-born (OECD, 2008b, p 89).[8] This ratio is above one in all countries, and above two for several countries (see Tables A-2.1 and A-2.2 at the end of this chapter for all country-level data). The ratio can be high even though the actual unemployment rate is low, that is, a high ratio means that immigrants perform worse than the native-born in the respective country but not that an immigrant is more likely to be unemployed in, say, Norway than in Germany. I assume that how immigrants perform relative to the native-born is what concerns voters the most; thus I rely on the ratio.

Results in column 6 show that a successful integration of immigrants in the labour market has important implications for the gaps between the groups. The gap between the pure Leftists and the cross-pressured increases by approximately three percentage points if the ratio increases by one standard deviation. Thus the voting decision of voters with cross-cutting preferences depends more on the successful integration of immigrants than the degree of fractionalisation. This interpretation is strengthened by the positive correlation between the unemployment ratio and the saliency of the immigration issue, although the correlation is not very strong. This result is of particular interest to the Nordic countries, given their relatively poor labour market integration of immigrants relative to the native-born, and suggests that improving the labour market situation of immigrants will reduce any negative effects of immigration on redistribution.

Conclusion

This chapter has examined two proposed mechanisms through which increasing ethnic heterogeneity can weaken the political support for redistributive policies in Europe. The anti-solidarity hypothesis says that ethnic fractionalisation will increase tensions between minority and majority groups and undermine the support for redistribution. The analysis does not support the anti-solidarity hypothesis. While it shows a positive, yet weak, relationship between level of 'racial' fractionalisation and the level of negative sentiment toward immigrants, this finding is sensitive to Greece (an influential outlier) and does not hold up when I use alternative fractionalisation indexes. Moreover, the analysis of anti-immigrant sentiment and support for redistribution between 2002/03 to 2008/09 yields insignificant effects of all the immigration variables. Thus I find no support for the claim that xenophobia undermines support for redistribution in the European electorates.

Next, I analyse the voting pattern of voters with cross-cutting preferences on the redistribution and immigration dimensions, that is, voters who support redistribution but who oppose a liberal immigration policy. This group of voters is substantial in most countries and if they grow and increasingly vote for non-Left parties, xenophobia among the voters might reduce the level of redistribution even though the demand for redistribution is unaffected by xenophobia. I call this the 'distraction' hypothesis. The size of this group of voters has been fairly stable from 2002 to 2006 in most countries and significantly less likely to vote for a Left party compared to voters with pure Left preferences. However, to what degree they differ from the pure Leftists varies substantially across countries. The distance between the moderate Left party (typically the Social Democratic party) and the most immigration-hostile party on the immigration dimension, and the level of unemployment among the foreign-born relative to the native-born decreases the probability that a voter with cross-cutting preferences will vote for a Left party.

The results in this chapter are highly relevant to the debate about immigration as a challenge to the Nordic welfare state model. Although the results suggest that ethnic heterogeneity neither constitutes a direct threat to the legitimacy of the Nordic welfare state, nor directly undermines support for Left political parties, they nonetheless suggest that a relatively high unemployment rate among immigrants (possibly seen as an unsuccessful labour market integration of immigrants) shrinks the support for Left parties. If one accepts that Left parties advocate and implement more welfare-friendly policies than Right parties – a fairly reasonable reading of the empirical literature – and that unsuccessful integration of immigrants undermines support for the Left because voters perceive the Left's welfare state policies to be 'part of the problem' (a more speculative, yet not entirely implausible, interpretation), the Left might change its policy position on welfare state policies to remain competitive. I find it highly unlikely that the Left will suddenly turn against the welfare state as such; however, advocates of a universalist welfare state might fear that pragmatic Social Democratic parties should be tempted to ease their opposition against a two-tier or dual welfare state to stay competitive in a setting where the saliency of the immigration issue is high. Although the results in this chapter suggest that there is a (at least short-term) electoral gain of this strategy, it does not appear to be large in most countries.

Notes

[1] I would like to thank the participants at the Democracy and Diversity workshop at Queen's University Kingston, Canada, the ESOP lunch seminar at the University of Oslo, Norway, the Comparative Politics seminar at the University of Oslo, the Friday lunch seminar at the Norwegian School of Management (BI), Patrick Emmenegger, Kåre Vernby and colleagues at NOVA (Norwegian Social Research Institute) for useful suggestions. The usual disclaimer applies.

[2] Typically understood as the probability that two randomly drawn people from the population have different ethnic backgrounds (Alesina et al, 2001).

[3] Alesina and Glaeser (2004) were not the first to argue that a potential tension exists between ethnic heterogeneity and generous welfare states (see, for example, Stephens, 1979; Freeman, 1986; Weede, 1986).

[4] Alesina and Glaeser (2004) use the term 'racial' heterogeneity and develop a cross-country index that they label 'racial' fractionalisation. The use of the word 'racial' is controversial. I follow the guidelines of The Policy Press and put the word in inverted commas to make it clear that these are social, not biological, distinctions. Alternatively, one could use the word ethnic fractionalisation; however, Alesina and Glaeser (2004) use this term for a related but different index of fractionalisation. Therefore, I rely on Alesina and Glaeser's (2004) term 'racial' fractionalisation to avoid confusion as to which index I am referring.

[5] The models are estimated using the lmer package (Bates, 2005) in R.

[6] See Tables A-2.1 and A-2.2 at the end of this chapter for a description of these variables.

[7] This result is to be expected because voters opposing redistribution might be attracted by the Left parties on non-economic issues, but the cost of following their non-economic attraction to Left parties is higher if polarisation on the redistributive dimension is high.

[8] Ideally, I would like to have the unemployment rate of non-Western immigrants rather than merely among the foreign-born, but such data is not available. The data is from 2000, except for Finland and Switzerland, for which I have had to use data from 2005.

References

Alesina, A. and Glaeser, E. (2004) *Fighting poverty in the US and Europe: A world of difference*, Oxford: Oxford University Press.

Alesina, A., Glaeser, E. and Sacerdote, B. (2001) *Why doesn't the US have a European-style welfare system?*, Brookings Papers on Economic Activity, No 2, Washington DC: Brookings Institution.

Alesina, A., Devleeschauwer, A., Easterly, W., Kurlat, S. and Wacziarg, R. (2003) 'Fractionalization', *Journal of Economic Growth*, vol 8, no 2, pp 155-94.

Allan, J.P. and Scruggs, L. (2004) 'Political partisanship and welfare state reform in advanced industrial societies', *American Journal of Political Science*, vol 48, no 3, pp 496-512.

Bates, D (2005) 'Fitting linear models in R using the lme4 package', *R News*, vol 5, no 1, pp 27-30.

Benoit, K. and Laver, M (2006) *Party policy in modern democracies*, London: Routledge.

Brüker, H., Epstein, G.S., McCormick, B., Saint-Paul, G., Venturini, A. and Zimmermann, K. (2002) 'Welfare state provision', in T. Boeri, G. Hanson and B. McCormick (eds) *Immigration policy and the welfare system*, Oxford: Oxford University Press, pp 66-90.

Causa, O. and Jean, S. (2006) *Immigrants' integration in OECD countries: Does labour market policy matter?*, OECD Economics Department Working Papers, No 564, Paris: OECD.

Crepaz, M. (2006) 'If you are my brother, I may give you a dime! Public opinion on multiculturalism, trust, and the welfare state', in K. Banting and W. Kymlicka (eds) *Multiculturalism and the welfare state*, Oxford: Oxford University Press, pp 92-117.

Crepaz, M. (2007) *Trust beyond borders: Immigration, the welfare state, and identity in modern societies*, Ann Arbor, MI: University of Michigan Press.

Cusack, T., Iversen, T. and Rehm, P. (2006) 'Risk at work: the demand and supply sides of government redistribution', *Oxford Review of Economic Policy*, vol 22, no 3, pp 365-89.

De La O, A.L. and Rodden, J.A. (2008) 'Does religion distract the poor? Income and issue voting around the world', *Comparative Political Studies*, vol 41, no 4-5, pp 437-6.

Eger, M.A. (2010) 'Even in Sweden: the effect of immigration on support for welfare state spending', *European Sociological Review*, vol 26, no 2, pp 203-17.

Esping-Andersen, G. (1990) *Three worlds of welfare capitalism*, Cambridge: Polity Press.

Finseraas, H. (2008) 'Immigration and preferences for redistribution: an empirical analysis of European survey data', *Comparative European Politics*, vol 6, no 4, pp 407-31.

Finseraas, H. (2009) 'Income inequality and demand for redistribution: a multilevel analysis of European public opinion', *Scandinavian Political Studies*, vol 32, no 1, pp 92-119.

Freeman, G.P. (1986) 'Migration and the political economy of the welfare state', *The Annals of the American Academy of Political and Social Science*, vol 485, pp 51-63.

Gelman, A. and Hill, J. (2007) *Data analysis using regression and multilevel/hierarchical models*, New York: Cambridge University Press.

Gelman, A., Park, D., Shor, B., Bafumi, J. and Cortina, J. (2008) *Red state, blue state, rich state, poor state: Why Americans vote the way they do*, Princeton, NJ: Princeton University Press.

Gilens, M. (1995) 'Racial attitudes and opposition to welfare', *Journal of Politics*, vol 57, no 4, pp 994-1014.

Hooghe, M., Reeskens, T., Stolle, D. and Trappers, A. (2009) 'Ethnic diversity and generalized trust in Europe: a cross-national multilevel study', *Comparative Political Studies*, vol 42, no 2, pp 198-223.

Huber, J.D. and Stanig, P. (2007) *Why do the poor support rightwing parties? A crossnational analysis*, Leitner Working Paper, No 17, New Haven, CT: Yale University.

Jæger, M.M. (2006) 'Welfare regimes and attitudes towards redistribution: the regime hypothesis revisited', *European Sociological Review*, vol 22, no 2, pp 157-70.

Korpi, W. and Palme, J. (2003) 'New politics and class politics in the context of austerity and globalization: welfare state regress in 18 countries, 1975–95', *American Political Science Review*, vol 97, no 3, pp 425-46.

Manow, P. (2009) 'Electoral rules, class coalitions and welfare state regimes, or how to explain Esping-Andersen with Stein Rokkan', *Socio-Economic Review*, vol 7, no 1, pp 101-21.

OECD (Organisation for Economic Co-operation and Development) (2006) *Counting immigrants and expatriates in OECD countries: A new perspective*, Paris: OECD.

OECD (2008a) *Growing unequal? Income distribution and poverty in OECD countries*, Paris: OECD.

OECD (2008b) *International Migration Outlook*, Paris: OECD.

Pierson, P. (1996) 'The new politics of the welfare state', *World Politics*, vol 48, pp 143-79.

Pontusson, J. (2006) 'The American welfare state in comparative perspective: reflections on Alberto Alesina and Edward L. Glaeser, fighting poverty in the US and Europe', *Perspectives on Politics*, vol 4, no 2, pp 315-26.

Putnam, R.D. (2007) '*E pluribus unum*: diversity and community in the twenty-first century', *Scandinavian Political Studies*, vol 30, no 2, pp 37-174.

Rehm, P. (2009) 'Risks and redistribution: an individual-level analysis', *Comparative Political Studies*, vol 42, no 7, pp 855-81.

Roemer, J.E. and van der Straeten, K. (2005) 'Xenophobia and the size of the public sector in France: a politico-economic analysis', *Journal of Economics*, vol 86, no 2, pp 95-144.

Roemer, J.E. and van der Straeten, K. (2006) 'The political economy of xenophobia and distribution: the case of Denmark', *Scandinavian Journal of Economics*, vol 108, no 2, pp 251-77.

Roemer, J.E., Lee, W. and van der Straeten, K. (2007) *Racism, xenophobia, and distribution: Multi-issue politics in advanced democracies*, Cambridge, MA: Harvard University Press.

Senik, C., Stichnoth, H. and van der Straeten, K. (2009) 'Immigration and natives' attitudes towards the welfare state: evidence from the European Social Survey', *Social Research Indicators*, vol 91, no 3, pp 345-70.

Soroka, S., Banting, K. and Johnston, R. (2006) 'Immigration and redistribution in a global era', in P. Bardhan, S. Bowles and M. Wallerstein (eds) *Globalization and egalitarian redistribution*, Princeton, NJ: Princeton University Press, pp 261-88.

Soroka, S., Johnston, R. and Banting, K. (2004) 'Ethnicity, trust, and the welfare state', in P. van Parijs (ed) *Cultural diversity versus economic solidarity*, Vancouver: University of British Columbia Press, pp 33-58.

Stephens, J.D. (1979) *The transition from capitalism to socialism*, London: Macmillan.

van der Brug, W. and van Spanje, J. (2009) 'Immigration, Europe and the "new" cultural dimension', *European Journal of Political Research*, vol 48, no 3, pp 309-34.

van Oorschot, W. (2006) 'Making the difference in social Europe: deservingness perceptions among citizens of European welfare states', *Journal of European Social Policy*, vol 16, no 1, pp 23-42.

Vernby, K. and Finseraas, H. (2010) 'Xenophobia and left voting', *Politics & Society*, vol 38, no 4, pp 490-516.

Weede, E. (1986) 'Rent-seeking or dependency as explanations of why poor people stay poor', *International Sociology*, vol 1, no 4, pp 421-41.

Appendix: Parties included in European Social Survey coded as Left by country

Austria: SP, KP, Green Party

Belgium: Agalev, SP, PS, PVDA-AE, Ecolo

Switzerland: Social Democrats, Swiss Labour Party, Green Party, Women's Parties

Germany: SPD, PDS, Die Gruenen

Denmark: Social Democrats, Socialist People's Party, Unity List

Spain: Partido Socialista, Izquierda Unida, Esquerra Rep, Iniciativa per Catal, Eusko Alkartasuna

Finland: Social Democratic Party, Left Alliance, Green League, Communist Party, The Communist Workers

France: PC, PS, LCR, LO, MDC, Les Verts, Autres mouvements co

Great Britain: Labour, Social Democrats, Green Party

Greece: PASOK, KKE, SYN, DIKKI

Ireland: Labour, Sinn Féin, Green Party

Italy: Dem Sinistra, Verdi e SDI, Partito Comunista Italiano, Rifond Comun, Nouvo PSI

Luxembourg: Parti Socialiste, Les Verts, La Gauche

The Netherlands: PvdA, Socialistische Partij, Groen Links, Animal Rights Party

Norway: Social Democrats, Socialist Left Party, Red Electoral Alliance

Portugal: PS, PCP/PEV, BE, PCTP/MRPP, PH

Sweden: Social Democrats, Left Party, Green Party

Table A-2.1: Descriptive statistics

Variable	Description	n	Mean	Std dev	Min	Max
Left	Voted for a Left party	16,903	0.45	0.50	0	1
Cross-cutting preference	Support redistribution and restrictive immigration policy	16,903	0.32	0.47	0	1
Oppose redistribution	Oppose redistribution	16,903	0.30	0.46	0	1
Income	Income	16,903	0.31		-8	8
Education	Education in years	16,903	0.40		-12	14
Male	Gender	16,903	0.49	0.50	0	1
Churchgoer	Participate in religious ceremonies monthly	16,903	0.26	0.44	0	1
Young	Below years of age	16,903	0.20	0.40	0	1
Old	Above years of age	16,903	0.29	0.45	0	1

Table A-2.2: Country-level data

Country	Redistribution distance	Immigration distance	Immigration saliency	'Racial' fractiona-lisation	Inequality	Unemploy-ment ratio
Austria	7.2	9.6	14	0.03	26	1.86
Belgium	7	14.3	14.1	0.05	28	2.82
Denmark	2.6	8	15.7	0.03	23	2.44
Finland	1	10.9	10.9	0.02	25	2.23
France	9.6	13	13.7	0.10	28	1.78
Germany	-2	12.1	14.1	0.06	28	1.70
Greece	3.9	5.3	13.5	0.10	33	1.32
Ireland	7.2	6.1	11.6	0.03	31	1.33
Italy	5.8	12	14.3	0.02	33	1.11
Luxembourg	4.5	12	15	0.05	26	1.45
Netherlands	8.2	10.7	14	0.11	23	2.74
Norway	8.7	9.8	12.7	0.06	25	1.85
Portugal	7.9	7.6	13	0.05	37	1.15
Spain	9.3	9.2	14.3	0.03	34	1.14
Sweden	10.6	3.6	12.4	0.05	25	2.47
Switzerland	8.6	16.5	14.7	0.05	27	2.77
UK	7.2	4.8	13.3	0.10	35	1.66

Do we all (dis)like the same welfare state? Configurations of public support for the welfare state in comparative perspective

Mads Meier Jæger[1]

Introduction

Does equality in outcomes lead to a preference for equality? Compared to other OECD (Organisation for Economic Co-operation and Development) countries, the Nordic countries have welfare systems characterised by high levels of redistribution, universal coverage and generous cash benefits and social services. This welfare state architecture has resulted in high levels of equality in socioeconomic and social outcomes. However, while conventional wisdom has it that the populations in the Nordic countries have 'a passion for equality' that matches the high level of actual equality, results from comparative research on welfare attitudes suggest otherwise. Indeed, when compared to other OECD countries, the populations in the Nordic countries do not stand out in terms of their support for redistribution and other core welfare state functions (see, for example, Coughlin, 1980; Svallfors, 1997, 1999, 2003, 2006; Gelissen, 2000; Andress and Heien, 2001; Arts and Gelissen, 2001; Blekesaune and Quadagno, 2003; Linos and West, 2003; Lipsmeyer and Nordstrom, 2003; Mehrtens, 2004; Fraile and Ferrer, 2005; Jæger, 2006a, 2006b, 2009; Pfeifer, 2009).

What might explain why the populations in the Nordic countries are less supportive of the welfare state than we would expect? First, findings from existing comparative research may be correct: the populations in the Nordic countries are *not* more supportive of the welfare state than others. Second, existing empirical research may measure support for the welfare state in a manner insufficiently detailed for capturing the presumed Nordic passion for equality. This second scenario calls for a more comprehensive approach to measuring welfare state support.

In this chapter I address the second point by proposing a new approach to measuring public support for the welfare state that addresses two limitations in previous research. The first limitation is that most studies analyse *single* dimensions of welfare attitudes such as deservingness criteria (see, for example, van Oorschot,

2000; Jæger, 2007; Larsen, 2008), income redistribution (see, for example, Svallfors, 1997; Linos and West, 2003), or attitudes towards specific welfare programmes (see, for example, Nordlund, 1997; Edlund, 1999). Consequently, most studies do not consider the *interrelatedness* between different attitudinal dimensions and in so doing, may have failed to identify a particular Nordic configuration of welfare attitudes (if indeed such a configuration exists). A second limitation in existing research is that it almost exclusively addresses *quantitative* differences in welfare state support (that is, who supports the welfare *how much?*) and disregards *qualitative* differences (that is, who supports *which type* of welfare state?). By taking the interrelatedness of different dimensions of welfare attitudes into account, that is, how they might comprise an overall attitudinal 'package', as well as their different manifestation across countries and over time, we may gain new insights into the link between institutional contexts and attitudinal outcomes.

The new approach presented in this chapter builds on a latent variable method that may help us discover new patterns of welfare attitudes ignored in previous research. I analyse data from 12 countries from the International Social Survey Programme (ISSP) 'Role of Government' (RoG) modules (1985, 1990, 1996 and 2006). These countries approximate a wide range of welfare regime types, including the Social Democratic type found in the Nordic countries. I use five items (included in all survey waves) that measure the extent to which respondents believe that the government should be responsible for: redistributing income, providing jobs, providing a decent standard of living for those who are unemployed, providing healthcare for those who are sick and providing a decent standard of living for older people. Together, these five items touch on not only whether respondents support income redistribution (a core function in the welfare state), but also whether respondents think the government should be responsible for providing for social groups traditionally perceived to be deserving (older people and those with sickness or ill health) or undeserving (those who are unemployed). When treating all five items as partial manifestations of respondents' underlying welfare attitudes, I find that three prototypical types of welfare attitudes exist in all the 12 countries under study (Denmark, Norway, Sweden, Finland, Germany, France, Spain, Portugal, Italy, Great Britain, United States and Australia). I label these three prototypical attitudinal types, which capture particular configurations (rather than levels) of welfare state support: supporters of an 'unconditional welfare state model', supporters of a 'conditional welfare state model' and welfare state 'sceptics'.

Findings also show that countries differ with regard to the relative proportion of the population that belongs to each of the three types of welfare attitudes. To some extent, results follow expectations from welfare regime theory. The majority of the populations in the Nordic countries believe that the state should be responsible for redistributing income, providing jobs for everyone, providing a decent standard of living for older people and those who are unemployed, and providing healthcare for those who are ill. Consequently, the populations in the Nordic countries tend to support an unconditional welfare state model similar to the one that they already have. By contrast, the majority of North Americans and Australians (that is, respondents in Anglo-Saxon countries resembling the Liberal welfare regime) do not believe that the state should be responsible for redistributing income and providing jobs for everyone. They do, however, believe that the state should be responsible for providing for older people and those with ill health and thus they can be described as supporting a 'conditional' welfare state model. Finally, respondents in countries resembling the Continental European welfare regime fall somewhere in between these two groups. Interestingly, as the populations in the Southern European countries have the highest overall proportion of supporters of an unconditional welfare state model, the 'passion for equality' indeed appears most outspoken in Southern Europe.

In addition to cross-national differences, I also analyse within-country changes in the likelihood of belonging to each of the three prototypical types of welfare attitudes over the period 1985-2006. This analysis is informative about change in welfare state support in each country as measured qualitatively, not quantitatively. I find that support for the welfare state, as expressed by the probability of belonging to the latent group that supports an unconditional welfare state model, has stayed high over time in Norway, stayed low but stable in the Anglo-Saxon countries, and declined or fluctuated in the Continental and Southern European countries. The observed decline in welfare state support in some countries is driven mostly by people changing their attitudes from being supportive of an unconditional welfare state model to being supportive of a conditional welfare state model.

Theoretical background

This chapter draws on two types of literature in the conceptual framework. The first concerns the dimensionality and abstraction of welfare attitudes, that is, the different dimensions of the welfare state which go into people's total 'package' of welfare attitudes and their level of abstraction. This literature concerns the operational measurement of my dependent variable. The second literature concerns institutional differences across countries, particularly differences in welfare regimes and their impact on welfare state support and changes in support over time. Drawing on both strands of literature, I present a set of hypotheses for testing in the empirical analysis.

Attitudinal abstraction and dimensions of welfare attitudes

Previous research shows that two conceptual distinctions are important for analysing public support for the welfare state: level of abstraction and welfare state dimension. First, for level of abstraction one may distinguish between popular support for welfare state *principles* and *programmes* (see, for example, Roller, 1992; van Oorschot, 2000). Support for welfare state *principles* concerns core beliefs about the overall desirability of the welfare state (should we have a welfare state and what should this welfare state do?). At a lower level of abstraction support for welfare state *programmes* concerns attitudes towards specific schemes, for example, social assistance and family benefits. Research shows that survey questions on general welfare state principles tend to elicit ideologically charged attitudes, while questions addressing specific welfare state programmes elicit much more pragmatic ones (Free and Cantril, 1968; Coughlin, 1980). Consequently, the most promising avenue for identifying cross-national differences in public support for the welfare state is to analyse ideologically charged items. The items that I use from the ISSP as my dependent variables – government responsibility for income redistribution and provision for those who are unemployed, older people and those with ill health – arguably tap into people's beliefs about the overall desirability of the welfare state and thus their attitudes towards fundamental welfare state principles.

Second, it is important to distinguish between attitudes towards two different dimensions of the welfare state: redistribution and provision of social security for needy groups. Redistribution of income constitutes one of the most fundamental functions of the welfare state; it also affects everyone and is a source of ongoing political and social conflict (Esping-Andersen, 1990; Korpi and Palme, 1998).

Therefore, support for government responsibility for redistribution is a key component of welfare attitudes (see, for example, Edlund, 1999, 2003; Svallfors, 1999; Jæger, 2009). Furthermore, the question of *who* should be entitled to welfare benefits and services constitutes a second key component in welfare attitudes. A rich literature on deservingness criteria identifies the rules that people use when deciding which types of social needs are worthy of state welfare (see, for example, Will, 1993; van Oorschot, 2000; Jæger, 2007; Larsen, 2008). Based on evaluative criteria such as control over whether the need arose, the severity of the need and the extent to which people can identify with the needy group, research shows that certain social groups are consistently perceived as more deserving than others. In particular, people perceive those with ill health and older people as deserving needy groups while those who are unemployed, poor and those on social assistance are perceived as being much more in control of their own situation and thus not equally deserving.

Hence, in addition to support for redistribution, the distinction between deserving and undeserving social needs is the second key component of welfare attitudes. In the empirical analysis I combine the redistribution and deserving/ undeserving dimensions to study qualitative configurations of welfare attitudes and how these configurations differ across countries and over time.

In the next section I cover the independent variable dimension and present welfare regime theory as a possible explanation of, first, cross-national differences in public support for the welfare state and, second, within-country socioeconomic cleavages in welfare state support.

Welfare regime theory

Several institutionalist theories attempt to explain cross-national differences in public support for welfare state principles and programmes. The most prominent of these theories, welfare regime theory, proposes that welfare states can be divided into a number of distinct clusters and that each cluster is characterised by a particular level of attitudinal support (Esping-Andersen, 1990, 1999). Three ideal-typical welfare regimes are usually identified: *Social Democratic*, *Conservative* and *Liberal* welfare regimes (Esping-Andersen, 1990). In addition to these prototypical welfare regimes I also consider the *Southern* welfare regime (see, for example, Arts and Gelissen 2002).

First, in the Social Democratic (or *Nordic*) welfare regime the public sector is the main provider of social security; entitlement is universal and based on citizenship status or legal residence; benefits are generous by comparative standards; and the public sector offers a comprehensive range of social services. Furthermore, the level of vertical redistribution is high.

Second, in the *Conservative* (or *Continental*) welfare regime social insurance is the defining source of social security, and entitlement to the major social security programmes (for example, unemployment, sickness, retirement) is based on occupational rather than on citizenship status. Consequently, redistribution is predominantly horizontal, not vertical, and this regime fosters strong cleavages between well-protected 'insiders' (the core work force) and poorly protected 'outsiders' (for example, women, young people, immigrants and workers with weak labour market affiliation).

Third, in the *Liberal* (or *Anglo-Saxon*) welfare regime the market is the primary provider of social security. Hence, the role of the state is to provide targeted, low-quality cash benefits to individuals and families who are unable to provide for themselves. The level of both horizontal and vertical redistribution is low in this regime.

Fourth, in the *Southern* (or *Latin Rim*) welfare regime the family is the principal source of social security; entitlement to the major cash benefit schemes is tied to occupational status (as in the Conservative regime); and the public sector plays only a minor role in welfare provision. As a result, levels of horizontal redistribution are low, and social security coverage is poor for those who lack familial networks or strong labour market attachment (Arts and Gelissen, 2002).

As the four regime types are theoretical ideal types, countries may resemble each regime type to a higher or lesser degree. An important hypothesis in welfare regime theory is that welfare regimes produce and reproduce their own legitimacy. Thus regimes not only comprise sets of formal welfare state systems but also institutionalised solidarity and social belief systems (see, for example, Hall, 1986; Rothstein, 1998). Consequently, welfare regimes are hypothesised as shaping citizens' support for the welfare state in a systematic way. A rank order is often hypothesised in which support for the welfare state is expected to be *quantitatively* highest in the Social Democratic regime, second highest in the Conservative regime and lowest in the Liberal regime (Esping-Andersen, 1990; Gelissen, 2000, p 290; Andress and Heien, 2001, p 343; Arts and Gelissen, 2001, p 291; Jæger, 2006b, 2009). The relative position of the Southern welfare regime within this hierarchy is unclear. Some scholars argue that, with the Southern European countries being 'laggards' in terms of welfare state development, their citizens are likely to be strong supporters of public responsibility for welfare provision (see, for example, Gelissen, 2000; Arts and Gelissen, 2001). Others argue that given the strong tradition of family provision of social security, the opposite scenario is more plausible (Bonoli, 2000).[2] Consequently, while theory does not provide clear-cut expectations for the relative position of the Southern regime, the most likely scenario is that public support for the welfare state is higher in this regime than in the Conservative and Liberal regimes but not necessarily higher than in the Social Democratic regime. In summary, support for the welfare state should be highest in the Social Democratic welfare regime, lower in the Conservative regime and lowest in the Liberal regime. The position of the Southern regime remains unclear.

Change in welfare state support over time

Little systematic research exists on change in welfare state support over time. Longitudinal research has studied, first, how changing social and economic conditions affect public opinion (see, for example, Durr, 1993; Blekesaune, 2007); second, how public opinion drives policy (see, for example, Soroka and Wlezien, 2005; Brooks and Manza, 2006); and third, how public support for the welfare state has changed over time in response to the presumed 'crisis' of the welfare state (see, for example, Papadakis and Bean, 1993; Bean and Papadakis 1998). Results from this research suggest that changes in economic conditions do appear to affect welfare state support *in general* but also that observed changes in quantitative levels of welfare state support in different countries follow no consistent pattern. Given the lack of consistent results in previous research, I adopt a descriptive approach and present results from my cross-national analysis of changes in welfare state support over time by using a new approach to conceptualising welfare attitudes. As the empirical analysis shows, using a *qualitative* approach to measuring welfare state support yields somewhat more consistent cross-national results than the previous quantitative research.

Hypotheses

The hypotheses to be tested in the empirical analysis concern (1) the qualitative dimensionality of welfare attitudes and (2) cross-national differences in welfare attitudes. In addition, I explore the socioeconomic correlates of different types of welfare attitudes and changes over time in qualitative patterns of welfare attitudes.

For *dimensionality*, I expect individuals to cluster in well-defined groups based on attitudinal similarity along two dimensions. The first dimension pertains to *overall welfare state support*, that is, (high or low) support for government responsibility for income redistribution and for comprehensive social security provision. The second dimension pertains to *conditionality*, that is, the perceived importance of distinguishing between the deserving needy (those with ill health and older people) and the undeserving needy (those who are unemployed) recipients of state welfare.

For *cross-national differences*, I expect a large share of citizens in countries resembling the Social Democratic regime to support an unconditional welfare state model. By contrast, in countries resembling the Conservative and Liberal regimes I expect citizens to be generally less supportive of an unconditional welfare state model and more inclined to support a conditional welfare state model in which some social needs (for example, old age and sickness) are considered more worthy than others (for example, unemployment). As previously explained, the relative position of the Southern regime remains unclear.

In addition to these hypotheses, I explore the socioeconomic correlates of different types of welfare attitudes (in terms of respondents' education, income and socioeconomic status) and, for the countries in which I have time-series data, I analyse change in support for the welfare state over time. I carry out these additional analyses for two reasons: the first is, through using my new approach, to identify socioeconomic cleavages in welfare attitudes and compare the findings with results from previous research. The second reason is to contribute to the limited literature on change over time in public support for the welfare state.

Data, variables and methods

Data

I analyse data from the ISSP RoG modules carried out in 1985, 1990, 1996 and 2006. The ISSP includes nationally representative samples of the adult population in each country. I analyse data from four Nordic countries (Denmark, Finland, Norway and Sweden), two Continental European countries (France and Germany), three Southern European countries (Italy, Portugal and Spain) and three Anglo-Saxon countries (Australia, Great Britain and the US). These countries approximate the four different welfare regime types presented earlier. The number of available time points for each country varies: one each for Denmark, Finland and Portugal (2006), two each for France, Spain and Sweden (1996, 2006), three each for Italy and Norway (respectively, 1985-96, 1990-2006), and four each for Australia, Germany, Great Britain and the US (1985-2006).

Dependent variables

I use five items included in all ISSP RoG modules as my dependent variables. The RoG asks respondents how much they support government responsibility for income redistribution, job creation and provisions for several types of social needs. Respondents were asked: 'On the whole, do you think it should be or should not be the government's responsibility to...' for a list of topics. The five topics about government responsibility were:

- 'Reduce income differences between the rich and the poor'
- 'Provide a job for everyone who wants one'
- 'Provide a decent standard of living for the unemployed'
- 'Provide a decent standard of living for the old'
- 'Provide healthcare for the sick'

Respondents stated their opinion on all five statements using a four-point scale with the response categories: 'definitely should not be', 'probably should not be', 'probably should be' and 'definitely should be'. To simplify the empirical set-up, I recode each of the five dependent variables into dummy variables by assigning the value 1 if respondents answer 'probably should be' or 'definitely should be', and 0 otherwise. This recoding has no substantive impact on my results. Respondents answering 'don't know' were treated as missing values.

Independent variables

I include several individual-level demographic and socioeconomic variables in the analysis to account for socioeconomic correlates of different types of welfare attitudes. The demographic variables include gender (with a dummy variable for women) and age in years. Variables measuring socioeconomic position include respondents' education (measured by years of completed schooling), socioeconomic status (measured by the International Socio-Economic Index [ISEI] of Occupational Status; see Ganzeboom et al, 1992), family income (in national currencies but standardised within countries), a dummy variable for being employed in the public sector and a dummy variable for being married. I also include dummy variables to account for missing data on education, socioeconomic status and family income.

Methodological set-up

The idea in my analysis is to treat respondents' answers on each of the five dependent variables as partial manifestations of their true underlying welfare attitudes. Unlike previous research, which treats welfare attitudes either as a manifest (see, for example, Svallfors, 1997; Linos and West, 2003) or as a latent continuous variable (see, for example, Gelissen, 2000; Arts and Gelissen, 2001), I apply latent class analysis (LCA), which treats respondents as belonging to one of several categorical latent groups (see, for example, McCutcheon, 1987; Hagenaars and McCutcheon, 2002). The only previous application of LCA in the literature on welfare attitudes of which I am aware of is Edlund (2006), who analysed Swedish data. Each latent class is characterised by a set of conditional probabilities of agreeing with each of the five binary items used as dependent variables. Respondents belonging to a certain latent class thus share a common *configuration* of welfare attitudes and, consequently, the latent class methodology is designed to capture *qualitative* rather than *quantitative* differences in welfare attitudes.

In terms of model estimation, I determine the number of latent classes needed to explain the empirical association between the five dependent variables by estimating LCA models with increasing numbers of latent classes and by evaluating relative improvements in model fit. In the present analysis I use the Akaike Information Criterion (AIC) and the Bayesian Information Criterion (BIC) to determine the appropriate number of latent classes in each of the 12 countries. This is the standard method.

In addition to LCA models, I also estimate latent class regression (LCR) models to analyse socioeconomic correlates of welfare attitudes. The LCR is an extension of the LCA model, in which the probability of belonging to each of the latent classes is allowed to depend on a set of explanatory variables (in my case, respondents' demographic and socioeconomic characteristics). The results from the LCR are interpreted in the same way as a multinomial logit regression model.

Results

The results section is divided into three parts. The first presents results from the LCA analysis of the qualitative dimensionality of welfare attitudes in my sample of 12 countries. In this part I also explore the socioeconomic correlates of different types of welfare attitudes. The second part analyses whether the distribution of the qualitatively different types of welfare attitudes differs across countries in a way that welfare regime theory predicts. The third part analyses changes over time for the probability of belonging to the different types of welfare attitudes and interprets these changes in the context of welfare regime theory.

How many types of welfare state supporters can be identified?

The first substantive question is how many qualitatively different types of welfare attitudes can be identified from respondents' answers to the five dependent variables. To answer this question, I ran LCA models with 2-4 latent classes on the pooled ISSP sample for 2006 (which includes all countries except Italy) and on each country individually (models for Italy pertain to 1996, the most recent year in which Italy participated in the ISSP RoG). To save space I do not report model diagnostics from all models and for all countries (see the Appendix at the end of this chapter). Nonetheless, the analyses show quite consistently that LCA models with three latent classes fit the data best. In no country is a four-class model preferable to a three-class model. The Southern European countries (Italy, Portugal and Spain) show little difference in model fit between LCA models with two or three latent classes, mostly because the third latent class includes only a very small proportion of the respondents in these countries (I discuss this result later). The general conclusion, however, is that in all 12 countries three latent classes are needed for fully capturing the statistical association between respondents' responses to the five dependent variables.

Figure 3.1 shows, first, the estimated conditional probability of agreeing with each of the five attitudinal items (given that a person belongs to each latent class) and, second, the estimated proportion of respondents belonging to each class. The figure portrays three latent groups, which I label supporters of an *'unconditional'* welfare state model, supporters of a *'conditional'* welfare state model and welfare state *'sceptics'*.

The first group, supporters of an *unconditional* welfare state model, has a very high probability (85 per cent or higher) of agreeing with the statements that the government should be responsible for redistributing income, providing jobs for everyone, providing a decent standard of living for those who are unemployed and older people, and providing healthcare for those with ill health. Consequently, this latent class captures respondents who support an unconditional welfare state model and therefore do not distinguish between deserving and undeserving social needs.

The second group, supporters of a *conditional* welfare state model, have a much lower probability of believing that the government should be responsible for redistributing income, providing jobs and providing a decent standard of living

Figure 3.1: Conditional response probabilities for different welfare state support types, 2006

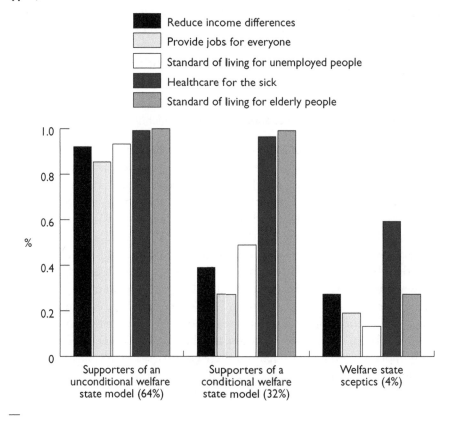

for those who are unemployed. However, they also believe that the government should be responsible for providing for older people and those with ill health, both of which groups that are typically classified as the 'deserving needy' (see, for example, van Oorschot, 2000; Jæger, 2007). Consequently, this latent group captures respondents who believe in a conditional welfare state model.

Finally, welfare state *sceptics* have the lowest overall probability of believing that the state should be responsible in *any* of the policy areas that the five items cover. I do not classify this group as being against the welfare state, because members have a non-trivial probability of believing that the government should be responsible for providing healthcare for those with ill health. Consequently, the term 'welfare state sceptics' is appropriate for this group.

The results from the LCA analysis corroborate the hypothesis that welfare attitudes cluster along two dimensions: (1) support (or non-support) for overall government responsibility for income redistribution and for providing core social security coverage and (2) the distinction between deserving and undeserving social needs. The group that supports an unconditional welfare state model and the 'sceptic' group capture two extremes of the 'more or less welfare state' dimension, while the conditional supporter group exemplify the 'deserving/undeserving needy' dimension. Figure 3.1 also shows the proportion of respondents that, based on their response patterns on the five attitudinal items, can be classified as most likely to belong to each of the three latent classes. It shows that the majority of respondents (64 per cent) can be classified as belonging to the group that supports an unconditional welfare state model. Furthermore, 32 per cent of respondents belong to the group that supports a conditional welfare state model, while only 4 per cent are welfare state sceptics. Together, these figures convey the impression that supporters of the welfare state outweigh sceptics across the 12 countries under study.

Socioeconomic correlates of welfare attitudes

Previous research has found significant socioeconomic cleavages in *quantitative* levels of support for the welfare state, based on, for example, education, income and social class position (see, for example, Svallfors, 1997; Linos and West, 2003; Jæger, 2006b). The question now is whether similar cleavages exist with respect to the *qualitative* differences in welfare attitudes that my alternative approach captures. Table 3.1 shows results from a LCR model of the pooled 2006 ISSP data. This model estimates the likelihood of belonging to either (1) the latent group supporting a conditional welfare state model or (2) the group that is sceptical of the welfare state relative to the group supporting an unconditional welfare state model (the reference group). The explanatory variables in the model are gender, age, level of education, family income, socioeconomic status (ISEI score), employment in the public sector and marital status.

Results from the LCR analysis show highly significant socioeconomic cleavages in welfare attitudes. Compared to supporting an unconditional welfare state

Table 3.1: Results from latent class regression

	Supporter of a conditional welfare state model	Welfare state sceptic
Gender (female)	−0.433 (0.050)***	−0.457 (0.091)***
Age (divided by 10)	0.011 (0.017)	0.022 (0.034)
Years of schooling	0.104 (0.008)***	0.120 (0.014)***
Family income	0.354 (0.036)***	0.439 (0.048)***
Socioeconomic status	0.020 (0.002)***	0.017 (0.003)***
Public employee	−0.369 (0.064)***	−0.679 (0.124)***
Married	0.123 (0.053)*	0.081 (0.100)
Constant	−2.169 (0.155)***	−4.254 (0.315)***
Log-likelihood	−32,081	
Number of observations	17,854	

Notes: Reference group is: supporters for an unconditional welfare state model. Log-odds estimates with standard errors in parenthesis.
*** $p<0.001$, ** $p<0.01$, * $p<0.05$. Model run on ISSP 2006 (excluding Italy, which was not included in 2006).

model (the reference group), the likelihood of supporting a conditional welfare state model or being sceptical of the welfare state increases with educational level, family income and socioeconomic status. Consequently, in line with previous research the findings show that the highly educated and those in advantaged socioeconomic positions are less likely to support an unconditional welfare state model compared to those in less advantaged positions.

In additional analyses not reported here, I find that the socioeconomic variables discriminate primarily between those who support an unconditional welfare state model and those who support a conditional welfare state model (and only to a lesser extent those who are sceptical of the welfare state). When using the supporters of a conditional welfare state model as the reference group, I also find that the socioeconomic variables for the most part do not discriminate between this group and the welfare state critics (the small relative size of the sceptic group might explain this finding). Finally, the analysis shows that women (more than men) and public employees are more supportive of an unconditional welfare state model. These results are similar to those found in previous research.

Cross-national patterns of welfare state support

The first part of the empirical analysis has shown that three prototypical types of welfare attitudes exist in all the 12 countries under study and that each attitudinal group is associated with certain socioeconomic characteristics. This second part of the analysis investigates cross-national differences in the share of the adult population (in each country) belonging to each of the three attitudinal groups. This analysis addresses the second hypothesis, which states that the share of the population in a country supporting an unconditional or conditional welfare state model, or the share which is sceptical of the welfare state, should vary systematically with the degree to which countries resemble the different welfare regime types (see, for example, Svallfors, 1997; Arts and Gelissen, 2001; Jæger, 2006b). As Figure 3.2 shows, I investigate this hypothesis by plotting for each country the share of the population belonging to each of the three attitudinal groups in the 2006 ISSP data (the data for Italy is from 1996). I am particularly interested in the distribution of the three groups in the Nordic countries vis-à-vis the other countries. Figure 3.2 reveals mostly expected patterns but also several interesting deviations.

First, the Nordic countries display somewhat heterogeneous attitudinal patterns. In Denmark and Sweden almost 60 per cent of the population support an unconditional welfare state model, about 40 per cent support a conditional welfare state model and only 2-3 per cent are sceptics. In Finland almost 70 per cent of the population support an unconditional welfare state model, while in Norway this proportion is almost 80 per cent. These results suggest not only that support for the welfare state is generally high in the Nordic countries but also that attitudinal patterns are quite diverse (previous studies also report this finding). As I discuss later, while the Nordic countries (except Denmark) used to be more similar, Sweden in particular has experienced a decline in welfare state support

Figure 3.2: Marginal distribution of welfare state support types across countries, 2006

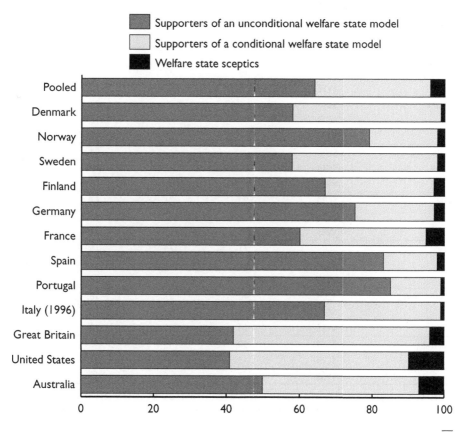

in recent years. In 1996, 73 per cent of the Swedish population supported an unconditional welfare state model (see Table 3.2), while in 2006 only 58 per cent of the population supported this type of welfare state model. The 1996 level for Sweden is similar to the 2006 level for Finland and Norway, while support for an unconditional welfare state model appears lowest in Denmark (unfortunately, no time-series data exist for Denmark and Finland).[3]

Second, the two Continental European countries, France and Germany, differ significantly in support for the welfare state. In Germany 75 per cent of the population support an unconditional welfare state model, 22 per cent support a conditional welfare state model and 3 per cent are welfare state sceptics.

Interestingly, while these figures are similar to those in the Nordic countries, the high level of support for the unconditional welfare state model is quite recent in Germany (see Table 3.2). In France 60 per cent support an unconditional welfare

Table 3.2: Time trends in levels of support for the welfare state (% of population that belongs to each attitudinal type)

Country	Type	1985	1990	1996	2006
Norway	SUM		73	79	79
	SCM		26	20	19
	WSS		1	1	2
Sweden	SUM			73	58
	SCM			24	40
	WSS			3	2
Germany	SUM	77	61	56	75
	SCM	19	32	40	22
	WSS	4	7	4	3
France	SUM			72	60
	SCM			18	35
	WSS			10	5
Spain	SUM			84	83
	SCM			15	15
	WSS			1	2
Italy	SUM	90	71	67	
	SCM	9	27	32	
	WSS	1	2	1	
Great Britain	SUM	71	74	76	42
	SCM	27	25	19	54
	WSS	2	1	5	4
United States	SUM	40	37	38	41
	SCM	44	50	52	49
	WSS	16	13	10	10
Australia	SUM	50	43	43	50
	SCM	43	49	47	43
	WSS	7	8	10	7

Notes: SUM = Supporters of an unconditional welfare state model; SCM = supporters of a conditional welfare state model; WSC = welfare state sceptics.

state model, 35 per cent a conditional model and 5 per cent are sceptics. These results suggest that, as in the Nordic countries, support for the welfare state is quite diverse in the Continental European countries. However, I would need more countries in the Continental European cluster to draw inferences about overall trends in this regime.

Third, support for the welfare state is generally high in the Southern European countries of Italy, Portugal and Spain. In Portugal and Spain the share of the population supporting an unconditional welfare state model exceeds 80 per cent and is higher than in the Nordic countries. In Italy, in which just below 70 per cent of the population prefer an unconditional welfare state model, popular support is somewhat lower but still high compared to the others (keeping in mind that the figures for Italy are from 1996). Generally, results from the Southern European countries support the observation of Arts and Gelissen (2001) that people in Southern Europe, living in countries which are 'welfare laggards' compared to the rest of Western Europe, strongly support the welfare state.

Fourth, the three Anglo-Saxon countries – the Australia, Great Britain and the US – also form a distinct cluster, with comparatively low levels of support for the welfare state. In all three countries supporters of an unconditional welfare state model comprise less than half the population. Thus the Anglo-Saxon countries are the only countries in which supporters of a conditional welfare state model and welfare state sceptics outnumber supporters of an unconditional welfare state model. This attitudinal pattern testifies to a substantively lower level of welfare state support in these countries and to the existence of a distinctly liberal attitudinal cluster.

In summary, my cross-national analysis suggests that countries cluster in ways somewhat consistent with expectations from welfare regime theory. The highest level of support for an unconditional welfare state model is in the Southern European countries, with levels of support also mostly high in most Nordic countries. In the Continental European countries the results are mixed, while in the Anglo-Saxon countries the majority of the populations support a conditional welfare state model or are critical of the welfare state.

Change in welfare state support over time

This final section analyses changes in welfare state support from 1985 to 2006. As previously described, the analysis is motivated by the lack of consistent results in previous comparative research, which uses a purely quantitative approach to measuring welfare state support. Here, I take a different approach, instead analysing whether the relative shares of the population belonging to either the latent group supporting an unconditional welfare state model, the group supporting a conditional welfare state model or the group sceptical of the welfare state have increased or decreased over time within countries. I estimate LCA models for each country and available time period. The analysis is limited by the number of ISSP waves in which each country has participated. I have long time-series (at least 15 years) for Australia (1985-2006), Germany (1985-2006), Great Britain (1985-2006), Norway (1990-2006) and the US (1985-2006). I have medium-length time-series (at least 10 years) for France (1996-2006), Italy (1985-96), Spain (1996-2006) and Sweden (1996-2006). I do not have time-series data for Denmark, Finland and Portugal. Table 3.2 shows cross-time trends.

The time-series data for Norway suggest a high and stable level of support for the welfare state over the period 1990-2006. During the entire period around 75 per cent of Norwegians supported an unconditional welfare state model, while only a minority supported a conditional welfare state model or were sceptical of the welfare state. This stable trend might be attributable to the stable economic climate in Norway at this time. By contrast, support in Sweden for the welfare state declined considerably from 1996 to 2006. The proportion of the population supporting an unconditional welfare state model decreased from 73 per cent in 1996 to 58 per cent in 2006, while the proportion supporting a conditional welfare state model rose from 24 to 40 per cent. This trend might be attributable to the economic crisis that hit Sweden in the early 1990s and its effect on public opinion (Blekesaune, 2007). This crisis led to significant cuts in welfare spending, which in turn might have fuelled a higher demand for public social security, as my results for 1996 show. By 2006 Sweden's economy was back on track, and the demand for social security decreased.

Time trends in the Continental European countries are mostly characterised by a gradual decrease in public support for the welfare state. In Germany, the proportion of the population supporting an unconditional welfare state model decreased from 77 per cent in 1985 to 56 per cent in 1996, while the proportion supporting a conditional welfare state model increased from 19 to 40 per cent. However, by 2006 public support for the welfare state surged, with 75 per cent now supporting an unconditional welfare state model. France shows a gradual decline in support for the welfare state in that the proportion of the population preferring an unconditional welfare state model decreased from 72 to 60 per cent between 1996 and 2006.

In the Southern European countries trends are also country-specific. In Spain public support for an unconditional welfare state model remained very high between 1996 and 2006. Italy showed a quite substantial decline in support for an unconditional welfare state model between 1985 and 1996 and an increase in support for a conditional welfare state model.

Finally, time trends in the Anglo-Saxon countries display remarkable stability. In the US and Australia the likelihood of belonging to the group supporting an unconditional welfare state model, the group supporting a conditional welfare state model or the group which is sceptical of the welfare state hardly changed between 1985 and 2006. While trends are likewise very stable in Great Britain from during this period, I find a decline in welfare state support from 1996 to 2006. Interestingly, before 2006 levels of support for the welfare state in Great Britain were similar to those found in the Nordic countries (with about 75 per cent of the population supporting an unconditional welfare state model).

However, by 2006 support for the welfare state had declined in Great Britain to the level found in the other Anglo-Saxon countries. Consequently, the Anglo-Saxon countries are characterised by very stable and comparatively low levels of support for the welfare state.

In summary, keeping the significant limitations of the data in mind, the cross-time analysis suggests that, first, different countries have experienced different trends and, second, with some noteworthy exceptions it is difficult to identify regime specific trends in the development in welfare attitudes. Support for the welfare state has remained relatively stable (at high or low levels) in Norway, Spain, the US and Australia. A decline in support for the welfare state is evident in France, Germany, Great Britain, Italy and Sweden. The only consistent pattern which might be attributed to welfare regimes is the stability in attitudinal patterns over time in the Anglo-Saxon countries.

Conclusion

This chapter was motivated by the empirical finding that the populations in the Nordic countries, despite the comprehensive welfare state systems in these countries, do not stand out from other populations in terms of expressing a 'passion for equality'. The questions asked were whether the Nordic populations share a particular passion for equality or whether the measurement tools used in previous research are inadequate for capturing this passion.

To analyse these questions, the chapter introduces a new approach to conceptualising and measuring popular support for the welfare state. This approach focuses on qualitatively different configurations of welfare attitudes rather than on purely quantitative attitudinal differences that are dominant in previous research. Furthermore, the chapter applies the new approach to analysing cross-national patterns in welfare state support and changes in these patterns over time.

Results from the empirical analysis can be summarised as follows. I use five items from the ISSP surveys and identify three types of latent welfare attitudes. These three types include one group that prefers an unconditional welfare state model, one group that prefers a conditional welfare state model catering only to certain social needs and one group that is sceptical of the welfare state. These three attitudinal types exist in all 12 countries under study, and each group comprises a different share of the population in each country. I also find that attitudinal beliefs are correlated with respondents' socioeconomic characteristics. The propensity to prefer a conditional welfare state model over an unconditional model increases significantly with level of education, income and socioeconomic position. Conversely, women and those employed in the public sector are more likely to prefer an unconditional welfare state model.

The comparative analysis shows that the majority of the populations in the Nordic and (particularly) the Southern European countries support an unconditional welfare state model. A smaller proportion of the populations in the Continental European countries support this type of welfare state model, and the majority of the populations in the Anglo-Saxon countries support a conditional welfare state model. Consequently, while the Nordic countries exhibit a high overall level of support for the welfare state (and a significantly higher level than the Anglo-Saxon countries), there is little evidence that they stand out in terms of having a passion for equality. In this regard my findings – based on a new conceptualisation of welfare attitudes – corroborate results from previous research.

Furthermore, I find interesting country-specific changes in welfare state support over time, in particular a remarkable stability in support for the welfare state in Australia, Norway, Spain and the US. These nations consistently display either positive or negative public sentiment toward the welfare state. I observe attitudinal volatility, and in particular trends toward lower support for the welfare state, in France, Germany, Italy, Great Britain and Sweden. In general, my results suggest that country-specific factors rather than welfare regime factors drive changes in public opinion over time.

Results from this chapter feed into ongoing discussions in comparative research on welfare state support. I show that several distinct 'packages' of welfare attitudes may be discerned, and that these packages exist in all 12 countries under study. These results suggest that people's welfare attitudes cluster into well-defined groups based on the redistribution and 'deservingness' dimensions. This finding is new. My approach also demonstrates that while the Nordic countries are not in the lead in terms of having a passion for equality, their populations nonetheless appear more supportive of the welfare state than in previous comparative research. Although this empirical result would be expected from welfare regime theory, most existing research, and especially that focusing on support for redistribution, typically does not find the populations in the Nordic countries to exhibit strong support for the welfare state. Consequently, my approach, which conceptualises welfare state support by taking into account both redistribution and public responsibility for providing social protection for all needy groups, appears particularly well suited for capturing the Nordic notion of the (comprehensive) welfare state.

Notes

[1] The ISSP data used in this chapter was downloaded from the ZACAT online system hosted by the GESIS – Leibniz Institute for the Social Sciences. I thank participants at previous book seminars and the editors for excellent comments and suggestions.

[2] Even when taking differences in methodology into account, the existing empirical evidence on the Southern regime is mixed. Gelissen (2000), analysing Eurobarometer data, finds that people in the Mediterranean countries are less supportive of the welfare state than people in the Liberal regime. Arts and Gelissen (2001), analysing data from the ISSP and the European Values Study, reach the opposite conclusion. Papadakis and Bean (1993) find Italy to be somewhere in the middle, while Evans (1996) and Bean and Papadakis (1998) find Italians to be more in favour of the welfare state than other Europeans.

[3] The five ISSP questions that I use as my dependent variables were asked in an almost identical fashion in the 2008 round of the European Social Survey (ESS); however, the

response categories were a 0-10 scale instead of the ISSP 1-5 scoring. When I run the three-class LCA model for Sweden using the ESS 2008 data, I find that 74 per cent of Swedes can be classified as supporting an unconditional welfare state model, 22 per cent as supporting a conditional welfare state model and 4 per cent as being welfare state sceptics. While these figures are similar to the ISSP figures for Sweden in 1996 and for Finland and Norway in 2006, they deviate from the ISSP figures for Sweden in 2006. However, differences in the designs of the ISSP and ESS mean that one should be careful about directly comparing results from the ISSP and the ESS.

References

Andreß, H.-J. and Heien, T. (2001) 'Four worlds of welfare attitudes? A comparison of Germany, Norway, and the United States', *European Sociological Review*, vol 17, no 4, pp 337-56.

Arts, W. and Gelissen, J. (2001) 'Welfare states, solidarity and justice principles: does the type really matter?', *Acta Sociologica*, vol 44, no 4, pp 284-99.

Arts, W. and Gelissen, J. (2002) 'Three worlds of welfare capitalism or more? A state-of-the-art report', *Journal of European Social Policy*, vol 12, no 2, pp 137-58.

Bean, C. and Papadakis, E. (1998) 'A comparison of mass attitudes towards the welfare state in different institutional regimes, 1985-1990', *International Journal of Public Opinion Research*, vol 10, no 3, pp 211-36.

Blekesaune, M. (2007) 'Economic conditions and public attitudes to welfare policies', *European Sociological Review*, vol 23, no 3, pp 393-403.

Blekesaune, M. and Quadagno, J. (2003) 'Public attitudes toward welfare state policies: a comparative analysis of 24 nations', *European Sociological Review*, vol 19, no 5, pp 415-27.

Bonoli, G. (2000) 'Public attitudes to social protection and political economy traditions on Western Europe', *European Societies*, vol 2, no 4, pp 431-52.

Brooks, C. and Manza, J. (2006) 'Social policy responsiveness in developed democracies', *American Sociological Review*, vol 71, no 3, pp 474-94.

Coughlin, R. (1980) *Ideology, public opinion, welfare policy: Attitudes towards taxing and spending in industrialized countries*, Berkeley, CA: Institution of International Studies.

Durr, R.H. (1993) 'What moves policy sentiment?', *American Political Science Review*, vol 87, no 1, pp 158-70.

Edlund, J. (1999) 'Trust in government and welfare regimes: attitudes to redistribution and financial cheating in the USA and Norway', *European Journal of Political Research*, vol 35, no 3, pp 341-70.

Edlund, J. (2003) 'The influence of the class situations of husband and wives on class identity, party preference and attitudes towards redistribution: Sweden, Germany and the United States', *Acta Sociologica*, vol 46, no 3, pp 195-214.

Edlund, J. (2006) 'Trust in the capability of the welfare state and general welfare state support: Sweden 1997-2002', *Acta Sociologica*, vol 49, no 4, pp 395-417.

Esping-Andersen, G. (1990) *Three worlds of welfare capitalism*, Cambridge: Polity Press.

Esping-Andersen, G. (1999) *Social foundations of postindustrial economies*, Oxford: Oxford University Press.

Evans, G. (1996) 'Cross-national differences in support for welfare and redistribution: an evaluation of competing theories', in B.Taylor and K.Thomson (eds) *Understanding changes in social attitudes*, Aldershot: Dartmouth, pp 185-208.

Fraile, M. and Ferrer, M. (2005) 'Explaining the determinants of public support for cuts in unemployment benefits spending across OECD countries', *International Sociology*, vol 20, no 4, pp 459-81.

Free, L.A. and Cantril, H. (1968) *The political beliefs of Americans*, New York: Simon & Schuster.

Ganzeboom, H.B.G., de Graaf, P.M. and Treiman, D.J. (1992) 'A standard international socio-economic index of occupational status', *Social Science Research*, vol 21, no 1, pp 1-56.

Gelissen, J. (2000) 'Popular support for institutionalised solidarity: a comparison between European welfare states', *International Journal of Social Welfare*, vol 9, no 4, pp 285-300.

Hagenaars, J.A. and McCutcheon, A.C. (2002) *Applied latent class analysis*, Cambridge: Cambridge University Press.

Hall, P. (1986) *Governing the economy: The politics of state intervention in Britain and France*, New York: Oxford University Press.

Jæger, M.M. (2006a) 'What makes people support public responsibility for welfare provision: self-interest or political ideology?', *Acta Sociologica*, vol 49, no 3, pp 321-38.

Jæger, M.M. (2006b) 'Welfare regimes and attitudes towards redistribution: the regime hypothesis revisited', *European Sociological Review*, vol 22, no 2, pp 157-70.

Jæger, M.M. (2007) 'Cross-cultural heterogeneity and public support for the "deserving needy" in eight Western countries', in S. Mau, and B. Veghte (eds) *Social justice, legitimacy and the welfare state*, Aldershot: Ashgate, pp 73-94.

Jæger, M.M. (2009) 'United but divided: welfare regimes and the level and variance in public support for redistribution', *European Sociological Review*, vol 25, no 6, pp 723-37.

Korpi, W. and Palme, J. (1998) 'The paradox of redistribution and strategies of equality: welfare state institutions, inequality, and poverty in the Western countries', *American Sociological Review*, vol 63, no 5, pp 661-87.

Larsen, C.A. (2008) 'The institutional logic of welfare attitudes: how welfare regimes influence public support', *Comparative Political Studies*, vol 41, no 2, pp 145-68.

Linos, K. and West, M. (2003) 'Self-interest, social beliefs, and attitudes to redistribution. Re-addressing the issue of cross-national variation', *European Sociological Review*, vol 19, no 4, pp 393-409.

Lipsmeyer, C.S. and Nordstrom, T. (2003) 'East versus West: comparing political attitudes and welfare preferences across European countries', *Journal of European Public Policy*, vol 10, no 3, pp 339-64.

McCutcheon, A.C. (1987) *Latent class analysis*, Beverly Hills, CA: Sage Publications.

Mehrtens, F.J. (2004) 'Three worlds of public opinion? Values, variation, and the effect on social policy', *International Journal of Public Opinion Research*, vol 16, no 2, pp 115-43.

Nordlund, A. (1997) 'Attitudes towards the welfare state in the Scandinavian countries', *Scandinavian Journal of Social Welfare*, vol 6, no 4, pp 233-46.

Papadakis, E. and Bean, C. (1993) 'Popular support for the welfare state: a comparison between institutional regimes', *Journal of Public Policy*, vol 13, no 3, pp 227-54.

Pfeifer, M. (2009) 'Public opinion on state responsibility for minimum income protection', *Acta Sociologica*, vol 52, no 2, pp 117-34.

Roller, E. (1992) *Einstellungen der Bürger zum Wohlfahrtsstaat der Bundesrepublik Deutschland*, Opladen: Westdeutscher Verlag.

Rothstein, B. (1998) *Just institutions matter. The moral and political logic of the universal welfare state*, Cambridge: Cambridge University Press.

Soroka, S.N. and Wlezien, C. (2005) 'Opinion-policy dynamics: public preferences and public expenditure in the United Kingdom', *British Journal of Political Science*, vol 35, no 4, pp 665-89.

Svallfors, S. (1997) 'Worlds of welfare and attitudes to redistribution: a comparison of eight Western nations', *European Sociological Review*, vol 13, no 3, pp 283-304.

Svallfors, S. (1999) 'Political trust and attitudes towards redistribution. A comparison of Sweden and Norway', *European Societies*, vol 1, no 2, pp 241-68.

Svallfors, S. (2003) 'Welfare regimes and Western opinions: a comparison of eight Western countries', *Social Indicators Research*, vol 64, no 3, pp 495-520.

Svallfors, S. (2006) *The moral economy of class. Class attitudes in comparative perspective*, Stanford, CA: Stanford University Press.

van Oorschot, W. (2000) 'Who should get what, and why?', *Policy & Politics*, vol 28, no 1, pp 33-48.

Will, J. (1993) 'The dimensions of poverty: public perceptions of the deserving poor', *Social Science Research*, vol 22, no 3, pp 312-32.

Appendix

Table A-3.1: Model fit for different latent class models

	Number of latent classes	AIC	BIC		Number of latent classes	AIC	BIC
Pooled*	2	66,735	66,735	Spain	2	5,884	5,948
	3	66,190	66,322		3	5,872	5,971
	4	66,131	66,310		4	5,877	6,011
Denmark	2	4,946	5,004	Portugal	2	3,625	3,696
	3	4,932	5,020		3	3,601	3,695
	4	4,938	5,058		4	3,609	3,736
Norway	2	3,848	3,905	Italy	2	3,722	3,777
	3	3,811	3,899		3	3,718	3,803
	4	3,816	3,935		4	3,726	3,841
Sweden	2	4,447	4,503	Great Britain	2	3,545	3,598
	3	4,403	4,490		3	3,534	3,616
	4	4,395	4,512		4	3,541	3,652
Finland	2	3,812	3,867	United States	2	7,262	7,321
	3	3,767	3,853		3	7,119	7,209
	4	3,776	3,892		4	7,128	7,250
Germany	2	6,406	6,465	Australia	2	11,280	11,345
	3	6,364	6,455		3	11,231	11,331
	4	6,355	6,479		4	11,236	11,372
France	2	7,367	7,428				
	3	7,328	7,422				
	4	7,326	7,452				

Notes: AIC = Akaike Information Criterion; BIC = Bayesian Information Criterion; * Pooled models are unweighted.

Socioeconomic correlates of welfare attitudes

Figures A-3.1, A-3.2 and A-3.3 are based on latent class regression (LCR) models that show predicted probabilities of belonging to each of the three attitudinal types as a function of educational level, family income or ISEI score. In each graph all predictors in the LCR model except the predictor of interest are fixed at their means, and categorical variables are set at male, employed in the private sector and married.

Figure A-3.1: Effect of education on welfare support types

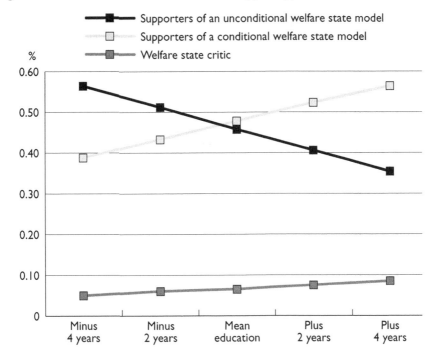

Figure A-3.2: Effect of family income on welfare support types

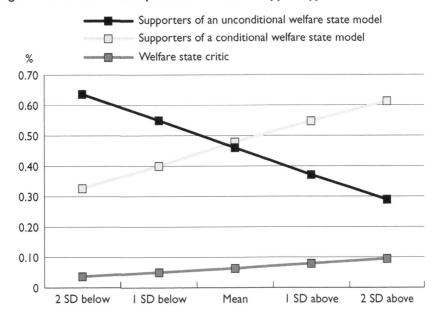

Figure A-3.3: Effect of socioeconomic status on welfare support types

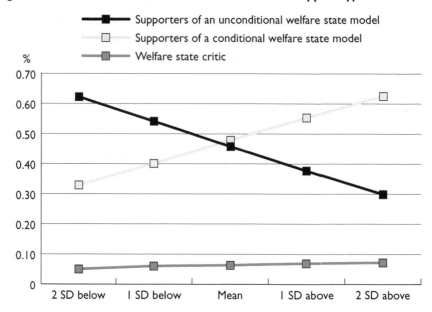

Eroding minimum income protection in the Nordic countries? Reassessing the Nordic model of social assistance

Susan Kuivalainen and Kenneth Nelson

Means-tested social assistance and minimum income benefits mitigate financial hardship and alleviate poverty. Whereas social insurance aims to provide protection against loss in work-related income, and family or child benefits are intended to compensate households for additional child-related costs, social assistance is meant to provide a safety net for households that have insufficient incomes and that do not qualify for other types of public support. Several scholars point to the necessity of a system of well-functioning minimum income benefits. According to Marshall (1950), the provision of a certain minimum income for all members of society is among one of the core elements of social citizenship. Rawls (1971) acknowledged the role of social minimums for the creation of just societies, because these minimums guarantee the meeting of short-term basic needs. More recently Leibfried (1993) has argued that the most appropriate test of full social citizenship for all is to ask what the welfare state does for the poor and destitute. Whatever their justification, minimum income benefits constitute important social policy means of reducing inequality.

Nordic social assistance and minimum income benefits have had a relatively marginal role compared with other welfare policy schemes. Nonetheless, benefit levels have been high, something that is of relevance for effective poverty alleviation. However, as last-resort social safety nets are changing, this chapter analyses whether the Nordic countries still have such a helpful model. We compare changes from 1990 to 2010 in Denmark, Finland, Norway and Sweden with those of Germany, the Netherlands and the United Kingdom (UK). As a last-resort benefit, social assistance does not exist in isolation from other welfare state structures: its role and importance depends on the organisation and functioning of other forms of social protection. This dependence is one reason why comparisons of social assistance must focus on both institutional structures and their outcomes. More precisely, the chapter asks and answers the following three questions.

First, is Nordic social assistance moving in the direction we would expect from the recognition of an encompassing or universalist Nordic model (Korpi and Palme, 1998)? This model suggests that means-tested social support, such as social assistance, is comparatively generous and has a marginal and diminishing role for income protection, both in terms of expenditure and caseloads.

Second, to what extent does Nordic social assistance help to prevent and alleviate poverty? Given the historical legacy of means-tested poor relief, social assistance tends to have had a limited and ambiguous role in relation to promoting clear rights and providing relative market independence (Esping-Andersen, 1990, 1999). Even so, some scholars have argued that Nordic social assistance has tended to be comparatively generous, and hence effective, for alleviating poverty for the relatively small share of the population receiving it (Lødemel and Schulte, 1992).

Third, have institutional and other changes in Nordic social assistance promoted convergence with other advanced welfare states? Over the last two decades Nordic income protection arrangements have undergone substantial reforms. Have these social protection reforms introduced greater institutional conformity in both the set-up and outcomes of social assistance across a broader spectrum of welfare states? Whether social policy converges between countries is a continuous subject of discussion in the European Commission and among scholars (European Commission, 1998; Threlfall, 2003; Nelson, 2008, 2010a).

The chapter is structured as follows. The first section reviews earlier comparative work on Nordic social assistance and describes some major trends in the Nordic welfare states. The next section discusses available data, followed by the empirical results and a concluding discussion.

Nordic social assistance

Although social assistance shows high degrees of country-specific characteristics and substantial variation within countries (Ditch, 1999), several studies categorise countries in different groups by their organisation of minimum income benefits (Lødemel and Schulte, 1992; Leibfried, 1993; Eardley et al, 1996; Gough et al, 1997; Lødemel, 1997; Gough, 2001). For example, Gough et al (1997) identify eight different types of social assistance arrangements in the OECD (Organisation for Economic Co-operation and Development) countries, based on the extent, structure and generosity of benefits. The extent of benefits involves the relative role of social assistance in the overall system of social protection. Here Nordic social assistance was characterised as having strong residual traits, in part due to the tradition of nearly full employment and the accomplishment of an encompassing welfare state that together reduced the demand for means-tested protection. Developments in Sweden are illustrative: before the Swedish old age pension reform and the introduction of universal child benefits in the late 1940s, social assistance accounted for 16 per cent of social policy expenditure. After the reforms this share plummeted to 4 per cent (Korpi, 1975). Similar developments occurred in the other Nordic countries (see, for example, Lødemel, 1997, for Norway; and Jaakkola et al, 1994, for Finland).

The structure of social assistance refers to the legal and administrative framework, the ways of means-testing income and assets, and the degree of discretion. Characteristic for the Nordic countries was the existence of a single general scheme defined by national law, but for which local governments had the administrative responsibility. The high degree of local discretion allowed decisions concerning benefit eligibility to vary across municipalities, and sometimes even between social workers within the same social welfare agency (Minas and Stenberg, 2000). The harshness of means testing was another distinct feature, where eligibility used to be determined by both income and assets. Another peculiarity of Nordic social assistance was the close link between cash and care (Bradshaw and Terum, 1997). This integration of economic protection and treatment in Nordic social assistance is closely related to the specific target group for minimum income benefits – for a long time the very poorest of the able-bodied population (Fridberg et al, 1993). In addition to low income, many of these individuals often had multiple or complex social problems, involving, for example the combination of low income and ill health (Korpi, 1975). This composition of the traditional social assistance clientele explains why Nordic social assistance tends to be more controlled, discretionary and perhaps even more stigmatised than corresponding schemes in other countries (Lødemel, 1997).

The generosity of social assistance concerns the level of benefits and ultimately the effects of benefits on poverty. The Nordic countries shared similarities in outcomes, with low levels of income inequality and poverty and a high degree of gender equality (Kautto et al, 2001). These egalitarian structures in the Nordic welfare states are not solely the consequence of the functioning of social assistance. Perhaps more important are female labour force participation, low unemployment and the organisation of social insurance and child benefits. Nonetheless, the Nordic countries appear to have succeeded comparatively well in providing minimum income benefits to citizens in need. Gough et al (1997) ranked Denmark, Finland, Norway and Sweden among the top eight OECD countries in the early 1990s in terms of social assistance benefit levels. Nordic social assistance has also achieved comparatively high levels of redistribution. In the early 1990s, for example, social assistance in Denmark, Finland and Sweden on average reduced poverty by more than twice the amount of several other European countries (Sainsbury and Morrissens, 2002). Similar results on the level and effectiveness of Nordic social assistance appear in Nelson (2003) and Kuivalainen (2004).

While Nordic social assistance has been described as harsh and less rights-based than in several other countries, once eligibility for social assistance had been established, benefits were often of high quality and comparatively effective for alleviating poverty among benefit recipients. However, in the early 1990s, under a severe recession, the pressure on social assistance to ensure people against poverty increased. At this time social policies also underwent reform. Some of the consequent social policy changes involved cutbacks in legislated public benefits, tighter eligibility criteria for social insurance and greater reliance on means-tested benefits (Hvinden et al, 2001). The number of social assistance recipients increased the most in Finland and Sweden, where the recession was particularly deep. The Nordic countries also reinforced their orientation toward employment-promoting measures, a change partly resembling (if not inspired by) ideas usually associated with the active or inclusive welfare state (Giddens, 1998).

The reorganisation of the Nordic welfare states had some notable consequences for social assistance. In Denmark social assistance was heavily affected by reformed tax and labour market policies in the mid-1990s: the labour market reforms had strengthened the activation principles of labour market policy and tightened the eligibility criteria for membership in an unemployment insurance fund. Along with these changes, social assistance became taxable in 1994 and tied to the level of unemployment insurance. Thus, even if Nordic social assistance has always strongly focused on control, treatment and correction, elements of activation and individual moral choice have become even more prominent in the Danish system of benefits (Cox, 2001). One reason for this development might be changes in the composition of the client group, as a larger share of recipients are now seen as having low income as their primary or even sole problem. During the years of prosperity following the 1990s, activation was used also as a response to the problems of structural unemployment and shortage of labour supply (Goul Andersen, 2002).

In the 1990s principles of activation were also reinforced in Swedish social assistance, particularly in connection with young people (Johansson, 2000; Salonen, 2000; Bergmark, 2003). Similar developments occurred in Norway, primarily in connection with long-term social assistance recipients (Lorentzen and Dahl, 2005). In Finland rehabilitative working activity was introduced in 2001, and a policy of sanctions enacted against people not accepting activation offers was put forward in 1996 and further strengthened in 1998. According to Lødemel and Trickey (2001), this reinforcement of activation has altered the balance between rights and obligations in social assistance. For example, the traditional Nordic employment strategy placed less emphasis on exclusively individual factors for welfare dependency and focused on measures for stimulating both the supply and demand of labour, combined with job matching. But the renewed activation paradigm places stronger emphasis on individual responsibilities for self-support rather than on the structural determinants of poverty. Several of the 1990s measures for increasing activation in connection with social benefits appear preventive, deterring potential claimants from applying for benefits, or involving, for example, harsher assessments of availability, increased use of sanctions and wider redefinitions of what constitute 'suitable' jobs (Serrano Pascual, 2007).

Benefits have likewise been curtailed. Policy makers have cut benefits in absolute terms or the value of benefits has eroded because of so-called 'non-decisions' and an insufficient updating of benefits over the longer run (Nelson, 2010b). Due to fiscal constraints in the 1990s, several Swedish municipalities began to exclude some of the budgetary items included in the national guideline norms for the Social Welfare Allowance, whereby benefit levels were adjusted downwards in absolute terms. Although the 1998 revisions of social assistance strengthened the right to benefits by introducing nationally defined standard amounts, some budgetary items previously included in the recommendations that the National Board of Health and Welfare issue annually were excluded from the national regulations. Nonetheless, many municipalities continued to pay for these excluded budgetary items on an almost regular basis.

Finland introduced a new Social Assistance Act in 1998, lowering the level of benefits in particular for families with children. The Act also introduced a 7 per cent self-liability portion of housing costs, a policy abolished in 2006. Another major change of relevance for the provision of minimum income benefits in Finland was the 1994 introduction of a third means-tested tier in the unemployment benefit system. The new means-tested benefit was intended for young people entering the labour market for the first time and for people whose maximum period of payment for the unemployment allowance had ended.

In Denmark the introduction of taxable social assistance benefits, together with changes in housing benefits, had negative consequences for the relative income position of single people and single parents receiving benefits. The changes in Denmark were more beneficial for two-parent families who lacked work income and had no access to social insurance. The new individualised benefits entitled both parents to a benefit claim, thereby substantially improving the income position of those households. Yet both single people and two-parent families experienced absolute cuts in benefits in the mid-2000s, due to changes introduced in the calculation of housing benefits.

In addition, the localised and discretionary character of Nordic social assistance has changed. We see a trend towards centralisation and standardisation of the basic scale rates, thereby making eligibility less dependent on local and professional judgements. Finland has been a forerunner among the Nordic countries in this regard, introducing national social assistance scale rates in 1989, with a five-year transition period. Denmark tied social assistance benefits to the maximum unemployment benefit in 1994, thereby individualising social assistance. While Sweden introduced a national standard for social assistance in 1998, some budgetary items in the Swedish Social Welfare Allowance were left out of the national benefit norms and continue to be subject to the discretion of the local welfare offices. Norway strengthened its centralised coordination structures in 2001 by introducing national guideline rates for social assistance, although substantial administrative discretion in Norwegian social assistance remains, including some local resistance. Despite the Norwegian national norms having reduced local variation in social assistance benefit levels, only half the municipalities appear to comply with the national guideline rates. Both political and economic factors explain parts of this local variation (Brantzaeg et al, 2006). Thus the scope for local discretion in defining the level of benefits is greater in Norway and most restricted in Denmark and Finland, with Sweden in an intermediate position.

Finland and Denmark have also relaxed the harshness of the means test associated with social assistance, partly to facilitate transitions from benefit dependency into work. Whereas means testing in Norway and Sweden continues to be enforced in principle without tapers for work income, Finland and Denmark now exempt parts of work income from the means test as a way of increasing employment incentives.

These changes in Nordic social assistance call for a more systematised empirical investigation. The following section explains how we define and measure the extent, generosity and effects of social assistance in our analysis.

Data

We use different types of data to examine the development of Nordic social assistance. To study the extent of social assistance, we use data on social spending; to study generosity, we use data on benefit levels for stylised cases; and to study effects, we use household income data.

Although we could assess the extent of social assistance through the number of claimants, no such comparative data is available for the non-Nordic countries. Hence, we use the claimant data only for the Nordic countries, to assess whether social assistance is becoming more prominent or marginal in overall Nordic social protection. For comparisons with non-Nordic countries, we draw on the share of means-tested benefit expenditure in total social spending to analyse the extent to which these countries rely on minimum income benefits in their overall distributive systems.

Data on benefit levels are from the Social Assistance and Minimum Income Protection Interim Dataset (SaMip). SaMip includes comparable indicators reflecting the level of social assistance and related minimum income benefits available to households lacking both work income and entitlements to contributory benefits such as social insurance. It includes 34 countries and covers 1990-2009. Data in SaMip is based on a type-case approach, where benefit levels for pre-constructed families are calculated from national legislation (Nelson, 2007). SaMip uses three typical household types: a single person, a two-parent family and a single parent with two children. To increase comparability across countries with different types of systems, the minimum income benefit package includes all benefits available to low-income households: basic social assistance benefits, child benefits, housing benefits and refundable tax credits where relevant. All benefits are calculated net of taxes. The data for Norway should be treated with caution: for 1990-2000 they are based on social assistance expenditure levels disaggregated by family type and harmonised according to the 2001 national social assistance guideline rates. The harmonisation procedure has been to calculate yearly changes in expenditure levels and, for 1990-2000, to apply those change rates to the 2001 guideline rates. Using only expenditure data would clearly over-estimate the level of social assistance benefits in Norway.

Data on poverty and anti-poverty effects are from the Luxembourg Income Study (LIS), a collection of national household income surveys harmonised to enable comparative studies (see Smeeding, 2002). Researchers use the LIS datasets to analyse not only changes in poverty rates among households receiving minimum income benefits but also the ability of such benefits to alleviate poverty (the poverty reduction effect). Here we use the relative approach to measure income poverty, defining poverty as household income below 60 per cent of the median disposable equivalent income in the total population. To adjust for family size, we use the square root of household size. For some countries we cannot disaggregate the anti-poverty effect of single schemes in the LIS datasets (especially for earlier waves of income data). We therefore use the pre-constructed LIS income variable *MEANSI*, which includes all means-tested benefits that households receive. Where possible we have also used the variable *v25s1i*, which captures only general social assistance benefits, such as Income Support in the UK and *Ekonomiskt bistånd* (Economic Assistance) in Sweden.

We use standard methods to measure the anti-poverty effect of means-tested benefits by comparing the actual poverty rates to the counter-factual case of an income distribution lacking means-tested benefits. Thus, we assume that an absence of means-tested benefits has no behavioural effects. While this assumption appears unrealistic, it is a common one among scholars who assess the impact of social policy on poverty and income inequality. The relative reduction in poverty is the decline of the poverty rate after means-tested benefits are included in disposable income. The LIS dataset have income data for Denmark, Finland, Norway, Sweden, Germany, the Netherlands and the UK for various years, from the early 1990s to the mid-2000s.

To assess the changing character of Nordic social assistance, we examine two factors: trends and absolute differences between countries. Trends show the extent to which Nordic social assistance over the last two decades has followed either a unique regional path of development or an international one. Levels help assess the impact of these trends, that is, whether Nordic social assistance remains distinct. We analyse, in turn, the generosity of benefits, the extent of benefits, the prevalence of poverty, and redistribution.

The generosity of social assistance and minimum income benefits

Benefit generosity can be analysed both in absolute and relative terms. We begin this analysis by comparing the absolute value of benefits. Figure 4.1 shows the level of social assistance and minimum income benefits as averages of three family types for seven countries in 1990-2009. Benefits are expressed in US$ purchasing power parities (PPPs) and 2005 price levels. It shows that benefit levels have increased faster than prices in all the countries, particularly Germany and Norway, over the entire period. Finland and Sweden have the slowest increase rate, with the Netherlands and the UK in an intermediate position. Over time benefit levels have tended to diverge.

In 1990 the Nordic countries had the most generous benefits – above those of Germany, the Netherlands and the UK. By 2009, however, Finland and Sweden were providing less generous benefits than the three non-Nordic countries. Benefit levels are approximately the same in Germany and Denmark, and above those of the Netherlands and the UK. The decline of Swedish benefit levels in the second half of the 1990s is in part related to the 1998 Social Service Act, which changed

Figure 4.1: Levels of social assistance and minimum income benefits in US$ purchasing power parities (PPPs) and 2005 price levels (type-case data and averages of benefits for a single person, a lone parent and a two-parent family), 1990-2009

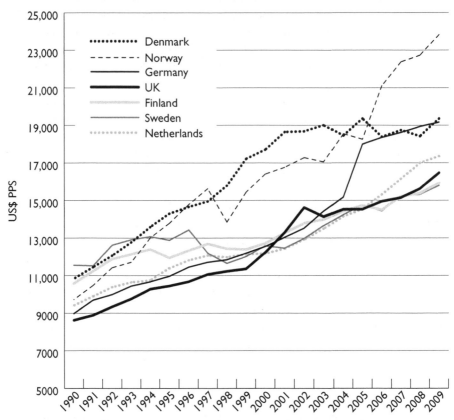

Source: SaMip

the 'basket of goods' used for benefit calculation and reduced benefits for certain items. The substantial increase in German benefit levels in 2005 is due to the Hartz IV reform, whereby the general social assistance scheme (*Sozialhilfe*) and the benefit for the long-term unemployed (*Arbeitslosenhilfe*) were replaced with a new means-tested benefit, *Arbeitslosenhilfe II*. Initially, the reform set benefits at levels slightly above those of *Sozialhilfe* but lower than the scale rates of *Arbeitslosenhilfe*.

The determinants for cross-national variation in the level of minimum income benefits and developments over time are complex, and a detailed exploration is beyond the scope of this study (see Nelson, 2006; van Mechelen, 2010). However, as different indexation mechanisms can be applied to social assistance, they can affect the analysis of the development of benefits over time, as well as (potentially) the amount of cross-country variation observed in the generosity of benefits. Although most countries use a formal adjustment mechanism to more or less automatically compensate households for increased prices and thus stabilise the purchasing power of social assistance over the longer term, governments occasionally bypass such indexation and change benefits according to ad hoc decisions (Cantillon et al, 2004). Finland, Sweden and the UK update benefits according to price development. Denmark (since the mid-1990s reforms) and the Netherlands index benefits to wages. Germany changed its indexation measures in the 1990s, so that social assistance is now partly related to changes in income and consumption patterns. However, in countries where social assistance is indexed according to wages, consumption or living standards, the benchmark is often set among the lower socioeconomic strata (Nelson, 2008).

Due to these practices for indexation, the relative value of social assistance benefits often has a tendency to decline over time. Even though benefits have increased faster than prices, both wages and living standards have generally increased even faster, thus placing beneficiaries in a more precarious position in the overall income distribution. One way of exploring this relative aspect of minimum income benefits is to relate the benefit package of low-income households to median incomes, where median incomes is strongly influenced by wage development. Figure 4.2 shows such adequacy rates of social assistance and minimum income benefits for 1990-2008. The adequacy rate is the equivalised level of benefits for the three typical family types as shares of the median disposable equivalent income in total population. We use the square root scale to standardise income to household size.

As Figure 4.2 shows, over the period 1990-2008 benefit adequacy decreased the most in Sweden, followed, in order, by the Netherlands, Denmark, Finland and last, the UK. The Norwegian path is more stable, especially since the late 1990s, with a slight overall increase of benefit adequacy. Germany also shows a modest increase of benefit adequacy over the period, a development that may relate to the overall design of social protection in Continental European countries with corporatist social policy structures. Some believe that corporatist social policy systems are particularly resistant to cutbacks and decline (Esping-Andersen, 1996), in part due to the involvement of the social partners in managing the schemes (Bonoli and Palier, 2000). Although social insurance replacement rates declined less in continental European countries than elsewhere in Western Europe from 1980-2000 (Montanari et al, 2008), whether the resilience of first-tier schemes spread to second-tier assistance benefits is beyond the scope of this chapter. Nonetheless, the German adequacy rates clearly fluctuate considerably over time. Since the sharp increase of benefit adequacy following the Harz IV reform, the relative value of benefits also drops substantially.

The low adequacy rates of Nordic minimum income benefits raise some concern in connection with the redistributive consequences of social assistance, another aspect of the Nordic welfare model sometimes highlighted in international comparisons. For example, in the early 1990s Sweden was one of the few European countries that provided benefits above the European Union (EU) 'at risk of poverty' threshold of 60 per cent of median disposable income. By 2008 Sweden has joined the rest of Europe by providing benefits clearly below that threshold (Nelson, 2010b). Similar but less marked developments characterise Denmark and

Figure 4.2: Adequacy of social assistance and minimum income benefits (type-case data and averages of a single person, a lone parent and a two-parent family), 1990-2008

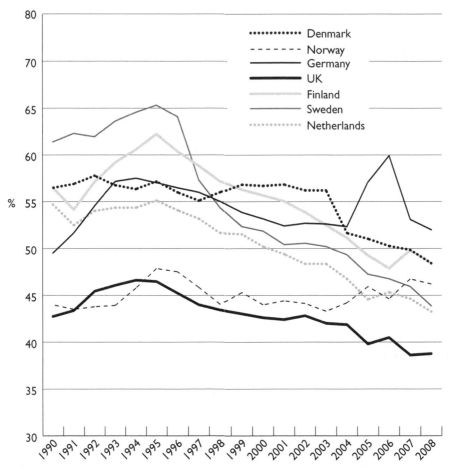

Note: Adequacy is defined as the level of the equivalised benefit as percentage of the level of equivalised median income in total population.

Source: SaMip

Finland. By 2008 Nordic social assistance reached levels only between 44 and 48 per cent of median disposable income. The Norwegian income levels made benefit adequacy quite moderate, that is, below 50 per cent of median disposable income throughout the entire period.

While predicting how benefit adequacy will develop over the coming years is difficult, the 2008 financial crisis may eventually cause benefit adequacy to increase, particularly if wage increases slow down and inflation continues to be low. The development of benefit adequacy in the early 1990s illustrates such a scenario. The adequacy of benefits in Finland, Norway and Sweden improved during much of the economic downturn of the early 1990s, an improvement largely attributable to the low inflation and the slowdown of wage increases during those years, rather than due to improvements in the basic rates of benefits per se. Similar developments have occurred in Germany and the UK in the first half of the 1990s, whereas Denmark and the Netherlands have shown a more stable path over these years.

In terms of absolute and purchasing power-adjusted benefit levels, the Nordic group appears on the verge of disappearing. Although benefits in Denmark and Norway are still generous (also by international standards), Germany, the Netherlands and the UK score better than Finland and Sweden. When we evaluate benefits in relative terms and in relation to median incomes, the Nordic countries appear more similar, even though Swedish adequacy rates have deteriorated substantially. In the ranking of adequacy rates the Nordic countries fall somewhere between Germany and the Netherlands, with the UK clearly lagging behind.

The extent of social assistance and means-tested benefits

Now we turn to the extent of social assistance and means-tested benefits, something that we begin to analyse in terms of social benefit expenditure. Figure 4.3 shows the development of means-tested benefit expenditure as a share of total social benefit expenditure for 1990-2008. Finding any clear common trend in the development of means-tested benefit expenditure is difficult, although the role of means-tested benefits in the overall system of social protection to a varying extent appears to vary over the business cycle. One example is Sweden, where the share of means-tested benefit expenditure increased with the financial crisis of the early 1990s. Another example is Finland, where the share of means-tested benefit expenditure increased in the mid-1990s when unemployment assistance was introduced.

The share of means-tested benefit expenditure also increased in the UK in the early 1990s, followed by a continuous decline until the 2000s, when the share of expenditure stagnated. This downward trend in the second half of the 1990s is likely attributable to a reduced demand for means-tested benefits and a greater enforcement of activation requirements that have had a deterrent effect on claim making. In Germany the share of means-tested benefit expenditure has been on the rise throughout almost the entire period, predominantly in the first half of the 1990s and in the 2000s. Unification and mass unemployment can explain part of this increase (Leibfried and Obinger 2003), whereas additional factors are necessary for providing a more complete explanation for the entire period.

The share of means-tested benefit expenditure continues to be comparatively low in the Nordic countries, despite increases during parts of the period. This share varies between around 3 per cent in Sweden and 4 per cent in Finland, with Denmark and Norway in intermediate positions. The share of means-tested benefit expenditure in the non-Nordic countries varies between 8 and 12 per cent.

Expenditure gives only a partial description of the extent of benefits. Another factor is caseloads, for example, measured in terms of the share of social assistance

Figure 4.3: Means-tested benefit expenditure as a percentage of total social benefit expenditure in different countries, 1990-2008

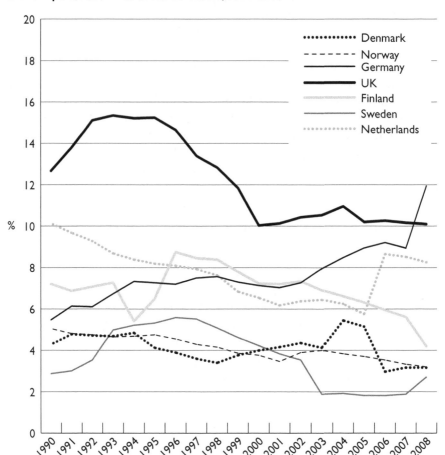

Source: Eurostat

beneficiaries in the total population. According to this indicator (not shown here), social assistance has not become more important in the Nordic countries. The share of social assistance beneficiaries has varied the most in Finland and Sweden, where substantial increases occurred during the economic crisis of the early 1990s, followed by significant drops in subsequent years. By 2009 the beneficiary ratio in Finland was back at the level of nearly 6 per cent observed for 1990, whereas the Swedish rate had declined from 5 per cent in 1990 to slightly less than 4 per cent in 2009. Similar downward trends can be observed for Denmark and Norway, where the share of social assistance beneficiaries in 2009 was about 4 and 3 per cent, respectively. The greater share of beneficiaries in Finland is due to institutional reforms in the first half of the 1990s, whereby social assistance gradually became a top-up to the basic unemployment benefit and unemployment assistance (OECD, 1998).

Poverty and redistribution

The first trend in outcomes to be monitored is poverty among beneficiaries. Figure 4.4 shows the poverty rate among recipients of means-tested benefits at four years between the early 1990s and mid-2000s. The poverty rate increased in the Nordic countries over the period, with the most dramatic development in Norway, where the poverty rate increased from 17 to 43 per cent between 1991 and 2004. The poverty rate in the other Nordic countries was around 35 per cent in the mid-2000s. Some notable differences exist between the Nordic countries, especially in the early 1990s, when the poverty rate increased in Norway, declined in Denmark and Sweden, and remained almost stable in Finland. At least for Sweden, one possible explanation is that the economic crisis led to a lowering of the level of the median income, thereby counteracting any poverty increases among the recipients of means-tested benefits. In the second half of the

Figure 4.4: Poverty rates among recipients of means-tested benefits at four-year intervals, 1990-2005

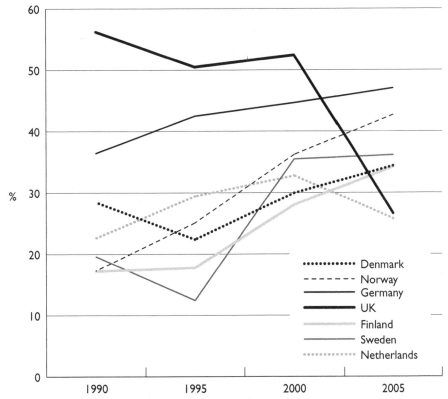

Note: Denmark (1992, 1995, 2000, 2004), Finland (1991, 1995, 2000, 2004), Germany (1989, 1994, 2000, 2004), The Netherlands (1991, 1994, 2000, 2004), Norway (1991, 1995, 2000, 2004), Sweden (1992, 1995, 2000, 2004) and the UK (1991, 1995, 2000, 2004),

Source: LIS

1990s, when their economies had improved, both Denmark and Sweden show the increasing trend observed in the other Nordic countries.

Poverty rates, as Figure 4.4 shows, also increased in Germany and the Netherlands over the period, whereas developments in the UK diverged from this general pattern. In the UK the poverty rate dropped from 52 per cent in 1999 to 27 per cent in 2004. This extraordinary development results not from changes in general social assistance benefits (particularly Income Support and Jobseeker's Allowance) but rather from a complex set of factors. One example is the introduction of various forms of in-work tax credits, which are accessible to low-income workers and to parts of the traditional UK social assistance clientele. The first wave of such in-work benefits in the UK occurred in 1999, with a second wave in 2003. For the UK we can disaggregate the analysis further, to include only those households that receive general social assistance benefits. The poverty rate among this narrower group has not similarly declined. To the contrary, the poverty rate among UK recipients of general social assistance benefits has remained stable since the mid-1990s. Approximately every second recipient of general social assistance benefits in the UK can be defined as poor (not shown here).

The second trend in outcomes to be analysed is redistribution, measured in terms of poverty alleviation linked to means-tested benefits. Figure 4.5 shows the share of poverty reduction attributed to means-tested benefits among beneficiaries between the early-1990s and the mid-2000s. In the first half of the 1990s, poverty alleviation generally increased in the Nordic countries, with the exception of Norway, where effectiveness somewhat declined. Poverty alleviation throughout the period has been the lowest in Norway among the Nordic countries, a development again indicating that comparatively high median incomes make the relative value of Norwegian benefits less impressive.

As Figure 4.5 shows, means-tested benefits have become less effective in reducing poverty among the Nordic countries since the mid-1990s. In Finland the effectiveness of means-tested benefits in reducing poverty decreased by more than one third, from 51 per cent to about 32 per cent. Effectiveness also substantially declined in Denmark and Sweden, whereas Norway had a more modest decline. Similar results appear when we measure the anti-poverty effectiveness of means-tested benefits in the total population, with the analysis producing somewhat lower reduction coefficients. The trend among the non-Nordic countries since the mid-1990s is the opposite of that of the Nordic countries, with increased anti-poverty effectiveness of means-tested benefits. In the early-1990s poverty alleviation in the Nordic countries was either more substantial or on a par with the levels for the non-Nordic countries. By the mid-2000s the pattern is more mixed, with the greatest reduction of poverty in Denmark, followed (in order) by the Netherlands, Sweden, the UK, Finland, Germany and Norway.

In sum the poverty rate among beneficiaries of means-tested benefits in the Nordic countries has increased and anti-poverty effectiveness has been reduced. These developments largely differ from the pattern observed for the non-Nordic countries, leading to convergence cross-nationally. However, one should

Figure 4.5: Percentage reduction of poverty attributed to means-tested benefits at four-year intervals, 1990-2005

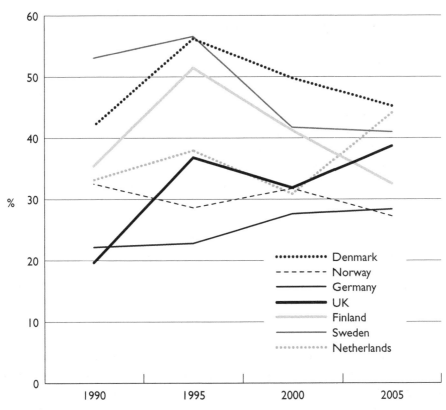

Note: Denmark (1992, 1995, 2000, 2004), Finland (1991, 1995, 2000, 2004), Germany (1989, 1994, 2000, 2004), The Netherlands (1991, 1994, 2000, 2004), Norway (1991, 1995, 2000, 2004), Sweden (1992, 1995, 2000, 2004) and the UK (1991, 1995, 2000, 2004),

Source: LIS

be careful about linking the poverty alleviation effect of means-tested benefits to the organisation of social assistance. One reason is that the final distribution achieved by the social transfer system depends on a number of factors, such as labour market behaviour, demographic patterns and the coverage and distribution of social insurance provision and family benefits. Nonetheless, the results for the four Nordic countries match expectations derived from the previous institutional analysis, with improved or stable adequacy rates in the first half of the 1990s and reduced adequacy thereafter.

Conclusion

This chapter has compared developments in social assistance and minimum income benefits in the Nordic countries from the early 1990s to the end of 2010 with those of other countries, with a particular focus on institutional characteristics and outcomes. We asked whether Nordic social assistance had departed from its traditional hallmarks of the encompassing, universalist Nordic welfare state, according to which typology social assistance plays a residual role in the overall welfare state machinery, paying out generous benefits that are effective for alleviating poverty. Thus our question was whether Nordic social assistance still differs from that of other European countries in terms of three factors: the extent of benefits in the overall system of social protection, the levels of benefits provided and poverty outcomes.

Despite some differences between the Nordic countries, we show that overall the adequacy and effectiveness of benefits in reducing poverty have declined, and that poverty among beneficiaries has increased. The extent of social assistance showed less visible trends. In terms of benefit generosity and poverty outcomes Nordic social assistance has moved closer to international patterns, and the classification of Nordic social assistance into a separate model of social welfare is no longer as distinct as 20 years ago.

Our empirical analyses provide enough evidence for concern about the present state of the Nordic welfare model and the experiences of the most vulnerable share of the Nordic population. On most, if not all, dimensions analysed here, the situation in the Nordic countries has deteriorated. We can, of course, find positive sides to these recent developments in social assistance in the Nordic countries. The introduction of national social assistance standards or national guideline norms has made benefits more rights-based, and the high degrees of local discretion that used to characterise Nordic social assistance has declined. However, in terms of benefit levels and effectiveness, the development has been less positive.

The 2008 financial crisis gives us a good reason for reconsidering the redistributive strategies of the Nordic welfare states. Projections indicate that high unemployment rates are not going away. Lessons learned from the economic downturn in the early 1990s show that high unemployment rates may last even beyond 2015. Consequently, we expect the demand for social protection to be high. In this scenario social assistance is an important safeguard for people who slip through the net of first-tier benefits – the younger and the long-term unemployed, that is, people with a weaker foothold in the labour market and insufficient contribution records. To provide a more effective system of redistribution, the Nordic governments need to develop strategies for improving the adequacy of social assistance and minimum income benefits. This chapter has shown that current benefit levels do not provide enough money for families to escape poverty. If the deterioration of benefits continues, the Nordic countries will most likely experience poverty rates of a similar magnitude to those in several other Liberal and Corporatist welfare states. This increase of inequality means that one of the most significant hallmarks of the Nordic welfare states will disappear.

References

Bergmark, Å. (2003) 'Activated to work? Activation policies in Sweden in the 1990s', *Revue Française des Affaires Sociales*, vol 4, no 4, pp 291-306.

Bonoli. G. and Palier, B. (2000) 'How do welfare states change? Institutions and their impact on the politics of welfare state reform in Western Europe', *European Review*, vol 8, no 3, pp 333-52.

Bradshaw, J.R. and Terum, L.I. (1997) 'How Nordic is the Nordic model? Social assistance in a comparative perspective', *Scandinavian Journal of Social Welfare*, vol 6, pp 247-56.

Brantzaeg, B., Flermoen, S., Lunder, E.L., Løyland, K., Møller, G. and Sannes, J. (2006) *Fastsetting av satser, utmåling av økonomisk sosialhjelp og vilkårsbruk i sosialtjenesten* [*Setting of rates and payments for social assistance and the use of conditions in social services*], Rapport nr 232, Telemark: Telemarksforskin-BØ.

Cantillon, B., Marx, I., van den Bosch, K. and van Mechelen, N. (2004) *The evolution of minimum income protection in 15 European countries 1992-2001*, Antwerpen: Centrum voor Sociaal Beleid Herman Deleeck.

Cox, R.H. (2001) 'The social construction of an imperative: why welfare reform happened in Denmark and the Netherlands but not in Germany', *World Politics*, vol 53, no 3, pp 463-98.

Ditch, J. (1999) 'Full circle: a second coming for social assistance', in J. Clasen (ed) *Comparative social policy: Concepts, theories and method*, Oxford: Blackwell, pp 114-35.

Eardley, T., Bradshaw, J., Ditch, J., Gough, I. and Whiteford, P. (1996) *Social assistance in OECD countries: Volume I Synthesis reports*, DSS Research Report No 46. London: HMSO.

Esping-Andersen, G. (1990) *Three worlds of welfare capitalism*, Cambridge: Polity Press.

Esping-Andersen, G. (1996) *Welfare states in transition. National adaptions in global economies*, London: Sage Publications.

Esping-Andersen, G. (1999) *Social foundations of postindustrial economies*, Oxford: University Press.

European Commission (1998) *Report on the implementation of the Recommendation 92/441/EEC of 24 June 1992 on common criteria concerning sufficient resources and social assistance in social protection systems. Commission report to the Council, European Parliament, Economic and Social Committee, and Committee of the Regions. COM (98) 774 Final*, Brussels: European Commission.

Fridberg, T., Halvarson, K., Hove, O., Julkunen, I., Marklund, S. and Tanninen, T. (1993) *On social assistance in the Nordic capitals*, Copenhagen: Danish National Institute for Social Research.

Giddens, A. (1998) *The third way. The renewal of social democracy*, Cambridge: Polity Press.

Gough, I. (2001) 'Social assistance: a cluster analysis', *Journal of European Social Policy*, vol 11, no 2, pp 165-70.

Gough, I., Bradshaw, J., Eardley, T. and Whiteford, P. (1997) 'Social assistance in OECD countries', *Journal of European Social Policy*, vol 7, no 1, pp 17-43.

Goul Andersen, J. (2002) 'Work and citizenship: unemployment and unemployment policies in Denmark, 1980-2000', in J. Goul Andersen and P.H. Jensen (eds) *Changing labour markets, welfare policies and citizenship*, Bristol: The Policy Press, pp 59-84.

Hvinden, B., Heikkilä, M. and Kankare, I. (2001) 'Towards activation? The changing relationship between social protection and employment in Western Europe', in M. Kautto et al (eds) *Nordic welfare states in the European context*, London: Routledge, pp 168-97.

Jaakkola, J., Pulma, P., Satka, M. and Urponen, K. (eds) (1994) *Armeliaisuus, yhteisöapu, sosiaaliturva. Suomalaisen sosiaalisen turvan historia [Mercifulness, local support, social security. History of the Finnish social security]*, Helsinki: Sosiaaliturvan keskusliitto.

Johansson, H. (2000) *Ungdomar med socialbidrag – ett politiskt problem för 1990-talet [Youth on Social Assistance – a political problem for the 1990s]*, SOU 2000:40, Stockholm: Fritzes.

Kautto, M., Fritzell, J., Hvinden, B., Kvist, J. and Uusitalo, H. (eds) (2001) *Nordic welfare states in the European context*, London: Routledge.

Korpi, W. (1975) 'Poverty, social assistance and social policy in postwar Sweden', *Acta Sociologica*, vol 18, no 2-3, pp 120-41.

Korpi, W. and Palme, J. (1998) 'The paradox of redistribution and strategies of equality: welfare state institutions, inequality and poverty in the Western countries', *American Sociological Review*, vol 63, no 5, pp 661-87.

Kuivalainen, S. (2004) *A comparative study on last resort social assistance schemes in six European countries*, Research Report 146, Helsinki: Stakes.

Leibfried, S. (1993) 'Towards a European welfare state', in C. Jones (ed) *New perspectives on the welfare state in Europe*, London: Routledge, pp 245-79.

Leibfried, S. and Obinger, H. (2003) 'The state of the welfare state: German social policy between macroeconomic retrenchment and microeconomic recalibration', *West European Politics*, vol 26, no 4, pp 199-218.

Lorentzen, T. and Dahl, A. (2005) 'Active labour market programmes in Norway: are they helpful for social assistance recipients?', *Journal of European Social Policy*, vol 15, no 1, pp 27-45.

Lødemel, I. (1997) *The welfare paradox: Income maintenance and personal social services in Norway and Britain, 1946-1966*, Oslo: Scandinavian University Press.

Lødemel, I. and Schulte, B. (1992) 'Social assistance: a part of social security or the Poor Law in new disguise?', in European Institute of Social Research (ed) *Reforms in Eastern and Central Europe: Beveridge 50 years after*, Leuven: Acco, pp 515-38.

Lødemel, I. and Trickey, H. (2001) *An offer you can't refuse: Workfare in international perspective*, Bristol: The Policy Press.

Marshall, T.H. (1950) *Citizenship and social class*, Cambridge: Cambridge University Press.

Minas, R. and Stenberg, S.-Å. (2000) 'På tröskeln till bidrag. Mottagningen av nya socialbidragsansökningar på sju socialkontor i Sverige', CUS-skrift 2000:1, Socialstyrelsen, Stockholm.

Montanari, I., Nelson, K. and Palme, J. (2008) 'Towards a European social model? Trends in social insurance among EU countries 1980-2000', *European Societies*, vol 10, no 5, pp 787-810.

Nelson, K. (2003) *Fighting poverty, comparative studies on social insurance, means-tested benefits and income redistribution*, Stockholm: Swedish Institute for Social Research.

Nelson, K. (2006) 'The last resort: determinants of the generosity of means-tested minimum income protection policies in welfare democracies', in E. Carroll and L. Ericsson (eds) *Welfare politics cross-examined: Eclecticist analytical perspectives on Sweden and on the developed world*, Amsterdam: Aksel Atland Printers, pp 85-116.

Nelson, K. (2007) *Introducing SaMip: The Social Assistance and Minimum Income Protection interim dataset*, S-WoPEc No 11/2007, Stockholm: Swedish Institute for Social Research.

Nelson, K. (2008) 'Minimum income protection and European integration: trends and levels of minimum benefits in comparative perspective 1990-2005', *International Journal of Health Services*, vol 38, no 1, pp 103-24.

Nelson, K. (2010a) 'Social assistance and minimum income benefits in old and new EU democracies', *International Journal of Social Welfare*, vol 19, no 4, pp 367-78.

Nelson, K. (2010b) 'Social assistance and EU poverty thresholds 1990-2008. Are European welfare systems providing just and fair protection against low income?', Forthcoming in *European Sociological Review*.

OECD (Organisation for Economic Co-operation and Development) (1998) *The battle against exclusion. Social assistance in Australia, Finland, Sweden and the United Kingdom*, Paris: OECD.

Rawls, J. (1971) *A theory of justice*, Cambridge, MA: Harvard University Press.

Sainsbury, D. and Morrissens, A. (2002) 'Poverty in Europe in the mid-1990s: the effectiveness of means-tested benefits', *Journal of European Social Policy*, vol 12, no 4, pp 307-28.

Salonen, T. (2000) *Ungdomars socialbidragstagande och försörjningsvårigheter under 1990-talet* [*Social assistance receipts and economic hardships among young people during the 1990s*], SOU 2000:40, Stockholm: Fritzes.

Serrano Pascual, A. (2007) 'Reshaping welfare states: activation regimes in Europe', in A. Serrano Pascual and L. Magnusson (eds) *Reshaping welfare states and activation regimes in Europe*, Brussels: P.I.E. Peter Lang, pp 11-34.

Smeeding, T. (2002) *The LIS/LES Project: Overview and recent developments*, Luxembourg Income Study Working Paper No 294. Luxembourg: Luxembourg Income Study.

Threlfall, M. (2003) 'European social integration: harmonization, convergence and single social areas', *Journal of European Social Policy*, vol 13, no 2, pp 121-39.

van Mechelen, N. (2010) *Barriers to adequate social safety nets*, Antwerpen: Universiteit Antwerpen.

FIVE

Equality in the social service state: Nordic childcare models in comparative perspective

Gabrielle Meagher and Marta Szebehely

Introduction

The Nordic countries are renowned for high levels of both equality and tax-funded social service provision. Equality and services are linked by the roles that extensive provision of services plays in enabling women's labour market participation and in ensuring that the capacity to pay does not determine access to services. The connection between institutional structures and equality achievements led Jorma Sipilä to argue in the mid-1990s that social care services are the key to the Scandinavian welfare model. Although Sipilä's argument has since been challenged (see, for example, Rauch, 2007), any reassessment of the Nordic welfare model would not be comprehensive without some analysis of social services.

   This chapter examines the place of childcare in the Nordic welfare model since the 1990s. We recognise that a more encompassing assessment of social services as a *system* would include care of older people and those with disabilities, and would reveal complex patterns of differential development between care fields (Anttonen et al, 2003; Rauch, 2007). However, as such a comprehensive analysis is beyond the scope of this chapter, we focus on change in the organisation and distribution of childcare and related measures in the four largest Nordic countries. We also use data from the European Union Statistics on Income and Living Conditions (EU-SILC) to compare the Nordic situation to developments in other European countries with different family policy systems. Our aims are to understand whether and, if so, how policy-induced shifts in the boundaries between the state, market and family have affected social groups differently and to assess the equality achievements and challenges of the Nordic model from a comparative perspective.

Childcare and equality: making the links

Tax-funded services certainly lie at the centre of the Nordic response to family needs for support in caring for children, as Sipilä suggests. However, in Nordic countries and elsewhere, other policy measures also contribute to meeting care needs. The scale, design and mix of these other measures, along with childcare services, together determine the overall equality outcomes of family policies. In addition to services, which provide directly for care needs, governments use one or more of the following measures to make provision for care: monetary benefits, employment-related benefits and incentives for employment creation or market provision (Daly, 2002). This chapter focuses on two of these measures: services and financial benefits (specifically, care allowances).

Along with attention to the choice and design of measures for meeting care needs, the influence of political structure on policy settings and equality outcomes is also important. In the Nordic countries, for example, the division of financing between state and municipal government can affect policy decision making at the local level, and we discuss these effects where relevant.

Policies for meeting the care needs of families with children can play an important role in promoting class and gender equality and equality between ethnic groups. The extent to which policy institutions reduce inequality depends on the extent to which measures are (a) universal (that is, accessible to all citizens according to need), thereby reducing inequalities arising from differential access to economic resources, and (b) promote defamilialisation (that is, relieve family members of care obligations), thereby reducing care-related inequalities (Rauch, 2007, drawing on Lister, 2003, among others). Policies may be universal, defamilialising or both, and combinations of the two dimensions correspond reasonably well with Walter Korpi's typology of gender policy institutions (2000; later developed by Ferrarini, 2006). Systems in which policies are both universal and defamilialising offer what Korpi (2000) calls 'dual-earner support'; those that are universal but not defamilialising tend to offer 'general family support'; and those that are neither universal nor defamilialising tend to be 'market oriented'. In turn, institutional types, and policy settings within them, promote or reduce inequalities of class and gender.

Thus, as a measure for promoting *gender* equality, universal childcare services can promote defamilialisation by enabling high levels of female labour force participation (Korpi, 2000; Mahon, 2002; Lister, 2009; Plantenga and Remery, 2009; de Henau et al, 2010). Childcare can also promote *class* equality, broadly defined, by two different mechanisms. First, by enabling high labour force participation among mothers, particularly lone mothers, universal childcare can significantly reduce child poverty and the associated risks to child development and well-being (Ferrarini and Duvander, 2010). Second, as children spend more time in centres where family differences in cultural capital are not reproduced, high-quality universal childcare can reduce the impact of parents' social status on their children's futures (Esping-Andersen, 2005).

Several recent studies confirm the positive effects of participation in high quality childcare, especially for children from disadvantaged families (Swedish National Institute of Public Health, 2009). Moreover, the benefits may not be short-lived: Norwegian research on the long-term effects of childcare has found that, overall, attendance has 'strong positive effects' on educational attainment, labour market participation and reduced welfare dependency, with positive effects particularly pronounced for children of low-educated mothers (Havnes and Mogstad, 2009). In the same vein, attendance at childcare can promote *ethnic* equality by supporting the educational integration of children from immigrant families, thereby reducing educational gaps that contribute to inequality (Ferrarini and Duvander, 2010). One recent Swedish study found that attendance at childcare centres significantly narrowed the language gap between immigrant and native-born children (Hall et al, 2010). To fulfil their potential for reducing inequalities of gender, class and ethnicity, universally available services need to be of high quality so that they are attractive to most parents, irrespective of social position, and affordable for poorer parents.

Employment-related benefits, such as parental (or other) care leave or reduction of workhours, provide time to family care-givers. The consequences for gender and class equality are related to the length of the leave and compensation level, as well as whether certain segments of the leave are earmarked for mothers or fathers (see, for example, Leira, 2006).

Care allowances for parents are typically flat-rate monetary benefits offered in lieu of a publicly funded childcare place for children under three years of age. Parents can use a care allowance as an (inevitably partial) replacement for labour income after parental leave entitlements are exhausted or (if programme design permits) for purchasing private childminding services. In general, policy analysts regard such cash benefits as moves to refamilialisation with a strongly gendered impact: care allowances tend to decrease female labour force participation because care at home for children is overwhelmingly provided by mothers (Mahon, 2002; Leira, 2006; Lister, 2009; Sipilä et al, 2010). Further, because payment rates of care allowance are typically lower than wages, they are more attractive to low-income families (although not to lone parents), among which immigrant families are over-represented. Hence, care allowances are likely to increase gender, class and ethnic inequalities (Ferrarini, 2006; Lister, 2009; Ferrarini and Duvander, 2010).

In the childcare domain, incentives for employment creation or market provision take a variety of forms, such as vouchers, subsidies for social security costs or tax rebates for private purchases. The equality impacts of this class of measures are somewhat sensitive to programme design, for example, the extent to which benefits meet the real costs of purchases or the extent to which voucher systems permit consumers to top up the public contribution with personal funds. Overall, however, the logic of marketisation is towards increasing inequality among service users, as the capacity to pay determines the amount and quality of services received. Market promoting measures can also promote inequality on the supply side of childcare provision, through creation of poor quality jobs for childcare workers (Mahon, 2002).

Care for children in Nordic countries

The Nordic countries have a long-standing commitment to meeting the childcare needs of all parents. The main measures have been provision of tax-funded services after a relatively long and generous parental leave and, in some countries, monetary benefits, primarily in the form of home childcare allowances (HCA).

Today, all Nordic countries except Iceland give parents the legal right to tax-funded childcare (Eydal and Rostgaard, 2011). Finland was the first to introduce a service guarantee for preschool as part of a larger political compromise in 1984. The Social Democrats argued for childcare services while the Centre and National Coalition parties argued for cash-for-care benefits. The resulting legislation combined two different care rights: municipal childcare services and a HCA for children under three (Repo, 2010). The next country to introduce a childcare guarantee was Sweden, in 1995, when a Social Democratic government obligated municipalities to provide full-time childcare to all children between the ages of one and twelve if their parents were working or studying. The guarantee was extended to include 15 hours of childcare a week to children of unemployed parents in 2001 and to children whose parents are on parental leave with a younger sibling in 2002. Thus the legal right to childcare in Sweden is still not fully universal (Szebehely, 2005).

Similar but more encompassing policies were enacted in Denmark in 1999, when a Social Democrat-led government prompted the Danish municipalities to guarantee a childcare place for all children from the age of six months (Rauch, 2007, p 254). While Norway was a laggard in this respect, in 2008 a Social Democrat-led coalition introduced an individual right to childcare for children one year or older, starting in 2009 (Norwegian Government, 2008).

By the end of the first decade of the new millennium, in Denmark, Norway and Sweden participation in childcare by children aged two years is very high, and for three- to five-year-olds, it is basically universal. Nonetheless, despite service guarantees, participation in childcare is not universal in all Nordic countries (see Table 5.1).

Moreover, the pace of development of provision has differed between the Nordic countries. Coverage rates remain considerably lower in Finland than elsewhere.

Table 5.1: Children in childcare, Nordic countries, percentage of different age groups, 2009

	Denmark	Finland	Norway	Sweden
0 years	15.1	0.90	4.40	0.00
1 year	88.0	29.0	69.8	49.5
2 years	92.4	50.3	85.8	90.9
3 years	97.6	67.1	96.1	95.0
4 years	97.5	73.5	97.0	97.7
5 years	95.1	77.1	97.9	98.0

Source: Nordic Statistics (2010)

Figure 5.1, which presents changing participation for children aged one to five since 1990, shows that participation in Norway also lagged well behind Denmark and Sweden until very recently.

Previous studies have analysed in detail the differential development of childcare services in Nordic countries (Rauch, 2005, 2007; Ellingsæter and Leira, 2006; Ellingsæter and Gulbrandsen, 2007; Eydal and Rostgaard, 2011). This chapter highlights three notable differences or changes: the current variance in the rates of participation of children under three years; the convergence in overall rates of childcare participation in Denmark, Norway and Sweden from 1990-2009; and the relatively low rates of participation in Finland. These differences are related to the interaction of childcare policies with other family policy measures (including employment-related benefits and monetary benefits). Other factors include political structures (especially state–municipality relationships), the institutional structure of the childcare sector (especially the role of non-government providers) and the nature and extent of labour market opportunities for women.

We can largely explain current differences in participation rates among infants to one-year-olds in Denmark, Norway and Sweden by the interaction of direct childcare service provision and employment-related benefits, in the form of parental leave entitlements. The period of paid parental leave in Sweden is longer than that in Norway or Denmark, and in Denmark the municipalities are obliged to offer daycare places to all children from the age of 26 weeks, whereas in Sweden places are offered from the age of one year (NOSOSCO, 2009, p 55).[1] These differences explain the much higher rates of participation in childcare

Figure 5.1: Childcare coverage, children aged 1-5, Nordic countries, 1990-2009

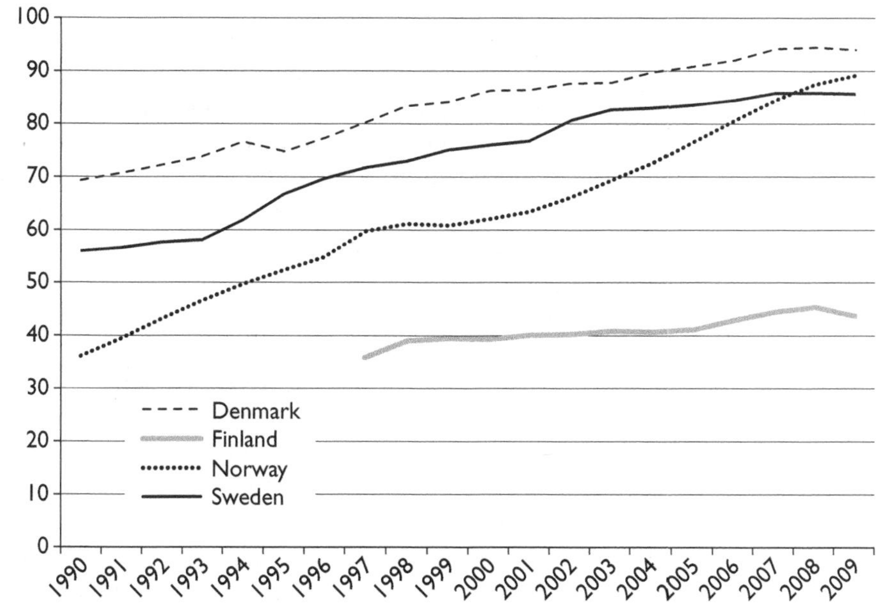

Source: Nordic Statistics (2010)

among Danish infants under one, and the absence of infants and the lower level of participation by one-year-olds in Sweden. In Finland, as we discuss later, interaction between childcare provision and a financial benefit – specifically, the HCA – is also critical to explaining the relatively low uptake among children under three. As Norway did not catch up until later and Finland took a different turn altogether, the next two subsections discuss these two countries separately.

Norway: a laggard catching up

In 2002, participation by Norwegian one- and two-year-olds stood at 30 and 51 per cent respectively, compared to 72 and 84 per cent in Denmark, and 45 and 85 per cent in Sweden (Nordic Statistics, 2010). In 2009, as Table 5.1 shows, participation of Norwegian children had grown to 70 per cent for one-year-olds and 86 per cent for two-year-olds. Given the prevalence of the idea of a common model in the Nordic countries – and the critique of this idea (Ellingsæter and Leira, 2006; Rauch, 2007) – both the lag and the catching up in Norway need explanation.

The slower rate of development of Norwegian childcare has generally been attributed to two ways in which it differs from Sweden and Denmark. First is the relative lack of coordination of economic policies with social policies in Norway, compared with Sweden and Denmark (Leira, 1993). In Norway, policy has emphasised only the social-pedagogical role of childcare (Leira, 1993; Ellingsæter and Gulbrandsen, 2007), while in Sweden and Denmark, childcare has always been understood *both* as a social-pedagogical measure for the benefit of children *and* as a support for maternal employment that fosters gender equality. Levels of public spending on childcare were also lower in Norway than in Denmark and Sweden, especially during the 1970s and 1980s (Rauch, 2005).

Second is the dominant role of conservative non-government organisations in Norwegian childcare services during the 1970s, 1980s and 1990s, in the context of relatively weak steering by and support from the central state of municipal provision (Rauch, 2005). These organisations, which promoted a child-focused rationale for childcare services, tended to offer part-time care in line with their conservative values. The combination of ideological resistance to full-time childcare among a large proportion of provider organisations and significant opportunities for municipalities to resist central state demands to develop services held back the development of Norwegian childcare.

More recently, however, the childcare gap in Norway has closed, as the result of positive feedback effects between the rising provision of and the rising demand for public childcare. Even before the Social Democrats introduced the childcare guarantee in 2009, a broad political compromise in 2003 during the previous Right-Centre government had led to parliament setting a goal of full childcare coverage, encouraged by a maximum fee reform and increased state subsidies (Norwegian Government, 2008). On the demand side, according to Ellingsæter and Gulbrandsen (2007, p 663), 'a radical shift in cultural ideas of motherhood and early childhood' has occurred in Norway since the 1980s, so that centre-based childcare has become parents' most preferred form of non-parental care. This shift is the consequence of rising education and employment opportunities for women, both of which have combined with a growing supply of high quality childcare to underpin increasingly supportive attitudes to childcare among successive cohorts of mothers of preschool children. If centre-based care has become the preferred option, then there is no longer any conflict between a child-focused rationale and support for parental employment.

Finland: new familialism?

Relatively low participation in childcare in Finland is attributable to feedback effects between ideas, preferences, policies and economic realities. One crucial policy measure has been the HCA, introduced in 1984 by the previously mentioned political compromise between the Social Democrats and two Right-Centre parties. This compromise combined a legal entitlement to childcare with the right to a care allowance for those who do not take up a childcare place at the end of the period of parental leave (Leira, 2006; Repo, 2010). The allowance has quickly become popular, and a majority of families use the allowance instead of childcare services when the child is one or two years old. In 2006, the allowance was used by 57 per cent of children aged nine months to two years (Plantenga and Remery, 2009, p 60).

In 2010, the national rate of this taxable allowance was set at €314 per month (Kela, 2010). As municipalities are able to top up the national rate, many do so to reduce the demands for the more costly municipal daycare (Plantenga and Remery, 2009, p 60). Finnish municipalities have a stronger incentive to do so than those in Sweden and Denmark, because the loss of a tax base (the result of fewer women in paid labour) affects the Finnish state rather than the municipal budget in Finland, where the proportion of taxes paid to municipalities is considerably lower than in Sweden and Denmark.[2]

The existence of the HCA does not in itself explain its high uptake relative to participation in childcare. In 1998 a similar allowance was introduced by a Conservative Coalition government in Norway (Aassve and Lappegård, 2009), where municipalities also rely more on state funds than in Sweden and Denmark (Department of Municipalities and Regions, 2009). Yet, as we have seen, the use of childcare has risen dramatically in Norway, while the Norwegian HCA has fallen significantly (Ellingsæter, 2006). Why, then, is the uptake of the HCA so high among Finnish parents? Apparently, the feedback effects in Finland work in the opposite direction to those in Norway. In Finland the idea that family care is best is undergoing a resurgence, and the use of childcare is decreasing (Repo, 2010) in the context of both constrained labour market opportunities (in both type and availability) and a hybrid family policy regime offering dual-earner, general family and market-oriented support.

Finnish parents make decisions about work and care in a labour market in which the norm of full-time work has been very strong, and this is likely to make the choice between work and care starker. Finnish women are more likely than women in the other Nordic countries to work full time (35 hours or more), at 79 per cent compared to 64 per cent in Sweden, 63 per cent in Denmark and 62 per cent in Norway (OECD Family database 2010, Table LMF2.1.A, data for 2007). Further, for at least that subset of Finnish mothers who did not have a job before having a baby, the HCA is a source of income that provides an alternative to both unemployment and childcare (Salmi, 2006, p 163).

Another factor that helps explain the contrast between Norway and Finland in recent years is the state of the economy. Unemployment has been high in Finland, and labour market opportunities for women have been limited, while employment opportunities for women in Norway have burgeoned since the mid-1990s (Ellingsæter and Gulbrandsen, 2007, p 653). However, poor economic conditions do not always inhibit the growth of childcare provision and use: Sweden was experiencing a significant recession when the childcare guarantee was enacted in 1995 (Mahon, 2002).[3] Neither did the poor economic conditions in Denmark in the 1980s stem the increase of childcare services (Borchorst, 2002).

In Finland, the more difficult economic climate, combined with policy settings that provide support for family, private and public care for young children, has meant that the discourse framing political debate about care allowances has been very different from that in Norway and Sweden. The majority discourse on the HCA in Finland is that it provides 'freedom of choice', while in Sweden (where such allowances were introduced in 2008), the HCA has been regarded a 'gender trap' (Hiilamo and Kangas, 2009). One consequence of these interacting developments is evidence of a consolidation of a new norm in support of the stay-at-home mother in Finland (Hiilamo and Kangas, 2009; Repo, 2010).[4] Certainly the allowance is very popular in Finland, with a large survey finding that fewer than 1 per cent of mothers thought that the benefit should be abolished (Salmi, 2006). Nevertheless, the equality impacts of the hybrid family policy arrangements in Finland are cause for concern, as the vast majority of HCA recipients are women, and low-income and low-educated parents are over-represented (Rissanen and Knudsen, 2001; Sipilä et al, 2010).

Yet Finland is not the only Nordic country with an HCA. The next section briefly explores the legislation and impact of HCAs in Norway, Sweden and Denmark.

Home childcare allowances: does the timing of introduction matter?

As previously mentioned, an HCA has been offered in Norway since 1998. Legislated by a Centre-Right government, the measure was aimed at encouraging maternal care of young children and justified in terms of increasing parental choice and offering public subsidies to private childminders in the same way as to public childcare. In contrast to Finland, Norwegians can combine a reduced amount of the Norwegian HCA with part-time formal childcare (Ellingsæter and Gulbrandsen, 2007, p 661). As childcare provision has developed strongly since the introduction of the Norwegian HCA, uptake has fallen sharply but is still widely used: among children born in 1998, the allowance was used by 91 per cent (for an average of 20 months), compared to 62 per cent of children born in 2007 (for an average of 13 months), and an increasing proportion of those using the HCA are also in part-time childcare (Baken and Myklebø, 2010). However, as in Finland, mothers comprise 90 per cent of recipients of the allowance in Norway, and non-Western immigrants and low-educated mothers are strongly over-represented (Aassve and Lappegård, 2009; Baken and Myklebø, 2010).

Centre-Right governments in both Denmark (2002) and Sweden (2008) have also introduced an HCA, with the main argument being the increase of parental choice. In contrast to Finland and Norway, both Denmark and Sweden introduced their form of HCA when childcare was already widely in use, a situation that goes a long way towards explaining their much lower uptake of the allowance. In Denmark, the HCA was used by only 0.2 per cent of the children in 2006 (Plantenga and Remery, 2009). Beyond the popularity of centre-based childcare, the extremely low uptake is attributable mainly to strict eligibility criteria: the allowance is offered only to parents outside the labour market (Eydal and Rostgaard, 2011). In Sweden, the Centre-Right government predicted that 15 per cent of the households with children in publicly funded childcare would exchange it for the allowance. However, according to the first statistics available, in 2009 only 1 per cent of families with children one to three years old used the HCA, even though the uptake is higher in areas with many non-Western migrants and, as in the other countries, the allowance is used almost entirely by mothers (91 per cent of users) (Statistics Sweden, 2010).[5] Indeed, following the 2010 election, Christian Democrat leader Göran Hägglund admitted that the HCA, of which his party had long been the main proponent, was not popular with the Swedish electorate (Hägglund, 2010).

So what conclusions about policies for meeting care needs and equality in the Nordic countries can we draw at this stage? From the perspective of gender equality, the development of tax-funded service provision in Denmark, Norway and Sweden indicates continuing progress towards universalisation and defamilialisation, within a dual-earner model that supports high levels of labour market participation by women. Finland's trajectory away from the dual-earner model towards a 'new familialism', noted by Rianne Mahon nearly a decade ago (2002), appears to have been sustained. This latter finding suggests that increasing gender equality has not been supported by childcare policies in Finland, particularly by the monetary benefits in the form of the HCA. Overall the HCA also appears to be a threat to ethnic equality in the Nordic countries, because available evidence suggests that uptake is higher among non-European immigrant groups. In the next section, we explore in more detail the different class and gender equality outcomes of childcare policies in Nordic countries within a broader European context.

Nordic childcare in comparative perspective

This section uses the EU–SILC[6] 2006 and 2008 for analysing the relationship between childcare use and gender and class inequality. Along with the four Nordic countries we discuss, we include seven other European nations, altogether representing a variety of family policy models and levels of public expenditure on childcare. The other European nations are France (FR), Germany (DE), Greece (GR), Italy (IT), the Netherlands (NL), Poland (PL) and the United Kingdom (UK). We report use of three forms of care: formal care services (mainly centre-based), care by a privately paid childminder in the child's home or in the childminder's home and care by grandparents, other relatives or friends. Along with care by parents only, these alternatives form a spectrum of responses to family care needs from the most social to the most private. We report separately for children aged one to two[7] and three to five years, following Korpi's characterisation of formal services for children under two years as indicators of dual-earner support, and for children three and older as indicators of general family support (2000, p 145). In addition to comparing the structure and defamilialising potential of childcare use in the 11 countries, we also analyse patterns of use by class. In the concluding discussion, we explore the implications of our findings in the context of measures of system structure, outcomes for women and children and policy developments.

Childcare and gender equality

The top panel of Table 5.2 presents our findings on the use of non-parental childcare for one- to two-year-olds. We show coverage and mean hours of use of each form of care and, following Rauch (2007), use these to calculate the full-time equivalent (FTE) of care per 100 children.[8] When applied to formal care services, the FTE is a measure of defamilialisation. Table 5.2 shows that formal care is most developed as a defamilialising or dual-earner support measure in Denmark, Sweden and Norway, where the FTE is at least 50. Indeed, formal care is overwhelmingly the primary form of non-parental childcare in these countries, with childminders, relatives and friends playing a marginal role. The overall defamilialising potential of formal care is less well developed in Finland, France, Italy and the Netherlands. In the Netherlands the cause is relatively short *hours* of formal care (mean of 17). In the other countries, the cause is relatively low *coverage* (less than 40 per cent), that is, formal care appears to support defamilialisation only for the minority of families that use it. Support for defamilialisation is even lower in Germany, Greece, Poland and the UK – in the UK because hours tend to be very low (mean of 13), and in the other countries primarily because coverage is low, particularly in Poland (4.5 per cent).

Formal childcare is increasing in many countries. Most of the countries for which we have data show a measurable trend towards defamilialisation between 2006 and 2008. However, this finding does not hold for the two countries with the

Table 5.2: Forms of care: proportions receiving care, average hours in respective forms of care and FTE/100 children in the age group,[a] children 1-2 years (top panel) and 3-5 years (bottom panel), 2008[b]

	Formal care			Childminder[c]			Care by relatives or friends		
	Coverage (%)	Mean hours	FTE/100 children	Coverage (%)	Mean hours	FTE/100 children	Coverage (%)	Mean hours	FTE/100 children
				One- to two-year-olds					
DK	90.7	34	**88.1**	0		**0**	0.8	–	–
SE	70.7	29	**58.6**	3.2	–	–	2.0	–	–
NO	58.0	32	**53.0**	4.8	–	–	5.8	–	–
FI	34.1	34	**33.1**	1.7	–	–	1.9	–	–
NL	55.8	17	**27.1**	19.7	14	**7.9**	54.3	8	**12.4**
UK	45.3	13	**16.8**	13.0	20	**7.4**	37.4	14	**15.0**
FR	38.6	28	**30.9**	15.0	31	**13.3**	23.3	18	**12.0**
DE	24.0	23	**15.8**	5.2	(16)	**(2.4)**	1.1	–	–
IT	33.8	30	**29.0**	3.6	(10)	**(1.0)**	37.8	21	**23.7**
GR	15.2	29	**12.6**	5.9	–	–	52.6	32	**48.1**
PL	4.5	(38)	**(4.9)**	6.0	(30)	**(5.1)**	31.9	28	**25.5**
				Three- to five-year-olds					
DK	97.1	33	**91.6**	0	–	–	0.1	–	–
SE	92.8	32	**84.8**	3.3	–	–	0.5	–	–
NO	82.8	33	**78.1**	0.5	–	–	2.3	–	–
FI	67.9	34	**66.0**	0.8	–	–	4.2	18	**2.2**
NL	93.1	22	**58.5**	20.1	11	**6.3**	48.4	6	**8.3**
UK	87.4	21	**52.4**	10.2	18	**5.2**	37.0	12	**12.7**
FR	93.3	28	**74.6**	10.4	15	**4.5**	19.8	12	**6.8**
DE	92.2	23	**60.6**	1.1	–	–	0.4	–	–
IT	90.9	33	**85.7**	2.8	9	**0.7**	36.9	15	**15.8**
GR	67.4	27	**52.0**	3.7	–	–	38.7	23	**25.4**
PL	35.1	35	**35.1**	2.6	–	–	29.8	24	**20.4**

Notes: FTE = full-time equivalent; – Value not reported due to *n*<30. Values within brackets based on 30<*n*<40.
[a] Following Rauch (2007), FTE/100 children is calculated as mean hours/35 * coverage.
[b] Data for France and Germany available only for 2006.
[c] For Sweden the figures on childminders include tax-funded family daycare, which in other countries is reported as formal care.
Source: Authors' own compilations of EU-SILC

lowest coverage (Greece and Poland) or for the Nordic country with the lowest coverage (Finland) (see Table A-5.1 in the Appendix at the end of this chapter).

In some countries where formal childcare provision does not strongly support defamilialisation, other forms of non-parental care can play an important role in meeting family care needs. For example, childminders provide nearly half as many hours of care on average as children receive in formal care in France (13.3 compared to 30.9 FTE) and the UK (7.4 compared to 16.8 FTE), and while the role of childminders is small in Poland, it is about the same as formal care (5.1 compared to 4.9 FTE).

Care by relatives and friends is clearly important in many countries. In Greece and Poland it is by far the most common form of non-parental childcare, and in Italy and the UK, non-parental informal care is nearly as important as formal care. In the Netherlands and France it also plays quite an important role. Interestingly, in Germany, where formal care is relatively underdeveloped for this age group, childminders and non-parental informal care do not emerge as alternatives.

The bottom panel of Table 5.2 presents analogous findings for children aged three to five. Formal care is much more developed for children aged three to five than for younger children, as the higher FTEs in all countries compared to those for children aged one to two show. This finding is not surprising, because services for children in this age group are offered both in countries providing only general family support and in those offering dual-earner support.

In Denmark, Sweden, Norway, France and Italy, where the FTE is around 75 or higher, formal care for three- to five-year-olds has a clear defamilialising impact. The relatively high FTE in Finland (66.0) is also likely to have a defamilialising impact *among families using formal care*, because the average hours among those who do use it are among the highest anywhere. In Poland, while coverage is low, the mean hours are the highest recorded, likewise suggesting a strong defamilialising impact among the minority of families using formal care. Greece holds an in-between position, with moderate coverage and moderately long hours. In Germany, the Netherlands and the UK coverage is high but average hours are relatively low, suggesting that the defamilialising impact of formal care is less developed in these countries. Childminders, relatives and friends provide less care for older preschool children than for the younger age group. However, grandparents and other relatives play a relatively important role in Greece, Italy, Poland and the UK.[9]

Figure 5.2 offers a different perspective on childcare coverage. It shows the proportion of children in the two age groups in each country using each form of childcare, or combinations thereof, and of those who receive only parental care. For the younger age group, we highlight the more significant role of formal care in Denmark, Sweden and Norway: only in these three countries do the majority of younger children use formal care only. By contrast, in Finland and Germany, the majority are cared for only by their parents, while in Italy, Greece and Poland, the majority of small children receive some form of family care, either from parents alone or along with relatives. The Netherlands and the UK stand out for combinations of care: indeed, in the Netherlands more than 40 per cent of children use more than one form of non-parental care.

Among three- to five-year-olds, the Nordic countries, now joined by Germany, stand out as those where use of formal care only is overwhelmingly the norm. However, Table 5.2 shows that hours in Germany are considerably shorter than those in the Nordic countries, thereby reducing the defamilialising impact of high coverage in Germany. Care only by parents is much less common in this age

Figure 5.2: Combinations of care for children aged 1-2 (top panel) and 3-5 (bottom panel), coverage, 2008[a]

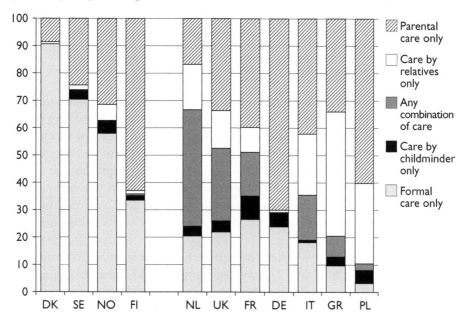

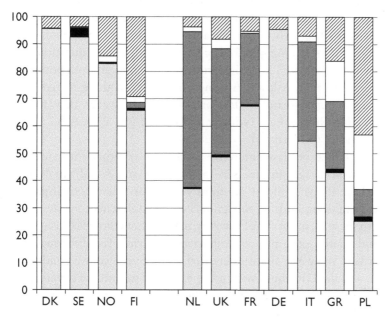

Note: [a] Data for France and Germany available only for 2006.
Source: Authors' own compilations of EU-SILC

group, although it remains relatively high in Finland (29 per cent) and Poland (43 per cent). Combinations of care are even more common among this age group, suggesting that formal care offerings are failing to meet the childcare needs or preferences of families in France, Greece, Italy, the Netherlands and the UK.

Childcare and class inequality

Thus far our focus has been the defamilialising potential of the Nordic countries, in comparative perspective. But as we argued earlier, policies for meeting family care needs can also promote or reduce class equality, and thus it is to the class dimension of changing inequalities that we now turn. We use education as a proxy measure of class and divide the sample into two groups: those in which at least one parent has a university education (high), and those in which neither has a university education (lower). The smaller the class gap in formal childcare use, the more the childcare system promotes class equality – or at least does not undermine it.

Figure 5.3 shows the class pattern of formal childcare use among one- to two-year-old children in 9 of the 11 countries, using the FTE measure. Among the Nordic countries, Sweden and Denmark show little or no class difference in use,[10] while both Norway and Finland show a strong pattern of higher use by those with higher education. In the other countries a similar strong class pattern is evident. France stands out as the country with the largest class difference in formal care for one- to two-year-olds, with 44.7 FTE among children of highly educated parents compared to 20.4 among children of parents with lower education. The exception is Germany, where FTE participation among children from both high and lower-educated families is low.[11] Among children aged three to five, class differences in use of formal care are less pronounced. However, they remain significant in Finland, Greece, Italy, Norway and Poland (see Table A-5.2 in the Appendix at the end of this chapter).

There is also evidence of class difference in the use of other forms of care among children in both age groups (see Tables A-5.1 and A-5.2). In Nordic countries, as we have shown, children are mostly cared for either by their parents or within formal childcare settings, so significant class differences in care relate almost entirely to these forms of care. However, in the other countries we analyse, childminders and relatives also play an important role, and class differences are evident in their use. Some key findings are that among very young children in the Netherlands and the UK, those with more educated parents are significantly more likely to use *both* formal care and childminders than are children of less educated parents. In Italy and Poland, very young children of parents with higher education are significantly more likely to be cared for by their grandparents, as well as to use formal care, than children of parents with low education (see Table A-5.1). Among older preschool children, we find significant class differences in the use of childminders in France, Greece, Italy, the Netherlands, Poland and the UK, and in the use of grandparent care in Greece and Italy. In each case, the

Figure 5.3: Formal care for children 1-2 years old by parents' educational background, FTE places per 100 children, 2008[a]

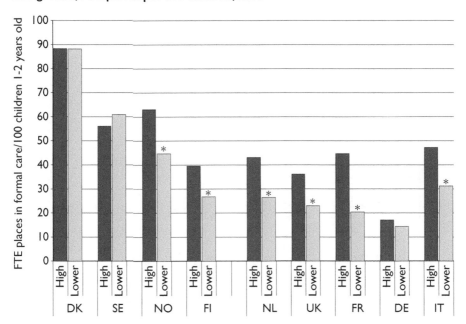

Notes: Significant difference between the two educational groups marked with * (*p*<0.05).
[a] Data for France and Germany available only for 2006; data not reported by educational groups for Poland and Greece due to *n*<30.
Source: Authors' compilations of EU-SILC

children of parents with higher education are those more likely to be using these forms of care in addition to formal care (see Table A-5.2).

The class differences in childcare use revealed in this section highlight an important threat to equality, along with the question of gender equality discussed earlier, and we discuss these issues in the following section.

Meeting family care needs: are all measures equal?

This section discusses our findings on patterns of childcare use in the countries we studied in light of the characteristics of the childcare systems of those countries, and links these to outcomes for women and children. Our aim is to assess the equality achievements and threats to equality in the Nordic countries, relative to the other seven European countries (see Table 5.3).

A recent body of research evidence shows that provision of childcare services for young children is crucial for enabling women's labour market participation, promoting gender equality and supporting fertility (Gupta et al, 2008; Stadelmann-Steffen, 2008; Plantenga and Remery, 2009; de Henau et al, 2010). Simply put, the more universal and defamilialising the childcare system, the more it supports gender equality. The data presented in Table 5.3 confirm these findings.

Table 5.3: Childcare systems, usage and outcomes

	DK	SE	NO	FI	NL	UK	FR	DE	IT	GR	PL
Care systems											
Formal care guarantee for children under 3	Yes	Yes	Yes	Yes	No	No	No	No	No	No	No
Public spending on formal services (% of GDP)[a]	1.8	1.7	1.3	1.4	1.0	1.0	1.6	0.7	0.7	0.4	0.3
Quality in formal care[b]	H	H	M-H	H	L-M	L-M	L	L	L	L	L
Affordability[c]	H	H	H	H	M	L	L	M	L	M	L-H
Childcare use											
Use of formal care FTE (1-2/3-5)[d]	88/92	59/85	53/78	33/66	27/59	17/52	31/74	16/61	29/86	13/52	5/35
Class difference in use of formal care (1-2/3-5)	N/N	N/N	Y/Y	Y/Y	Y/N	Y/N	Y/N	N/N	Y/Y	Y/Y	Y/Y
Parental care only (1-2/3-5)	9/4	24/4	31/14	63/29	17/4	34/8	40/5	70/4	42/7	34/16	60/43
Outcomes											
Mothers' employment (0-3/3-5)[d]	71/78	72/81		52/81	73/73	54/59	57/73	54/64	50/53	51/54	49/56
Part-time working hours (% of employed women working <30 hours per week)[e]	18	16	26	12	56	34	23	39	31	14	12
Child poverty rate (1-parent/2-parent families)[f]	7/2	8/3	13/2	14/3	39/6	24/6	19/6	42/9	26/14	27/12	44/18
Defamilialisation overall	H	H	H	M	M	L	M	L	L	L	L
Equality potential	H	H	M	M	L	L	L	L	L	L	L

Notes: Y = Yes, N = No, L = Low, M = Medium, H = High.
[a] OECD Family database 2010.
[b] Plantenga and Remery (2009, pp 43-4).
[c] Plantenga and Remery (2009, p 50).
[d] OECD Family database 2010, Chart LMF1.2B: Maternal employment rates by age of youngest child, 2007.
[e] OECD Family database 2010, Chart LMF2.1.A: Usual working hours per week by gender, 2007.
[f] OECD Family database 2010, Table CO2.2.C: Poverty rates (households with an equivalised income of less than 50% of the median) by household type, mid-2000s.
All others reported in the paper.

We begin by discussing care for children under three years of age. Table 5.3 shows that Denmark, Sweden and Norway, countries with high levels of participation in formal care among children under three, have guaranteed access to childcare services, backed by high public spending, high affordability[12] and high quality. These patterns of use and characteristics of the childcare system are associated, in turn, with high rates of full-time or long part-time labour market participation among mothers, and very low rates of child poverty in couple families. However, a clear difference exists in child poverty rates in single-parent families in Denmark and Sweden (where childcare coverage is highest) compared to Finland and Norway (where it is lower). These measures, taken in the mid-2000s, are evidence that high childcare coverage reduces poverty among single parents.

In Finland, use of formal childcare is lower than in the other Nordic countries, as is labour market participation among mothers of children under three, even though Finland has a service guarantee, and public spending on childcare and its affordability and quality are all high. As we discussed earlier, Finland's HCA plays an important role in explaining this finding, and has worrying implications for equality in that country. Indeed, Sipilä and colleagues argue that 'the political acceptance of CFC [cash-for-care] means quiet acquiescence of female poverty' (2010, p 38).

In the rest of the countries, where we found that use of formal childcare is medium or low among children under three, childcare guarantees are absent for this age group, and childcare systems are characterised by medium or low public spending (with the exception of France) and (at best) medium quality and affordability. These system characteristics support only low rates of employment among mothers of very young children in all countries except the Netherlands, which, however, shows the highest rate of short part-time work among women. Child poverty rates are also higher in all these countries than in the Nordic ones, particularly for children in single-parent families (see also Chapter Eight in this volume).

Among children aged three to five, *coverage* rates are high in all the countries except Finland and Greece, where they are medium, and Poland, where they are low. Higher coverage in this age group reflects the much more widespread development of pedagogically oriented services for older children in the preschool years. However, the pattern of FTE use in the three- to five-year-old group mostly resembles that for children under three, so that in the non-Nordic countries maternal employment remains relatively low, and the rates of part-time work among women tend to be higher than in the Nordic countries.

Overall, therefore, gender equality is strongly supported by childcare systems only in Denmark, Norway and Sweden, where dual-earner support is most highly developed. Moreover, our analysis of the EU-SILC data also reveals significant *class* differences in the use of formal childcare for children under three in all the countries except Denmark, Sweden and (for different reasons) Germany. Significant class differences persist among children aged three to five in Norway and Finland (where HCAs are likely to affect older preschool children whose parents are at home with a younger sibling), and in Greece, Italy and Poland. Class differences in childcare use are likely to be associated with class differences in women's employment, and with higher child poverty rates among families that do not use formal services. Explaining these class inequalities is critical to a broader understanding of the equality achievements and threats that family policy settings engender. In this respect, the widely used HCA in Finland and Norway appears to play a crucial role in explaining the class pattern we find in the use of formal childcare in these two countries.

To complement our previous analysis of the Nordic countries, the remainder of this section briefly explores how policy histories and differences in the non-Nordic countries have shaped the characteristics of their childcare systems and their class and gender outcomes.

Germany, the Netherlands and the UK share a history as male breadwinner models, in which short part-time work for women is common (the UK, Germany) or even dominant (the Netherlands), and childcare has been relatively underdeveloped. However, in recent years and in different ways, their governments have been active in the family policy area, and childcare coverage has been increasing in all three nations (Plantenga and Remery, 2009, p 58).

In the Netherlands, labour market policy has promoted part-time work over full-time, and childcare policy has promoted cash subsidies over service provision, with both approaches framed as measures for enhancing choice. Consequently, a 'one-and-a-half-earner model family' has become the norm (Lewis et al 2008, pp 272-3), as evident in the patterns of female labour force participation and childcare use in Table 5.3. In the childcare field, a series of policy measures since the early 1990s has shifted childcare from a 'welfare sector' to a 'market sector', culminating in 2005 when a Centre-Right Coalition government introduced a financing system in which parents pay the full price for childcare and receive compensation from their employers and government (Plantinga et al, 2010, p 403). This kind of funding system is more complex for parents to negotiate than publicly funded services and, along with only medium affordability and a propensity for higher employment rates among more educated women (Evertsson et al, 2009), the financing system helps explain the class difference in use of formal childcare for children under three.

In the UK during the 1980s, the Labour Party (then in opposition) decided that it needed to attract female voters and that women-friendly policies, including childcare, were likely to do so (Fleckenstein, 2010, p 800). Thus, after a long period of relative neglect under Conservative governments, childcare became a significant policy focus during the 'New Labour' years (1997-2010). The policy goals of Labour's 1998 and 2004 National Childcare Strategies included reducing child poverty, improving educational outcomes for children from low-income families and increasing maternal employment. Measures included an entitlement for three- and four-year-olds to 12.5 hours per week of free early education (increased to 15 hours in 2010), supply-side supports in the form of start-up grants to new facilities, and demand-side supports in the form of cash and tax subsidies to parents purchasing childcare (Fleckenstein, 2010, p 793). Significantly, the lack of a service guarantee for infants under three, the short part-time hours of the guaranteed offering for older children and the chosen funding mechanisms have combined to create a private sector-dominated mixed market in childcare, in which parents bear a considerable portion of the costs – when they can afford and gain access to services. The result is 'separate markets for the poor and better off' (Lloyd, 2008, p 479), relatively low overall use of childcare and a class divide in its use.

In Germany, the norm of maternal care for children at home has been strong, supported by an HCA introduced in 1986 (Evertsson et al, 2009) by a Centre-Right government. However, in 1992, a Centre-Right government legislated a legal entitlement to half-day care for children aged three and above (in effect in 1996) in a post-reunification political compromise over abortion laws (Fleckenstein, 2010, p 792). As Fleckenstein notes (2010, p 792), 'with this legislation, the government acknowledged the dual responsibility of parents *and* the state for care provision', as well as the need for policies to reconcile work and family. The beginnings of public support for care for children under three were offered by a Red-Green Coalition government in 2002. In 2007, the HCA was partially replaced by an earnings-related parental leave benefit (a basic rate is still paid to those without prior earnings). Since then, the 'Grand Coalition' of Christian and Social Democrats in 2008 has offered further funding to expand places, and plans to introduce a right to public childcare for one- and two-year-olds in 2013 (Fleckenstein, 2010, p 793). Interestingly, in the German case, the Christian Democrats now see the electoral benefits of women-friendly family policies (Fleckenstein, 2010).

Our findings on childcare use in Germany are drawn from data for 2006, when pedagogically oriented services for children over three had long been established, and formal care for children under three was still fairly undeveloped. Under this structure of provision, the male breadwinner model mitigates class inequalities in childcare use but also results in very high poverty rates among children in single-parent families. The German childcare system for children under three is now changing rapidly, and its defamilialising impact is likely to increase if the expanding system offers longer hours of care. If longer hours become more widely available, the class impact of growth in the number of childcare places will depend on the affordability of services and on the quality and quantity of labour market opportunities for women, particularly those with low education.

In France, while the level of spending on childcare is comparable with that in Nordic countries, the characteristics of the system, and outcomes for children and for equality, are quite different. Since the second half of the 1980s, the trajectory of childcare policy for children under three, under both Left- and Right-wing governments, has shifted away from the expansion of public childcare towards a cash benefit-oriented system, with the stated goal of increasing choice (Mahon, 2002; Martin and Le Bihan, 2009). An evolving system of benefits has offered a combination of an HCA with subsidies for the purchase of private childminders.

The consequences of this 'new policy paradigm' diverge significantly by class (Martin and Le Bihan, 2009). Uptake of the HCA has been much stronger among low-income families: among the poorest mothers, only 20 per cent are employed, compared to 70 per cent of mothers in high-income families (Plantenga and Remery, 2009, p 60). With the shift of public funds from formal childcare services to cash subsidies for privately purchased care, paid childcare services for those under three are decreasingly accessible to low-income families (Martin and Le Bihan, 2009, p 65). Thus young preschool children of parents with higher education in France are significantly more likely to use formal childcare or childminders than children of low-educated parents, who are significantly more likely to be cared for by their parents only (see Table 5.2).

In Italy, Greece and Poland formal care services are poorly developed for children under three, yet employment rates among mothers of very young children, while not high, are around 50 per cent in all three countries. These employment rates are made possible by the low employment among the *grandmothers* of these children: among women aged 55-64 only 21 per cent were employed in Italy in 2005, with similarly low proportions in Greece (26 per cent) and Poland (20 per cent), compared to the EU25 average of 34 per cent and 67 per cent in Sweden (Eurostat, 2008, p 207). Our analysis of the EU-SILC data confirms that care by relatives is the most widely used form of non-parental care in these countries for children under three years old (see Table A-5.2). This form of care may not be sustainable: these governments are seeking to raise both the official and effective retirement ages, which will shrink the pool of available grandmothers.

As in many of our comparison countries, almost all Italian children over three years old use formal childcare services, primarily the free state-run preschools offered under a universal programme and framed as education (Hohnerlein, 2009, p 89). However, services for younger children are underdeveloped, and those that exist are the responsibility of municipal and regional governments. In the absence of a state-mandated service guarantee, Italian local authorities have never been able to develop childcare for very young children as a universal service available on demand (Hohnerlein, 2009, p 100). A similar situation prevails in Greece, where municipalities offer early childhood education to children four years and older (compulsorily for five- and six-year-olds since 2006), while 'custodial care' is the less well-developed form of service offered to children under three (Petrogiannis, 2010). As elsewhere, class differences arise because of the much stronger incentive for educated women to continue working and the greater resources they are likely to have for accessing services.

Of all our comparison countries, Poland has the least well-developed childcare system. Expenditure is low, and coverage is negligible for children under three years of age. Even among older children, the use of formal services is low, despite a guarantee of five hours of free preschool education per day for three- to five-year-olds (Plomien, 2009, p 139). Low affordability, a lack of places, inflexible opening times, poor quality and the weak labour market position of women all play an explanatory role (Plomien, 2009). These characteristics of the system also explain the class differences observed in the EU–SILC analysis and the high rates of child poverty reported in Table 5.3.

Conclusion

To achieve the kind of universal childcare system that promotes equality, policy makers need to keep both benefits for children and benefits for parents in mind. If educational benefits for children are the sole focus, three hours a day for children three years and above may be sufficient, but at the considerable cost of mothers' employment, as the Dutch, German and UK cases so clearly show. If mothers' labour market opportunities are the sole focus, the quality of care is likely to suffer, and with it, children. Understood as 'educare', universal high quality public childcare can encompass pedagogical benefits for children while also giving both parents the opportunity to engage in paid work.

By contrast, significant threats to gender, class and ethnic equality are posed by the HCAs that have been introduced in Nordic countries and elsewhere, in the name of the dominant 'choice' rhetoric of the age. As we have shown, available research clearly shows that these allowances are mainly used by mothers (not fathers), and by less-educated mothers and mothers of non-Western descent in particular. Thus HCAs affect mothers with the weakest labour force participation and the children who would gain most from high quality childcare.

The threat to gender equality is clear, because HCAs enable or prolong mothers' absence from the labour market. Moreover, the gender inequality risk multiplies through the mechanism of statistical discrimination. This form of discrimination occurs when employers judge that the probability that *any* woman of childbearing age will take extended leave is high, and therefore offer *all* women worse jobs or advancement paths than they would offer men with the same qualifications. In this way, HCAs can have negative effects on all women of childbearing age, not only those who use them (Gupta et al, 2008).

The threat of HCAs to class equality is not only clear but also evident in the intra-Nordic difference in the class pattern of use of formal childcare: in Finland and Norway, where large proportions of the population use the HCA, children in families with lower education are significantly less likely to use formal childcare compared to children in families with higher education. In Denmark and Sweden, where very few families use the HCA, similar proportions of children in high- and low-educated families use formal childcare.

Finally, the threat that HCAs pose to ethnic equality is profound, even in countries such as Sweden, where uptake of the HCA remains low overall. Integration of non-Western immigrants has been cited as one of the most significant challenges facing Social Democratic welfare states, and measures that can compound existing disadvantages of immigrant groups demand particular attention. As parental care and formal childcare are substitutes in the Nordic countries, evidence that non-Western immigrant families are significantly less likely to use formal care in Norway (Sæther, 2010) means higher rates of care by parents only, encouraged by the HCA. Ferrarini and Duvander (2010) argue that the risks of poverty and poor educational outcomes are particularly high when immigrant children of low-educated parents are cared for at home rather than attending childcare. Our intra-Nordic comparison suggests that these risks are more serious when HCAs are introduced in societies where uptake of childcare is not yet universal (Finland and Norway). However, it is too early to evaluate the impact on class and ethnic inequalities of the newly introduced HCA in Sweden.

Overall, our analysis supports the general conclusion that while some equality achievements of some Nordic countries have been consolidated over the last two decades, real challenges remain. The universalisation of childcare in Denmark and Sweden represents an important achievement in the direction of gender, class and ethnic equality in those countries. In Norway, progress towards closing the childcare gap has been strong over the last decade but class and ethnic differences are worrisome. In Finland, the development of egalitarian family policy has stalled, with sweeping reform necessary if the country is to realign its path with those of its Nordic neighbours. Yet this is not the final word. Ferrarini and Duvander (2010) have argued that Swedish family policy is 'at a crossroads', as Sweden itself takes a step in the direction of Finland's hybrid family policy model by introducing an HCA. It would be unfortunate indeed if Sweden and Denmark were to undermine their relatively recent and hard-won equality achievements.

Notes

[1] The uptake of childcare among children around one year old in Sweden is affected by the 480 days of parental leave, with the final 90 days reimbursed at a much lower level than the rest of the leave (Ellingsæter and Leira, 2006, p 23).

[2] Municipal income taxes are levied at a flat rate that average about 18.6 per cent in Finland (Ministry of Finance, 2009, pp 19-20) and 31.6 per cent in Sweden (Swedish Tax Agency, 2010). In Finland the central government's contribution to municipal finances is considerably higher than that in Denmark and Sweden (NOSOSCO, 2009, p 230).

[3] The expansion of formal childcare in Sweden during the 1990s was not achieved without some compromise on quality (including falling staffing ratios and rising group sizes) and affordability (parent fees rose) (Bergqvist and Nyberg, 2002).

[4] In contrast to the other Nordic countries, a comparatively strong support for the male breadwinner, female carer model appears in Finland: while only 2-3 per cent of Danish and Swedish women aged 15-39 'agree totally' that '[i]deally a woman should stay at home to look after children', 20 per cent of Finnish women in the same age group do (the EU25 average is 15 per cent). And 27 per cent of Finnish women in the same age group 'agree totally' that '[b]oth men and women should contribute to the household income' (the lowest figure in EU), compared to 67 per cent in Denmark and 75 per cent in Sweden (Testa, 2006, p 60; no data on Norway).

[5] According to the latest available data (2005), there was no difference in take-up rates of formal childcare between children whose parents were migrants or born in Sweden (National Agency for Education, 2007, p 30).

[6] The EU-SILC is 'the EU reference source for comparative statistics on income distribution and social exclusion at the European level' (Eurostat, 2010). Tables A-5.1 and A-5.2 include sample sizes for the countries we study.

[7] To avoid the bias caused by the very different length of parental leave in the countries we study, we report childcare use for children aged 1-2 instead of the more common 0-2.

[8] FTE is calculated as follows: average weekly hours of care are divided by 35 and multiplied by the share using the services. Thus, for example, if 75 per cent of children use formal childcare and spend on average 30 hours a week in care, the FTE/100 children is, $30/35*75=64.3$.

[9] Less change has occurred between 2006 and 2008 in the defamilialisation of care for three- to five-year-olds, compared to younger children (Table A-5.2).

[10] In 2006, no class difference was evident between children of higher and lower-educated parents in Sweden. As the result of increased use of formal childcare in lower-educated families but not among higher-educated families, the data point towards significantly more children in lower-educated families using formal care services (see Table A-5.1). However, even if the proportion is higher, no significant difference exists between the two educational groups in FTE per 100 children (as reported in Figure 5.3).

[11] Given the small numbers using formal care services in Greece and Poland, we cannot calculate class-divided FTE measures. But, as Table A-5.1 shows, both countries exhibit a significant (or close to significant) class difference in the proportions using formal care services.

[12] Measured as a proportion of the average wage, childcare fees in 2004 for a two-year-old were 5 per cent in Sweden, 8 per cent in Finland, 8 per cent in Denmark and 9 per cent in Norway, compared to an EU24 average of 14 per cent (OECD Family database 2010, Chart PF3.4.A).

References

Aassve, A. and Lappegård, T. (2009) 'Childcare cash benefits and fertility timing in Norway', *European Journal of Population*, vol 25, no 1, pp 67-88.

Anttonen, A., Baldock, J. and Sipilä, J. (2003) *The young, the old, and the state: Social care systems in five industrial nations*, Cheltenham: Edward Elgar.

Baken, F. and Myklebø, S. (2010) 'Nedgang i bruk av kontantstøtte' ['Reduction in the use of childcare cash benefit'], *Arbeid og velferd*, Nr 1/2010, pp 45-51.

Bergqvist, C. and Nyberg, A. (2002) 'Welfare state restructuring and child care in Sweden', in S. Michel and R. Mahon (eds) *Child care policy at the crossroads: Gender and welfare state restructuring*, London and New York: Routledge, pp 287-308.

Borchorst, A. (2002) 'Danish child care policy: continuity rather than radical change', in S. Michel and R. Mahon (eds) *Child care policy at the crossroads: Gender and welfare state restructuring*, London and New York: Routledge, pp 267-86.

Daly, M. (2002) 'Care as a good for social policy', *Journal of Social Policy*, vol 31, no 2, pp 251-70.

de Henau, J., Meulders, D. and O'Dorchai, S. (2010) 'Maybe baby: comparing partnered women's employment and child policies in the EU-15', *Feminist Economics*, vol 13, no 1, 43-77.

Department of Municipalities and Regions (2009) *Rapport fra Det tekniske beregningsutvalg for kommunal og fylkeskommunal økonomi* [*Report from Committee for estimations of the municipal and regional finances*], Oslo: Department of Municipalities and Regions.

Ellingsæter, A.L. (2006) 'The Norwegian childcare regime and its paradoxes', in A.L. Ellingsæter and A. Leira (eds) *Politicising parenthood in Scandinavia*, Bristol: The Policy Press, pp 121-44.

Ellingsæter, A.L. and Gulbrandsen, L. (2007) 'Closing the childcare gap: the interaction of childcare provision and mothers' agency in Norway', *Journal of Social Policy*, vol 36, no 4, pp 649-69.

Ellingsæter, A.L. and Leira, A. (eds) (2006) *Politicising parenthood in Scandinavia*, Bristol: The Policy Press.

Esping-Andersen, G. (2005) 'Social inheritance and equal opportunities policies', in S. Delorenzi, J. Reed and P. Robinson (eds) *Maintaining momentum: Promoting social mobility and life chances from the early years to adulthood*, London: Institute for Public Policy Research, pp 31-53.

Eurostat (2008) *The life of women and men in Europe. A statistical portrait,* Luxembourg: Eurostat Statistical Books.

Eurostat (2010) *Description of target variables: Cross-sectional and longitudinal, 2008 operation*, Brussels: European Commission, Directorate F: Social Statistics and Information Society.

Evertsson, M., England, P., Mooi-Reci, I., Hermsen, J., de Bruijn, J. and Cotter, D. (2009) 'Is gender inequality greater at lower or higher educational levels? Common patterns in the Netherlands, Sweden, and the United States', *Social Politics*, vol 16, no 2, pp 210-41.

Eydal, G.B. and Rostgaard, T. (2011) 'Gender equality re-visited: changes in Nordic child-care policies in the 2000s', *Social Policy and Administration*, vol 45, no 2, pp 161-79.

Ferrarini, T. (2006) *Families, states and labour markets: Institutions, causes and consequences of family policy in post-war welfare states*, Cheltenham: Edward Elgar Publishing.

Ferrarini, T. and Duvander, A.-Z. (2010) 'Earner-carer model at the crossroads: reforms and outcomes of Sweden's family policy in comparative perspective', *International Journal of Health Services*, vol 40, no 3, p 373-98.

Fleckenstein, T. (2010) 'Party politics and childcare: Comparing the expansion of service provision in England and Germany', *Social Policy and Administration*, vol 44, no 7, pp 789-807.

Gupta, N.D., Smith, N. and Verner, M. (2008) 'The impact of Nordic countries' family friendly policies on employment, wages and children', *Review of Economics of the Household*, vol 6, no 1, pp 65-89.

Hägglund, G. (2010) 'KD ska förbli Sveriges familjparti' [Christian Democrats will continue to be Sweden's family party'], *Dagen*, 2 November.

Hall, C., Fredriksson, P., Johansson, E.-A. and Johansson, P. (2010) 'Do preschool interventions further the integration of immigrants? Evidence from Sweden', in C. Hall, *Empirical essays on education and social insurance policies, Dissertation Series 2010:2*, Uppsala: Department of Economics, Uppsala University and Institute for Labour Market Policy Evaluation.

Havnes, T. and Mogstad, M. (2009) *No child left behind: Universal child care and children's long-run outcomes*, Discussion Papers No 582, Oslo: Statistics Norway, Research Department.

Hiilamo, H. and Kangas, O. (2009) 'Trap for women or freedom to choose? The struggle over cash for child care schemes in Finland and Sweden', *Journal of Social Policy*, vol 38, no 3, pp 457-75.

Hohnerlein, E.M. (2009) 'The paradox of public preschools in a familist welfare regime: the Italian case', in K. Scheiwe and H. Willekens (eds) *Childcare and preschool development in Europe: Institutional perspectives*, Basingstoke: Palgrave Macmillan, pp 88-104.

Kela (2010) *Child home care allowance*, Helsinki: Kela – The Social Insurance Institution of Finland (www.kela.fi/in/internet/english.nsf/NET/150502155 459EH?OpenDocument).

Korpi, W. (2000) 'Faces of inequality: gender, class, and patterns of inequalities in different types of welfare states', *Social Politics*, vol 7, no 2, pp 127-91.

Leira, A. (1993) 'Mothers, markets and the state: a Scandinavian "model"?', *Journal of Social Policy*, vol 22, no 3, pp 329-47.

Leira, A. (2006) 'Parenthood change and policy reform in Scandinavia, 1970s-2000s', in A.L. Ellingsæter and A. Leira (eds) *Politicising parenthood in Scandinavia*, Bristol: The Policy Press, pp 53-78.

Lewis, J., Knijn, T., Martin, C. and Ostner, I. (2008) 'Patterns of development in work/family reconciliation policies for parents in France, Germany, the Netherlands, and the UK in the 2000s', *Social Politics*, vol 15, no 3, pp 261-86.

Lister, R. (2003) *Citizenship: Feminist perspectives*, New York: New York University Press.

Lister, R. (2009) 'A Nordic nirvana? Gender, citizenship, and social justice in the Nordic welfare states', *Social Politics*, vol 16, no 2, pp 242-78.

Lloyd, E. (2008) 'The interface between childcare, family support and child poverty strategies under New Labour: tensions and contradictions', *Social Policy and Society*, vol 7, no 4, pp 479-94.

Ministry of Finance (2009) *Taxation in Finland 2009*, Tax issues 7/2009, Helsinki (www.vm.fi/vm/en/04_publications_and_documents/01_publications/075_taxation/20090504Taxati26547/taxation_2009_netti%2Bkannet.pdf).

Mahon, R. (2002) 'Child care: toward what kind of "Social Europe"', *Social Politics*, vol 9, no 3, pp 343-79.

Martin, C. and Le Bihan, B. (2009) 'Public childcare and preschools in France: new policy paradigm and path dependency', in K. Scheiwe and H. Willekens (eds) *Childcare and preschool development in Europe: Institutional perspectives*, Basingstoke: Palgrave Macmillan, pp 57-71.

National Agency for Education (2007) *Barns omsorg 2005 [Care of children 2005]*, Stockholm: Skolverket.

Nordic Statistics (2010) Databank Table CHIL03: Children in day-care by reporting country, age, type and time (www.norden.org)

Norwegian Government (2008) *Om lov om endringer i barnehaveloven [On changes in the childcare legislation]*, Oslo: Norwegian Government.

NOSOSCO (Nordic Social-statistical Committee) (2009) *Social protection in the Nordic countries 2007/2008*, Copenhagen: NOSOSCO.

OECD (2010) *OECD Family database* (www.oecd.org/els/social/family/database).

Petrogiannis, K. (2010) 'Early childhood care and education in Greece: some facts on research and policy', *International Journal of Early Childhood*, vol 42, no 2, pp 131-9.

Plantenga, J. and Remery, C. (2009) *The provision of childcare services: A comparative review of 30 European countries*, Brussels: European Commission Directorate-General for Employment, Social Affairs and Equal Opportunities.

Plantinga, M., Plantenga, J. and Siegers, J. (2010) 'The relation between market forces and employee motivation: the consequences of the introduction of market forces in the Dutch childcare sector', *European Sociological Review*, vol 26, no 4, pp 401-14.

Plomien, A. (2009) 'Welfare state, gender, and reconciliation of work and family in Poland: policy developments and practice in a new EU member', *Social Policy and Administration*, vol 43, no 2, pp 136-51.

Rauch, D. (2005) 'Institutional fragmentation and Scandinavian childcare variations', *Journal of Public Policy*, vol 25, no 3, pp 367-94.

Rauch, D. (2007) 'Is there really a Scandinavian social service model?', *Acta Sociologica*, vol 50, no 3, pp 249-69.

Repo, K. (2010) 'Finnish child home care allowance – users' perspective and perceptions', in J. Sipilä, K. Repo and T. Rissanen (eds) *Cash for childcare: The consequences for caring mothers*, Cheltenham: Edward Elgar, pp 46-64.

Rissanen, T. and Knudsen, C. (2001) *The child home care allowance and women's labour force participation in Finland, 1985-1998: A comparison with Norway*, Oslo: NOVA Skriftserie 6/01.

Sæther, J.P. (2010) *Barn i barnehage – foreldrebakgrunn og utvilkling de seneste årene [Children in kindergarten: parental background and recent trends]*, Report 11/2010, Oslo: Statistics Norway.

Salmi, M. (2006) 'Parental choice and the passion for equality in Finland', in A.L. Ellingsæter and A. Leira (eds) *Politicising parenthood in Scandinavia: Gender relations in welfare states*, Bristol: The Policy Press, pp 145-70.

Sipilä. J. (ed) (1997) *Social care services: The key to the Scandinavian welfare model*, Aldershot: Avebury.

Sipilä, J., Repo, K. and Rissanen T. (eds) (2010) *Cash for childcare: The consequences for caring mothers*, Cheltenham: Edward Elgar.

Stadelmann-Steffen, I. (2008) 'Women, labour and public policy: female labour market integration in OECD countries. A comparative perspective', *Journal of Social Policy*, vol 37, no 3, pp 383-408.

Swedish National Institute of Public Health (2009) *Child day care center or home care for children 12-40 months of age – what is best for the child? A systematic literature review*, R2009:09, Östersund: Swedish National Institute of Public Health.

Statistics Sweden (2010) 'Nyttjande av kommunalt vårdnadsbidrag. Statistik för perioden 1 juli 2009-31 december 2009' ['Use of municipal child homecare allowance. Statistics for July 1-December 31, 2009'], Stockholm: Unpublished report for the Ministry of Health and Social Affairs.

Swedish Tax Agency (2010) *Taxes in Sweden, 2009: An English summary of the tax statistical yearbook of Sweden*, SKV 104 (www.skatteverket.se/download/18.233 f91f71260075abe8800021511/10410.pdf).

Szebehely, M. (2005) 'Care as employment and welfare provision: child care and elder care in Sweden at the dawn of the 21st century', in H.M. Dahl and T.R. Eriksen (eds) *Dilemmas of care in the Nordic welfare state: Continuity and change*, Aldershot: Ashgate, pp 80-97.

Testa, M. (2006) *Childbearing preferences and family issues in Europe*, l Eurobarometer 253/Wave 65.1 – TNS Opinion & Social. Brussels: European Commission.

Table A-5.1: Forms of care among children 1-2 years old by parents' highest education in 2008 (coverage and for formal care also mean hours and FTE places per 100 children in the age group and change in FTE places per 100 children since 2006)

	Education (n)	Parental care only (%)	Care by relatives or friends (%)	Care by child-minder (%)	Formal child-care (%)	Mean hours formal care	FTE formal care/100 children	Change in FTE formal care/100 children since 2006
DK	High (219)	7.9	0.9	0	91.2	33.9	88.3	+6.5
	Lower (141)	9.1	0.6	0	90.3	34.2	88.2	+5.9
SE	High (248)	**30.3**	2.1	2.3	**65.6**	29.9	56.1	+0.3
	Lower (262)	**17.3**	1.8	4.4	**76.6**	27.8	60.9	+11.2
NO	High (202)	**20.8**	7.5	3.7	**68.0**	32.5	**63.1**	+8.9
	Lower (164)	**40.0**	4.8	6.4	**48.8**	32.1	**44.7**	+12.3
FI	High (331)	**57.3**	1.3	1.8	**39.9**	34.6	**39.5**	+3.7
	Lower (231)	**70.2**	2.8	0.7	**27.2**	34.4	**26.8**	−1.6
NL	High (374)	**7.6**	**48.1**	**25.5**	**67.0**	22.5	**43.1**	+12.7
	Lower (256)	**27.3**	**60.3**	**13.5**	**43.4**	21.3	**26.4**	+10.4
UK	High (207)	**23.7**	39.3	**19.4**	**55.9**	22.6	**36.2**	+13.3
	Lower (247)	**42.9**	37.4	**8.8**	**35.8**	22.5	**23.0**	+11.8
FR	High (295)	**23.4**	27.5	*19.2*	**51.7**	30.3	**44.7**	–
	Lower (207)	**50.4**	20.7	*14.7*	**28.4**	25.1	**20.4**	–
DE	High (272)	68.1	**2.1**	6.5	24.1	24.9	17.1	–
	Lower (191)	71.9	**0**	3.9	24.0	21.0	14.4	–
IT	High (234)	**27.9**	**52.8**	4.9	**41.2**	40.1	**47.2**	+6.0
	Lower (698)	**47.3**	**32.3**	3.1	**31.2**	34.9	**31.1**	+6.6
GR	High (121)	**25.3**	57.0	**10.7**	*18.4*	29.0	12.6	+0.5
	Lower (144)	**41.3**	49.0	**1.4**	*12.5*			
PL	High (198)	**47.3**	**35.6**	**13.2**	**8.0**	(37.7)	(4.9)	(+1.1)
	Lower (518)	**68.4**	**29.2**	**1.4**	**2.5**			

Notes: Difference between the two educational groups: marked in bold if *p*<0.05, in italics if 0.05<*p*<0.10. Data for DE and FR available only for 2006.
SE: The figures on childminders include tax-funded family daycare, which in other countries is reported as formal care.
PL and GR: Mean hours and FTE not reported for the two educational groups due to *n*<30.

Table A-5.2: Forms of care among children 3-5 years old by parents' highest education in 2008 (coverage and for formal care also mean hours and FTE places per 100 children in the age group and change in FTE places per 100 children since 2006)

	Education (n)	Parental care only (%)	Care by relatives or friends (%)	Care by child-minder (%)	Formal child-care (%)	Mean hours formal care	FTE formal care/100 children	Change in FTE formal care/100 children since 2006
DK	High (340)	4.0	0.2	0	95.8	33.4	91.5	+2.5
	Lower (243)	4.2	0	0	95.8	33.2	90.9	−3.9
SE	High (301)	3.1	1.0	2.3	94.2	32.1	86.5	+4.8
	Lower (280)	4.2	0	4.4	91.4	32.1	83.7	+7.8
NO	High (319)	*11.0*	2.5	0.3	**86.2**	33.8	**83.2**	−3.6
	Lower (226)	*16.9*	2.3	0.8	**80.0**	32.5	**74.3**	+7.4
FI	High (521)	27.7	**3.4**	1.1	**70.2**	34.2	**68.5**	−1.8
	Lower (369)	31.3	**5.7**	0.4	**64.5**	33.9	**62.4**	−0.2
NL	High (679)	2.5	49.3	**25.2**	94.5	22.9	61.8	+3.1
	Lower (453)	5.3	47.1	**14.4**	91.5	21.7	56.7	+3.7
UK	High (288)	6.3	36.1	**14.7**	88.1	21.2	53.3	−6.1
	Lower (407)	9.2	37.9	**7.8**	86.8	20.9	51.9	+0.2
FR	High (449)	3.8	20.0	**15.5**	94.4	28.5	76.9	−
	Lower (414	4.9	19.9	**7.6**	93.9	27.4	73.7	−
DE	High (519)	6.7	**0.9**	*1.8*	93.2	23.7	63.2	−
	Lower (438)	8.8	**0.1**	*0.6*	91.2	22.6	59.0	−
IT	High (327)	4.1	**47.5**	**7.1**	93.3	35.2	**93.8**	+9.2
	Lower (1074)	7.4	**33.4**	**1.3**	90.7	32.5	**84.2**	+1.4
GR	High (181)	**6.4**	**44.8**	**7.5**	**76.7**	28.3	**62.0**	+5.4
	Lower (300)	**21.8**	**35.2**	**1.5**	**61.3**	26.0	**45.5**	+7.9
PL	High (271)	**26.1**	28.1	**4.8**	**54.1**	36.7	**56.6**	+4.1
	Lower (768)	**51.9**	30.7	**1.7**	**24.5**	32.1	**22.5**	+5.4

Notes: Difference between the two educational groups: marked in bold if *p*<0.05, in italics if 0.05<*p*<0.10. Data for DE and FR available only for 2006.
SE: The figures on childminders include tax-funded family daycare, which in other countries is reported as formal care.

SIX

Welfare state institutions, unemployment and poverty: comparative analysis of unemployment benefits and labour market participation in 15 European Union countries

M. Azhar Hussain, Olli Kangas and Jon Kvist

Introduction

Much intellectual effort has been expended on debating welfare state regimes – whether they exist (and, if so, how many), what their central characteristics are and whether they are becoming more similar or not. In his *Three worlds of welfare capitalism*, which launched an avalanche of welfare regime studies, Gøsta Esping-Andersen (1990) emphasised that a welfare state regime consists of a multifaceted interplay between labour markets and social policies. From this perspective he distinguished three clusters of welfare state: Nordic, Liberal and Corporatist regimes. The hallmark of the Nordic welfare state, consisting of Denmark, Finland, Norway and Sweden, is a high level of employment, with high income protection when one is unemployed, sick, disabled, elderly, etc. As a consequence of these interacting factors, poverty rates in all population categories – the employed, the unemployed, the retired, etc – are low.

In the Liberal welfare state means-tested or low flat-rate benefits dominate and, as a consequence of the low level of social protection, poverty among the welfare recipients is common. Typical examples of this welfare state model are: Australia, Canada, Ireland, New Zealand, the UK and the US. The third cluster, the Corporatist – typical of the Central European countries Austria, France, Germany, Belgium and the Netherlands – combines high social insurance benefits for the labour market insiders and a strong degree of familialism that supports traditional gender roles. To preserve class and status difference, social security is organised according to occupational lines. Esping-Andersen's triad has been expanded to include a fourth model, the Southern European welfare state (Greece, Italy, Portugal and Spain), characterised by generous entitlements for the core workers

– the replacement rates are among the highest in the EU hemisphere – while other forms of social protection are underdeveloped and the extended family plays a central role in care-giving. Female labour force participation is thus very low in comparison to the other regimes (Ferrera, 2010).

This chapter examines the interaction between the labour market, employment and social security in different welfare state regimes. More specifically, we investigate to what extent, if any, we can find regime-based differences in labour markets, in the generosity of unemployment insurance or in the economic consequences of being employed, becoming unemployed for a shorter or longer period and becoming employed again. Our study spans the mid-1990s to the late 2000s. While a decade is perhaps too short a period for seeing radical shifts in such rigid systems as welfare states, the Nordic countries – notably Finland and Sweden – underwent very deep recessions at the beginning of the period. The recession changed the way in which labour market and social policies work: unemployment increased, many welfare state benefits were cut, and the ability of the remaining benefits to mitigate the harmful effects of unemployment was circumscribed. Therefore, we find it worthwhile to examine whether the contours of the Nordic welfare state remain visible or whether the European nations have become more similar and regime differences more blurred in terms of the level of employment, the generosity of unemployment insurance and the incidence of poverty among people in different labour market positions.

The structure of the chapter is as follows. First, to put our study in a wider frame of reference, we briefly discuss the relationship between work and low income. At the end of this first section we also specify the aim of the study. The second section describes the databases at our disposal and the methods we use to analyse these data. The third section presents the labour market characteristics of the 15 countries in our study and briefly describes their unemployment protection systems. Due to data limitations we mainly concentrate on the generosity of income maintenance provided by unemployment insurance in the 15 countries. Following these institutional sections comes a longitudinal analysis of the economic consequences of changes in labour market status on individual income status (poor or not poor). The final section discusses our findings at a more general level.

Labour market and income: our research questions

Conventional wisdom states that work is the best form of social security and the most efficient guarantee against poverty and destitution. Certainly this adage contains much truth. In 2008, the poverty rate among the employed in 27 European Union countries (EU27) was 8 per cent. For those with permanent contracts the poverty risk was only 5 per cent, whereas almost half of the EU27 unemployed had incomes below the 60 per cent poverty line (Eurostat, 2010, p 4). Thus while work is good, employed people are not totally safe. A growing body of literature argues that changes in the labour market, the modes of production and even the very concept of work will result in growing numbers of employed people with income so low that they fall into poverty (Rifkin, 1995; Gray, 1998; Sennett, 2006; Standing, 2009).

Given the strong arguments about the increase of in-work poverty and the end of work (see Rifkin, 1995), it is surprising that empirical evidence does not give a unanimous picture of the development or magnitude of the problem. For example *The working poor in Europe* by Andreß and Lohmann (2008) shows that in most European countries the share of working poor has remained more or less constant during the last two decades or only slightly increased. Furthermore, it shows that no differences whatsoever exist among European welfare state regimes. Against all expectations, according to Andreß and Lohmann, the Nordic welfare states are not doing any better than the Central European or Liberal countries. Despite a slight tendency for the familistic Southern European regime to have higher poverty rates, even this pattern is not clearly delineated (see also Immervoll and Pearson, 2009; DiMarco, 2010). However, other studies are more in line with the regime-based interpretations. For example Airio (2008, p 80), who uses European Community Household Panel Survey (ECHP) data, shows that in-work poverty is the lowest in the Nordic region, followed by the Central European cluster, while the Liberal countries (Ireland and the UK) and the Southern European countries have higher poverty rates.

Thus competing research results exist on the importance of welfare regimes in explaining differences in poverty and labour market status. Not surprisingly, the problem with regime theory is the difficulty of defining the specific characteristics in 'the Nordic' that are 'good' or in 'the Liberal' that are 'bad'. One way of tackling this problem is to concentrate on specific social policy areas and to use various dimensions of social policy schemes instead of regimes (Korpi and Palme, 1998). In this chapter we therefore look at more specific indicators in the performance of the labour market, the generosity of unemployment insurance and the income status of individuals in different labour market positions. Countries are classified into four welfare state types: Nordic, Liberal, Central European and Southern European regimes.

Rather than focusing on poverty or income distribution per se (see Ritakallio, 2002; Smeeding, 2002; and Chapter Eight, this volume), we are interested in the dynamic relationships between shifts in employment and shifts in income status in different countries and groups of countries in the following ways:

- What happens in terms of poverty when a person is employed (employed both in year t and year $t+1$), becomes unemployed (employed in year t and unemployed in year $t+1$), is unemployed for two consecutive years (unemployed both in t and in $t+1$), or becomes employed again after unemployment (unemployed in t but employed in $t+1$)?
- Is finding employment enough to raise the individual above the poverty line?
- What is the effect of unemployment insurance on preventing poverty in different transitions?

• What kinds of country- or welfare regime-specific changes have taken place over time?

The 15 countries are clustered into four regimes: Nordic (Denmark, Finland, Norway and Sweden), Central European (Austria, Belgium, France, Germany and the Netherlands), Liberal (Ireland and the UK) and Southern European (Greece, Italy, Portugal and Spain). The rationale underpinning our comparisons is to analyse similarities and differences between and within regimes in the case of labour market and unemployment protection. For example, one could expect that due to the severe recessions in the 1990s and cuts in social benefits in Finland and Sweden, the Nordic cluster has lost some of its distinctiveness when it comes to low unemployment levels and high benefit levels.

Nonetheless, the hallmark of the Nordic welfare state model has perhaps been not only high income protection for those who are unemployed but also investment in active labour market policies (ALMPs) (Carroll, 1999; Drøpping et al, 1999) and in different kinds of welfare services facilitating the balancing of family and paid work (see Chapter Five, this volume). Consequently, female employment in particular has been the highest in the Nordic regime. However, in many other OECD (Organisation for Economic Co-operation and Development) countries policies aimed at increasing female labour force participation may have narrowed the gap between the Nordic and other regimes.

Data and methods

It is widely recognised that poverty and inequality measures based on cross-sectional annual income data far from fully explain the distribution of income in a society (see, for example, Aaberge et al, 1996; Goodin et al, 1999; Hussain, 2002). A shift from a cross-sectional research design to a more dynamic one allows us not only to better evaluate the interplay between labour market transitions, social policy and income dynamics, but also to cover wider issues of social justice – a crucial element for all social institutions (Goodin et al, 1999; Björklund and Jäntti, 2008).

The results on labour market transitions and income mobility in this chapter are based on the ECHP User Data Base (UDB) compiled by Eurostat. The ECHP contains data from waves 1-8, covering 1994 to 2001. For our purposes, one problem with the ECHP is that it lacks sufficient data for Sweden and does not include Norway. The second problem is that data gathering stopped in 2001 and was replaced by another Eurostat database, EU Statistics on Income and Living Conditions (EU-SILC), containing data for 2004 to 2008 (Wolff et al, 2010). Although about 20 countries are included in the EU-SILC, we have restricted our analyses to the 15 countries mentioned earlier. Because of problems with data we have, in some comparisons, also excluded Germany.

While the EU-SILC tries to mimic the ECHP, the databases are not totally comparable; therefore, strong conclusions about developmental patterns from 1994 to 2008 should be avoided. However, the databases are similar enough to allow comparisons between countries and country rankings within the time periods that the datasets cover (see Atkinson and Marlier, 2010). Some tentative analyses on general patterns in status dynamics between the two time periods can also be made. We test the reliability of our data against OECD data wherever possible.

The income measure we use is total annual disposable household income, including transfers and after deduction of income tax and social security contributions, with the household as the income recipient unit. We employ the 'modified OECD' equivalence scale, where the first adult in a household is given the value 1, each additional adult is given a value of 0.5 and each child is given a value of 0.3. We classify those whose income is below 60 per cent of the national median income as poor. In our analysis of labour market and poverty dynamics we use a balanced panel of 'survivors' who remained in the sample from one year to the next and use the 'base weight' as a longitudinal weight for this group, as specified by Eurostat.

The ECHP data for 1994-99 and the EU–SILC data for 2005-08 allow us to analyse transitions in the labour market and compare those changes with transitions in poverty status. The analysis goes as follows: the individual's labour market and income status in two consecutive years t and $t+1$ were recorded. The origin year t was either 1994, 1996 or 1998, while the destination year $t+1$ was the year after the origin, meaning 1995, 1997 or 1999. The same individual was thus followed from 1994-95, 1996-97 and 1998-99. The same approach was applied for 2005-08.

A discrepancy may exist between shifts in labour market status and shifts in income status (poor or not poor). Labour market status is an individual-level phenomenon, whereas income status pertains to a situation based on household income. Therefore, there may be mismatch between these two levels. First, an individual may become unemployed, be long-term unemployed or be employed at a very low wage and thus, on the basis of his or her own income, be poor. The individual may live in a household where the second earner has a good income, so that the first individual is not poor according to the household-based measure. Second, as changes in the composition of the household structure may affect poverty status, a mismatch may sometimes occur between the individual-level labour market status and household-level income. Nonetheless, while not all individuals with low income live in poor households, most individuals in poor households have both low income and weak labour market attachment (see, for example, Nolan and Marx, 1999; Cantillon et al, 2002; Andreß and Lohmann, 2008; Airio, 2008).

As our hypothesis is that micro-level phenomena (whether based on individual- or household-level data) are related to country- or regime-level units, we could use a multilevel approach. However, to properly carry out multilevel analyses, we should have a considerable number of higher-level units and a limited number of lower-level units (Rasbash et al, 2000; Goldstein, 2003). In our case the data situation is reversed: in the EU–SILC we have more than 140,000 lower-level units (individuals) and only 15 higher-level units (countries). Therefore, because the requirements for reliable multilevel analyses are not properly met, we apply a method called a two-step strategy (see a special issue of *Political Analysis*, 2005). For the first step we calculate micro-level parameters for each country through logistic regression models. For the second step, we regress the country-level parameters (odds ratios of being poor in different labour market transitions) against country-level indicators of the generosity of unemployment insurance. By so doing we control for confounding variables, which in our analyses are age, education, gender, household structure and subjective health. The country-level parameters represent characteristics of the unemployment systems plus all other nation-specific factors not captured by the covariates included in the logistic regressions.

Characteristics of the labour market: Nordic employment regime

An individual's position in the labour market has major impacts on his or her welfare. Therefore, before we proceed to labour market transitions and their economic consequences, we need to look at the characteristics of labour markets in the 15 countries in our study. Table 6.1 summarises some central features in 1987 and 2007. The first year pertains to the time period that the ECHP data cover, and the second to the EU-SILC. Countries are classified according to their welfare state regime types. In addition to the national scores, the table gives mean values and coefficient of variation (CV = standard deviation divided by the mean) for each regime and for the full sample of countries. CV reveals whether there is congruence within each regime or among all the countries. Changes in CV indicate whether countries have become more similar or dissimilar during the period under inspection.

The overall employment rates appear to more or less clearly divide according to regime type, with the Nordic cluster displaying the highest employment rates. In all regimes employment rates have gone up between the periods studied, and both the within- and between-regime dispersion has diminished. Differences among regimes are the largest for female employment. In 1997 the difference between the Nordic mean (67.7 per cent) and the Southern European mean (42.0 per cent) was 26 percentage points, while 10 years later it was 19 percentage points. Gender employment gaps also have decreased in all regimes, with a trend towards growing similarity among countries and welfare state regimes (as indicated by the decreased CVs). In that respect the Nordic model has lost some of its distinctiveness, not because the countries have abandoned their high employment but because the other countries are increasingly becoming 'Nordic'.

The Nordic countries – Denmark and Sweden, in particular – are renowned for their ALMPs. The OECD data (two right-hand columns in Table 6.1) show that on average the Nordic cluster is investing more than the other welfare models in ALMPs and that the pattern did not change considerably over the decade. Consequently, one could expect that unemployment rates and long-term unemployment would be lower in the Nordic countries than elsewhere. The

Table 6.1: Characteristics of the employment systems in 15 European countries in the mid-1990s and late 2000s

Country	Employment (%) 1997			Employment (%) 2007			Unemployment (%)		Long-term unemployment, % of all unemployment		ALMPs (% of GDP)	
	All	Male	Female	All	Male	Female	1997	2007	1997	2007	1997	2007
Nordic												
Denmark	75.4	81.3	69.4	77.3	81.3	73.3	6.8	3.8	26.9	18.2	1.66	1.85
Finland	62.8	65.2	60.4	70.5	72.4	68.5	15.1	6.9	27.5	23.0	1.40	0.89
Norway	77.0	81.7	72.2	76.9	79.7	74.0	5.5	2.6	8.2	8.5	0.90	1.00
Sweden	70.7	72.4	68.9	75.7	78.0	73.2	8.8	6.1	33.5	13.0	1.96	1.36
Mean/CV	71.5/0.09	75.2/0.11	67.7/0.08	75.1/0.04	77.9/0.05	72.3/0.03	9.1/0.47	4.9/0.41	24.0/0.46	15.7/0.40	1.48/0.30	1.28/0.34
Central European												
Austria	67.2	75.9	58.5	71.4	78.4	64.4	3.9	4.4	30.3	26.8	0.44	0.71
Belgium	57.0	67.1	46.7	61.4	68.2	54.9	9.7	7.5	61.7	50.0	1.22	1.09
France	58.9	66.3	51.7	64.4	69.1	59.8	11.0	8.3	44.2	42.2	1.35	0.92
Germany	63.8	72.1	55.3	68.0	74.8	62.9	8.0	8.4	52.6	56.6	1.27	0.88
Netherlands	67.5	77.9	56.9	74.1	80.0	68.1	6.6	3.2	47.9	41.7	1.58	1.22
Mean/CV	62.9/0.08	71.9/0.07	53.8/0.09	68.1/0.08	74.1/0.07	62.0/0.08	7.8/0.35	6.4/0.38	47.3/0.24	43.5/0.26	1.17/0.37	0.96/0.20
Liberal												
Ireland	56.3	67.8	44.7	69.0	77.4	60.3	12.3	4.5	56.0	30.3	1.60	0.62
UK	70.8	77.5	64.1	72.3	78.4	66.3	8.5	5.3	32.7	24.7	0.38	0.42
Mean/CV	63.6/0.16	72.7/0.09	54.4/0.25	70.7/0.03	77.9/0.01	63.3/0.07	10.4/0.26	4.9/0.12	44.4/0.37	27.5/0.14	0.99/0.87	0.52/0.25
Southern European												
Greece	54.8	71.9	39.1	61.6	74.9	48.1	9.0	8.3	54.9	50.3	0.44	0.07
Italy	51.6	66.8	36.4	58.7	70.7	48.6	11.2	6.1	59.6	49.9	0.40	0.53
Portugal	64.7	72.5	57.2	67.8	73.9	61.9	7.1	8.0	44.7	47.3	0.77	0.61
Spain	50.7	66.1	35.2	66.6	77.4	55.5	18.4	8.3	54.3	27.6	0.70	0.80
Mean/CV	55.5/0.12	69.3/0.05	42.0/0.25	63.7/0.07	74.2/0.04	53.5/0.12	11.4/0.43	7.7/0.14	53.4/0.12	43.8/0.25	0.58/0.62	0.50/0.62
All Mean/CV	63.3/0.13	72.2/0.08	54.4/0.22	69.1/0.08	75.6/0.05	62.7/0.13	9.5/0.40	6.1/0.33	42.3/0.36	34.0/0.45	1.07/0.50	0.84/0.51

Source: OECD (2000*, 2002, 2008)

expectation holds true for long-term unemployment, which in both time periods is lower in the Nordic regime than in the others. Nonetheless, variation among the Nordic countries is considerable, as the CVs indicate. The variation in 1997 is mainly attributable to the severe recession that hit Finland and Sweden in the early 1990s, and the unemployment rate in 1997 was still higher than in some Central European countries and the UK. Ten years later the Nordic unemployment level was the lowest (4.9 per cent), together with the Irish and the British. Although the overall unemployment rate was the same in the Nordic and Liberal countries, in the Liberal regime the incidence of long-term unemployment (28 per cent) was significantly higher than in the Nordic regime (16 per cent). The incidence of long-term unemployment was the highest in the Central and Southern European regimes (44 per cent).[1]

Results from investments in ALMPs are not clear-cut. Providing that ALMPs prevent people from becoming unemployed and help them find work when unemployed, a negative correlation should exist between the volume of ALMPs and the transition from work to unemployment, and the relationship between ALMPs and the shift from unemployment to work should be positive. We calculated correlations between investments in ALMPs (Table 6.1) and labour market transitions based on our Eurostat datasets. As a rule, the signs of the coefficients are in the expected direction but the associations are weak. In the ECHP data the coefficient for ALMPs and transition for work to unemployment is −0.29. But when we exclude the deviant case of Austria (displaying low fluidity into unemployment despite its low investment in ALMPs), the association becomes stronger (r=−0.45). There is virtually no correlation at all (r=0.01) between ALMPs and transition back to employment. However, here we also have one deviant case (Spain, with much transition and low ALMPs). When we exclude Spain, the correlation becomes somewhat higher (r=0.23).

In the EU-SILC data the situation looks very much the same. However, the association between ALMPs and the shift from employment to unemployment is somewhat higher (r=−0.33), and the exclusion of the two influential cases (Norway and the UK) improves the fit (r=−0.56★), indicating that ALMPs may diminish the flow from employment to unemployment. The association of ALMPs with the probabilities of finding employment is weak, and the sign is contrary to our expectations (r=−0.06). In this case the entire Southern European regime, with its low investment in ALMPs and high fluidity rates, deviates from the rest. The correlation is stronger and the sign is as expected if the Southern European countries are excluded from the model (r=0.52). According to our data, while investments in ALMPs are more efficient at preventing people from becoming unemployed than at helping them to find work when unemployed, the associations are not strong. Clearly ALMPs are merely one piece of a larger puzzle in which people are laid off, find work again or permanently exit from the labour market (see e.g. de Vreyer et al, 2000). Thus ALMPs alone do not sufficiently explain shifts in employment status in different welfare regimes.

——

Generosity of unemployment insurance: Nordic generosity for the low-income earners

Protection against unemployment and other social risks can take a number of forms, and a number of indicators measuring the characteristics of social insurance systems have been used. The most frequently used quality indicator is generosity of benefits.

Calculations are usually made for the average production worker (APW), who is supposed to earn the average national wage. Informative as those calculations are, the averages may conceal substantial differences in replacement levels at the lower and upper end of the income ladder. Therefore, complementary indicators are necessary.

Fortunately, the OECD provides a complete set of replacement rates for 2001-08 for six family types (no children – single person, one-earner married couple and two-earner married couple; and two children – lone parent, one-earner married couple and two-earner married couple) at three different income levels: 0.65 APW, APW and 1.5 APW (see www.oecd.org/els/social/workincentives). We calculated averages on the basis of the family types for each income level. The base year is 2007, that is, in the middle of the years that the EU-SILC covers. Because the OECD data dates back only to 2001, we had to use alternative data sources (Social Security Programs Throughout the World, 1995; OECD, 1996; Salomäki and Munzi, 1999) for the mid-1990s. The summary of country and regime replacements appears in Table 6.2.[2]

Generosity of unemployment protection varies considerably between income groups, and in most countries the compensations in relation to previous earnings are higher in low-income groups. On average the difference between 0.67 APW and 1.5 APW is about 20 percentage points. While in some countries generosity deteriorates rapidly when income increases (for example, in the 1990s the Danish compensation rate was as high as 93 per cent for the low-income earner but only 55 per cent for the high income-earner), in other countries – Portugal, France and Germany – income level does not play a role.

Despite these country variations, the congruence of different generosity measures is good. In 1995 the correlation of 0.67 APW to APW is 0.77★★, that of 0.67 APW to 1.5 APW is 0.56★ and that of APW to 1.5 APW is 0.82★★. In 2007 the corresponding figures are even higher: 0.78★, 0.62★ and 0.90★★. Some have argued that the countries that provide high-income replacements for average and higher income strata tend to have higher income protection for low-paid employees (see, for example, Korpi and Palme, 1998; Nelson, 2004). To some extent, that argument held true in 1995, when the Nordic regime had the highest replacement rates for all income groups (with the exception of the high income group, to whom the Central European countries paid higher compensations). But by 2007 the situation is somewhat different. The Nordic regime – which according to CV is homogeneous, as is the Liberal duo of Ireland and the UK – still provides the highest compensations for average- and low-income earners

Table 6.2: Replacement rates in different income levels, 1995 and 2007, in 15 European countries (net benefit/net income, %)

Country	1995			2007		
	0.67APW	APW	1.5APW	0.67APW	APW	1.5APW
Nordic						
Denmark	93	70	55	89	72	59
Finland	87	77	61	79	70	58
Norway	85	70	65	80	72	55
Sweden	80	78	63	84	71	55
Mean/CV	86.3/0.06	73.3/0.06	61.0/0.07	83.0/0.05	71.3/0.01	56.8/0.04
Central European						
Austria	65	63	62	70	67	53
Belgium	79	61	51	76	60	48
France	86	76	71	78	71	71
Germany	74	72	72	76	74	70
Netherlands	87	79	55	82	74	59
Mean/CV	78.2/0.12	70.2/0.11	62.2/0.15	76.4/0.06	69.2/0.09	60.2/17.0
Liberal						
Ireland	60	49	42	65	49	39
UK	58	38	43	67	53	39
Mean/CV	59.0/0.02	42.5/0.22	42.5/0.02	66.0/0.02	51.0/0.06	39.0/0.00
Southern European						
Greece	82	51	40	63	48	36
Italy	41	42	42	71	71	56
Portugal	88	78	80	81	85	85
Spain	72	74	59	81	73	54
Mean/CV	70.8/0.30	61.3/0.29	55.3/0.34	74.0/0.12	69.3/0.22	57.8/0.35
All Mean/CV	75.8/0.19	65.2/0.21	57.4/0.21	76.1/0.10	67.3/0.15	55.8/0.23

Source: Salomäki and Munzi (1999, pp 17-18, 26); Social Security Programs Throughout the World (1995); www.oecd.org/els/social/workincentives

but lags behind the Central and Southern European regimes when moving up the income ladder. These results are in line with the arguments of the status-preserving character of Esping-Andersen's Central European welfare state model (Esping-Andersen, 1990).

If we look at the development over time, we find a slight trend towards convergence between regimes in low- and APW-income groups, while regime differences in high-income groups are rather stable. Whereas all the compensations have gone down in the Central European and Nordic regimes, the Southern European countries show improvements across the entire income spectrum. In the UK and Ireland increases are targeted to low- and median-income groups. These changes explain the growing similarity among the regimes.

Consequences of changes in labour market positions: visible regime patterns

This section examines how changes in labour market status change the individual's income position. First, we calculate poverty risks for people with different labour market transitions for the initial year *t* and the destination year *t*+1; however, for space considerations, we present only destination year poverty rates here (see Table 6.3).

The category 'employed-employed' (Table 6.3) – people who are employed in two consecutive years – have the lowest threat of poverty. Our results for both time periods show quite consistent regime-based differences: in-work poverty is the lowest in the Nordic regime and the highest in the Southern European and Liberal regimes.[3] We find neither strong signs of greater similarities nor dramatic increases in the share of working poor in Europe. The average in-work poverty rate remained rather stable: 7.2 per cent in the 1990s and 6.9 per cent in the late 2000s. While this result is in line with Andreß and Lohmann's (2008) results, our table shows a higher degree of welfare state regime distinctiveness, with the Nordic regime having the lowest in-work poverty figures for both time points.

Losing one's job (the 'employed-unemployed' group) increases a risk of low income in all countries. While the average in-work poverty rate is less than 10 per cent, the incidence of low income is more than 20 per cent (23.1 per cent and 26.8 per cent, respectively) among those who in year *t* had employment but in *t*+1 were unemployed. Here we also find substantial and persistent differences among regimes. The poverty rate in the Nordic countries is less than 20 per cent but more than 30 per cent in the Southern European countries. Some countries deviate from their regime; for example, poverty rates in the Netherlands are lower than in the Central European countries on average, and often the Netherlands outperforms Finland and Norway.

The biggest poverty risk is associated with remaining unemployed for two years. In the 1990s about 32 per cent of those who were long-term unemployed were in poverty, while the share increased to close to 40 per cent by the late 2000s. The change in the Nordic regime is dramatic, and the regime no longer constitutes a homogeneous entity, as the high CV values indicate. This result is attributable mainly to a sharp increase in poverty among the Finnish long-term unemployed (as also documented by numerous national studies) and to the inclusion of Norway in the EU-SILC data. As for the high Norwegian poverty rates (66.4 per cent), the share of those who were unemployed for two years was extremely low; thus the group of long-term unemployed in Norway may be a much more selective group than in the other countries. Furthermore, the sample size in this combination of unemployment is very low for Norway (the lowest in the database); therefore, the associated poverty is determined with high uncertainty. All in all, differences among welfare regimes are not significant, and many countries do not 'fit' the regime in which they are categorised.

Table 6.3: Poverty rates for different labour market transitions (poverty in the destination year)

Regime/country	1994-99				2005-08			
	Employed-employed	Employed-unemployed	Unemployed-employed	Unemployed-unemployed	Employed-employed	Employed-unemployed	Unemployed-employed	Unemployed-unemployed
Nordic								
Denmark	3.4	10.6	8.1	8.5	3.5	6.8	9.0	25.0
Finland	3.8	20.9	12.3	24.1	3.7	21.2	17.9	44.9
Norway	md	md	md	md	2.7	36.1	21.0	66.4
Sweden	md	md	md	md	6.5	14.2	17.4	34.6
Mean/CV	3.6/0.08	15.8/0.46	10.2/0.29	16.3/0.68	4.1/0.40	19.6/0.64	16.3/0.31	42.7/0.42
Central European								
Austria	6.4	13.9	21.9	17.1	3.9	33.4	16.5	43.3
Belgium	5.1	19.6	12.0	28.5	4.5	35.7	24.1	19.9
France	6.3	25.3	23.3	37.1	7.0	6.1	13.9	34.2
Germany	4.7	19.3	15.7	44.7	md	md	md	md
Netherlands	4.3	12.9	17.9	25.5	3.8	20.8	18.3	40.0
Mean/CV	5.4/0.18	18.2/0.27	18.2/0.25	30.6/0.35	4.8/0.31	24.0/0.57	18.2/0.24	34.4/0.30
Liberal								
Ireland	5.2	25.6	17.0	44.6	5.8	17.5	12.3	27.7
UK	5.7	26.4	20.5	47.3	7.3	48.3	26.3	58.7
Mean/CV	5.5/0.07	26.0/0.02	18.8/0.13	46.0/0.07	6.7/0.16	32.9/0.66	19.3/0.51	43.2/0.51
Southern European								
Greece	14.8	27.0	18.8	30.6	13.4	36.5	18.3	33.9
Italy	10.4	42.9	29.2	47.3	11.4	41.2	24.0	37.5
Portugal	14.6	26.5	10.9	25.5	11.3	26.3	17.7	32.2
Spain	9.4	29.4	19.9	33.6	11.6	31.4	17.2	41.0
Mean/CV	12.3/0.23	31.5/0.24	19.7/0.38	34.3/0.27	11.9/0.08	33.9/0.19	19.3/0.17	36.1/0.11
All Mean/CV	7.2/0.54	23.1/0.37	17.5/0.33	31.9/0.38	6.9/0.52	26.8/0.48	18.1/0.26	38.5/0.32

Note: md = missing data.

As a rule, finding a job (the unemployed-employed group) is good for income: the average poverty rates for those who in year *t* were unemployed but in *t*+1 had jobs were 17.5 per cent in the 1990s and somewhat higher (18.1 per cent) 10 years later. Poverty rates of the long-term unemployed and of those who in *t* worked but in *t*+1 were unemployed are on average higher, with some exceptions. According to the ECHP, poverty for the employed-unemployed group was lower than for the unemployed-employed group in Austria (13.9 per cent versus 21.9 per cent) and the Netherlands (12.9 per cent versus 17.9 per cent). In the 2000s we find similar counterintuitive situations in Denmark (6.8 per cent versus 9.0 per cent), Sweden (14.2 per cent versus 17.4 per cent) and France (61 per cent versus 13.9 per cent). The somewhat surprising results for these countries may be caused by the annual income we use. To more closely analyse these cases we should have access to monthly income. Therefore, these data do not allow us to draw stronger conclusions on various work disincentives that the different welfare states possibly create. Nonetheless, finding employment appears to pay off better in the Liberal and Southern European regimes than in the Nordic and Central European countries, which offer high income protection for those who are unemployed.

Two-step approach: controlling for confounding variables blurs the regime boundaries

This section brings together the results of the preceding sections about the generosity of unemployment insurance and the transitional poverty rates to examine the strength of the association of poverty attached to changes in labour market status and the characteristics of unemployment insurance. As our insurance indicators are at the national level, we also use aggregate country-level poverty rates in our analyses. We are primarily interested in the connections between poverty and benefit generosity as measured separately for low- (0.67APW), middle- (APW) and high-income earners (1.5APW). The bivariate correlations for income status in different labour market transitions and generosity indicators appear in Table 6.4. Because unemployment protection does not involve those

Table 6.4: Correlations between unemployment protection generosity and poverty in different labour market status in the 1990s and 2000s

Replace-ment level	1990s			2000s		
	Employed-unemployed	Unemployed-unemployed	Unemployed-employed	Employed-unemployed	Unemployed-unemployed	Unemployed-employed
0.67APW	−0.64*	−0.68*	−0.71**	−0.56*/−0.76**	−0.09/57	−0.31/−0.68*
APW	−0.51	−0.52	−0.39	−0.31/−0.47	0.0/−0.35	−0.12/−0.50
1.5APW	−0.31	−0.33	−0.34	−0.43/−0.53	−0.11/−0.37	−0.23/−0.49

Note: Numbers to the right of the slash pertain to correlations when influential cases – Greece and Ireland – are omitted.

who have been steadily employed, the 'employed-employed' category is omitted from these analyses.

All the correlations in Table 6.4 go in the expected direction: the higher the income protection, the lower the poverty rate. Correlations are higher in the ECHP data than in the EU-SILC. For the EU-SILC data the results are highly sensitive to the deviant cases of Ireland and Greece – and the long-term unemployment category, Norway, with its extremely high poverty rates, also skews the association. If we exclude these three influential cases, the relationships turn out to be stronger. The strongest relation is between poverty rates and the 0.67 APW replacement levels, indicating that a sufficient level of minimum protection is crucial for protecting the unemployed from poverty.

Previous studies (see, for example, Kangas and Ritakallio, 2000; Fritzell and Ritakallio, 2004) have shown that differences in demography, employment patterns, family patterns, educational structures, and so on affect the incidence of poverty in advanced countries. To sort out the impacts of these confounding factors, we run logistic regressions controlling for age, gender, marital status, family structure, education and health status, and calculate poverty odds rates for each country. We use Austria as a benchmark. Odds rates higher than 1 indicate that the probability of low income in the country in question is higher than in Austria when the impacts of the confounding variables are taken into consideration. Correspondingly, numbers lower than 1 pertain to lower poverty rates than those in Austria.

Controlling for background factors somewhat changes the country rankings. For example, in the 2000s the gross poverty rates for the unemployed-unemployed category are almost the same in Austria and Finland (43.3 and 44.9 per cent, respectively). While the Finnish poverty rate is 1.03 higher than the Austrian, the relationship in odds rates is 1.66, indicating that if the Finnish population and employment structure were the same as in Austria, the long-term unemployed in Finland would have higher poverty rates as they de facto have. Similarly, the poverty rate among those who are long-term unemployed in Spain is 41.0 per cent, which in relation to the Austrian 43.3 per cent is 0.95. The relation between the odds rates for these two countries is 0.81, which, in turn, means that if Spain had the Austrian demographics and employment patterns, the Spanish poverty rate would be lower than it is. These comparisons show that much of the positive Nordic record in alleviating poverty stems from other factors (the dual-earner model) as from generous income maintenance programmes. Furthermore, the high incidence of poverty in the Southern European countries is not always caused by the poor level of income transfers but, rather, by the one-earner employment pattern (the male breadwinner model). If the Southern European male breadwinner becomes unemployed, the household income will fall below the poverty line, while in the Nordic regime dual earnership mitigates the detrimental income effects in situations where one spouse becomes unemployed.[4]

Table 6.4 shows that in poverty alleviation the most important characteristic of unemployment insurance is the level of protection at the lower end of the income ladder. Therefore, in the subsequent analyses (Figure 6.1) national level poverty odds rates generated by logistic regressions are projected against the 0.67 APW replacement rate. As unemployment protection is most important for those who in the year t were employed but in $t+1$ were unemployed (the employed-unemployed category), for those who were unemployed for two consecutive years (unemployed-unemployed) and to a lesser extent for those who found employment in $t+1$, we concentrate on those three crucial categories (Figure 6.1).

For the 1990s (the left-hand panels) a clear pattern emerges: the better the income-loss compensation for the low-income group, the lower the odds-rates. For the employed-unemployed and the unemployed-unemployed groups the compensation rates explain about 50 per cent of the variation in odds-rates (R^2 = 0.47 and 0.50, respectively). For the third group (unemployed-employed), the variance explained is somewhat lower ($R^2 = 0.38$).

The replacement rate explains much less of the country variations in the 2000s. At best the variance explained is 24 per cent (the upper right-hand panel, the 'employed-unemployed'). For the other categories the numbers are much lower, and the models perform less well. The fit slightly improves if Ireland, Norway and Spain are excluded from the models (see Table 6.4).

It is not surprising that the models work best for the employed-unemployed group. Those most recently unemployed are the most dependent on income transfers from the unemployment insurance system, whereas for the unemployed-employed group earnings from the new job should be the most important source of income and the correlation between poverty odds and the quality of social security should therefore not be very strong. That the level of income-loss compensations does not play a major role in the odds rates for those who are long-term unemployed is somewhat surprising – with three possible explanations. First, as the correlation changes when moving from 'gross' poverty rates to odds rates ('net' poverty), some degree of the variation is the result of differences in demographics and employment patterns. Second, labour markets, in particular the level of unemployment and the share of long-term unemployed, changed considerably from the mid-1990s to the late 2000s; therefore, the composition of the long-term unemployed may have also changed. Third, as a consequence of these changes, other income transfers such as housing allowances and social assistance are more important sources of income than the daily allowance from the unemployment insurance system.

All in all, the results from the two-step analysis show that controlling for the impact of the intervening variables makes the differences among welfare state regimes in net poverty much more blurred than looking directly at gross poverty rates. The Nordic model, which for gross poverty remains a distinct group (see Table 6.3), loses much of its distinctiveness for net poverty (see Figure 6.1).

Figure 6.1: Country-specific poverty odds-rates for the employed-unemployed and unemployed-unemployed in the 1990s and late 2000s

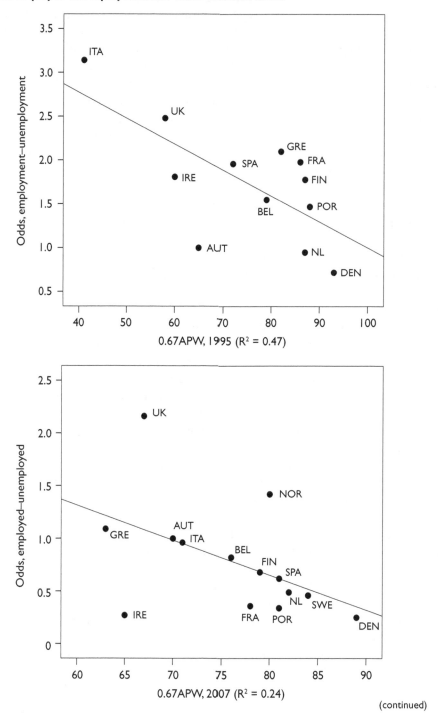

(continued)

Figure 6.1: Country-specific poverty odds-rates for the employed-unemployed and unemployed-unemployed in the 1990s and late 2000s (continued)

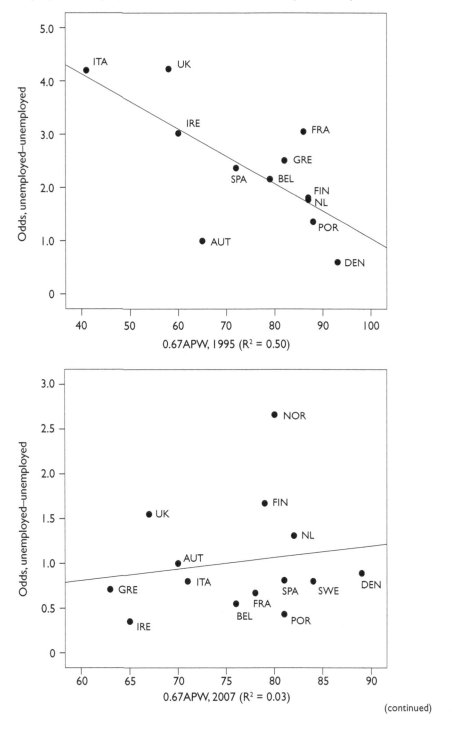

(continued)

Figure 6.1: Country-specific poverty odds-rates for the employed-unemployed and unemployed-unemployed in the 1990s and late 2000s (continued)

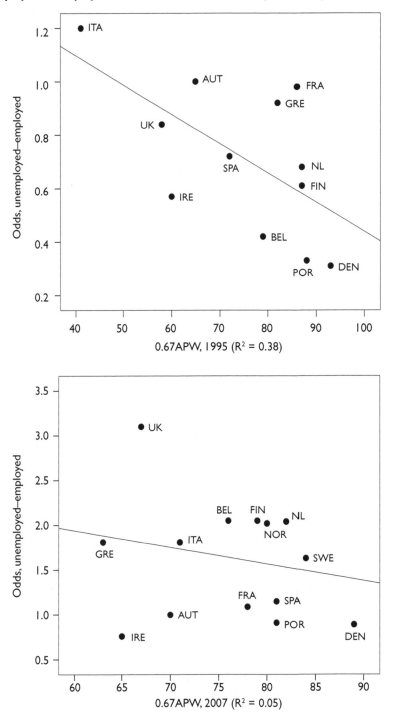

Discussion: diminishing differences but still a model of its own

The aim of this chapter was to analyse how changes in labour market status are reflected in shifts in poverty status in different countries and different welfare regimes. The underlying rationale was to analyse the distinctiveness of the Nordic model and possible shifts in the regime divide. To put our analyses in a wider frame, we first examined labour market characteristics and changes that have taken place since the mid-1990s. Detrimental impacts of the deep recession that hit Europe in the early 1990s was still visible in many countries in 1995, for example, unemployment rates remained exceptionally high in Finland and Sweden. By 2007 the situation had improved, so that with almost no exception employment rates were higher and unemployment rates lower than a decade earlier. The 2008 global recession was not yet visible, nor was it visible in our EU-SILC data.

Despite its many economic problems, the Nordic welfare regime – renowned for its high employment rates – in 1995 formed a cluster of its own. Since the mid-1990s, however, employment rates have increased not only in the Nordic countries but also in other countries. Moreover, as the expansion of women's entry into the labour market has grown faster in the other welfare regimes, the Nordic countries have lost their leading position in this respect – not from abandoning high employment but because the other countries are increasingly copying the Nordic employment pattern and because the dual-earner model is also gaining a foothold in the Southern European countries. Thus the European employment pattern has become more similar overall. Yet clear regime-based differences remain, in particular in female employment and in the incidence of long-term unemployment.

The next task was to examine the level of income-loss compensations that various national unemployment insurance schemes guarantee for the unemployed. To learn to what extent compensation levels vary between income groups, we calculated replacement rates for a low-income group (0.67 APW), middle-income group (APW) and a high-income earner (1.5 APW). In 1995, the Nordic countries offered the highest protection for the low- and average-paid employees. The well-off employees had and still have better compensation in the Central European regime. Compensations are the lowest in the Liberal regime. These results are very much in line with previous regime theories. A slight trend towards increasing convergence has taken place in compensation rates for the low and average earners, while differences have expanded in the higher income strata. This finding shows that when speaking of divergence or convergence in welfare arrangements, we must specify which factors we are examining. For example, the average income-receiver might show no changes at all, whereas considerable shifts may take place at the upper and lower income levels.

National unemployment schemes are buffers aimed at cushioning the harmful impacts of unemployment on the individual and preventing him or her from falling into poverty. We studied these effects by relating labour market transitions to the individual's income transitions through two parallel strategies. In the first analysis we used gross poverty rates, that is, we analysed the incidence of poverty in those groups that in consecutive years have been employed or unemployed, who in the year *t* had job but who in *t*+1 were unemployed and who in *t* were without work but who in *t*+1 had found work. We found clear and stable regime-related patterns for the period under investigation. The Nordic welfare state displays the lowest poverty rates for every status except long-term unemployment. Contrary to some earlier studies, our results show that European in-work poverty follows traditional regime characteristics. In-work poverty is the lowest in the Nordic regime, followed by the Central European and Liberal regimes. The working poor phenomenon is the most prevalent in the Southern European regime, the one that most relies on the traditional male breadwinner model (Ferrarini, 2003). The same pattern emerges when we look at the income situation among the employed-unemployed.

For the long-term unemployed, the Nordic countries do not perform comparatively well. One explanation might be that because the share of the long-term unemployed in the Nordic countries is lower than elsewhere, there is a stronger selection effect, that is, the Nordic unemployed may suffer more greatly from limited work capacity than the long-term unemployed elsewhere. There may also be some problems from which both the ECHP and EU-SILC suffer: in both databases household income pertain to annual income, which may in some cases cause problems for matching income status and labour market status. For example, two people in data are coded as being unemployed for two consecutive years. The first one, plagued by short-term unemployment, was unemployed both times that he or she was interviewed for the ECHP or EU-SILC; the second one has been unemployed for years. In our data both individuals fall into the same category, despite the probable differences in their income.

To better analyse such problematic cases, we should have access to monthly income. Furthermore, in future studies we need to analyse in greater detail the duration of unemployment spells and the income formation process of the long-term unemployed in different countries and regimes. A profitable task for future research is to more closely examine the composition of income packages among different groups of unemployed in European countries.

Although regime-based differences in the incidence of poverty are usually attributed to income transfers, much of the country variation in poverty rates results from demographic and labour market-related factors. To distinguish the net effect of the income transfer system from the gross effect, we applied a two-step method. We first run a logistic regression to control for confounding factors. The resultant country-specific odds ratios were then regressed against the replacement rates unemployment insurance guarantees in different countries. The experiment resulted in a decreased impact of income transfers, and differences among the welfare state regimes were blurred. The two-step approach showed that the welfare clusters are not as clear-cut as the gross poverty rates alone indicate. This finding does not mean that our results nullify the regime-based interpretations. A substantial part of the variance among the regimes may be explained by differences in family and employment patterns. However, family structures and employment configurations are also largely constructed by welfare state arrangements, that is, they are part of the regimes package. Indeed, as Esping-Andersen (1990) emphasises, the regime is created by a specific interplay between income transfers, social services and the labour market (see also Kangas and Palme, 2005).

Our study indicates that welfare state regimes may lose their distinctiveness in one of two ways. First, the countries in a regime may abandon the central aspect of the ideal model. Second, even though the countries in the regime may faithfully maintain and even fortify the central characteristics of the model, other countries adapting the same characteristics may catch up, thereby eroding the differences. We looked at three dimensions that are formative for the Nordic welfare state regime: high level of employment; high income protection in the case of unemployment; and the consequent low incidence of poverty in different labour market shifts. For the first dimension we find signs of the second type of convergence and a dilution of regime contours. While the Nordic countries are maintaining their high employment levels, other countries are gradually closing the gap. For the second dimension, while some convergence also exists in income replacements, the growing similarity is now a mixture of the two processes. On the one hand, income replacements have deteriorated in the Nordic countries (and in Central Europe) while they have improved in the UK, Ireland and the Southern European countries. For the third dimension, the incidence of poverty in specific transitions in the labour markets does not show radical changes in regime-based differences. Although the Nordic rates are increasing, so are the rates in the other regimes. Therefore, despite some signs of a piecemeal convergence, a high degree of welfare state 'regime integrity' remains.

Notes

[1] Here the overlap between OECD and Eurostat data is also more than satisfactory. The correlation coefficient for the overall unemployment rate in 1997 and our numbers for those who have been unemployed in two years was 0.91**. For the latter period the overall OECD unemployment level yields a correlation coefficient 0.43 to our long-term unemployment. Here the deviant case is the Netherlands, which has 'too high' shares of long-term unemployment in the EU-SILC data. The exclusion of the Netherlands considerably improves the fit of the datasets (r=0.72**). The fit between our long-term unemployment figures and the OECD ones is better (0.78**) (* = statistically almost significant, ** = statistically significant, and *** = statistically very significant).

[2] We cross-checked our APW calculations against Lyle Scruggs' data (http://sp.uconn.edu~scruggs/wp.htm). The correlation coefficient between our APW replacement levels and Scruggs' numbers is high (r=0.94**). As Scruggs provides compensation rates only for the APW, we could not cross-check replacement rates for 0.67 APW or 1.5 APW.

[3] The match between our total poverty rates for 2005-08 and Eurostat poverty rates for 2008 is reasonably high (r=0.75**).

⁴ However, it is too simplistic to argue that regime-based differences in the risk of poverty are totally explained by demographics and employment patterns or to conclude that characteristics of the regimes, that is, social policies, play no role. Social policies, more specifically family policy and services for families, have a huge impact on employment (see, for example, Ferrarini, 2003; Anttonen, 2005; and Chapter Five, this volume), and thus regime types indirectly explain the differences observed.

References

Aaberge, R., Björklund, A., Jäntti, M., Palme, M., Pedersen, P., Smith, N. and Wennemo, T. (1996) *Income inequality and income mobility in the Scandinavian countries compared to the United States*, Discussion Paper, no 168, Oslo: Research Department, Statistics Norway.

Airio, I. (2008) *Change of norm? In-work poverty in a comparative perspective*, Studies in Social Security and Health No 92, Helsinki: Kela.

Andreß, H.-J. and Lohmann, H. (eds) *The working poor in Europe: Employment, poverty and globalization*, Cheltenham: Edward Elgar.

Anttonen, A. (2005) 'Empowering social policy: the role of social care services in modern welfare states', in O. Kangas and J. Palme (eds) *Social policy and economic development in the Nordic countries*, Houndmills: Palgrave Macmillan, pp 88-117.

Atkinson, A. and Marlier, E. (eds) (2010) *Income and living conditions in Europe*, Luxembourg: Eurostat.

Björklund, A. and Jäntti, M. (2008) 'Intergenerational income mobility and the role of family background', in W. Salverda, B. Nolan, and T. Smeeding (eds) *Handbook of Economic Inequality*, Oxford: Oxford University Press, pp 491-521.

Cantillon, B., Marx, I. and van den Bosch, K. (2002) *The puzzle of egalitarianism: About the relationship between employment, wage, inequality, social expenditures and poverty*, LIS Working Paper Series no 337, Syracuse, NY: Syracuse University.

Carroll, E. (1999) *Emergence and structuring of social insurance institutions. Comparative studies on social policy and unemployment insurance*, Dissertation Series no 38, Stockholm: Swedish Institute for Social Research, Stockholm University.

de Vreyer, P., Layte, P., Wolbers, M. and Hussain, M.A. (2000) 'The permanent effects of labour market entry in times of high unemployment', in D. Gallie and S. Paugam (eds) *Welfare regimes and the experience of unemployment in Europe*, Oxford: Oxford University Press, pp 134-52.

DiMarco, M. (2010) 'Employment and social inclusion in the EU', A paper presented at the 2010 International Conference on Comparative EU Statistics on Income and Living Conditions, Warsaw, 25-26 March.

Drøpping, J.A., Hvinden, B. and Vik, K. (1999) 'Activation policies in the Nordic countries', in M. Kautto, M. Heikkilä, B. Hvinden, S. Marklund and N. Ploug (eds) *Nordic social policy: Changing welfare states*, London: Routledge, pp 133-58.

Esping-Andersen, G. (1990) *Three worlds of welfare capitalism*, Cambridge: Polity Press.

Eurostat (2010) 'Population and social conditions', *Statistics in Focus*, 9/2010, Luxembourg: European Commission.

Ferrarini, T. (2003) *Parental leave institutions in eighteen post-war welfare states*, Dissertation Series no 58, Stockholm: Swedish Institute for Social Research, Stockholm University.

Ferrera, M. (2010) 'The Southern European countries', in F. Castles, S. Leibfried, J. Lewis, H. Obinger and C. Pierson (eds) *The Oxford handbook of the welfare state*, Oxford: Oxford University Press, pp 616-29.

Fritzell, J. and Ritakallio, V.-M. (2004) *Societal shifts and changed patterns of poverty*, LIS Working Paper Series, no 393, Syracuse, NY: Syracuse University.

Gallie, D. and Paugam, S. (eds) (2000) *Welfare regimes and the experience of unemployment in Europe*, Oxford: Oxford University Press.

Goldstein, H. (2003) *Multilevel statistical models* (3rd edn), London: Arnold.

Goodin, R.E., Heady, B. and Dirven, H.J. (1999) *The Real Worlds of Welfare Capitalism*, Cambridge: Cambridge University Press.

Gray, J. (1998) *False dawn: The delusions of global capitalism*, London: Granta Books.

Hussain, M.A. (2002) 'Essays on income distribution', PhD dissertation, no 2002:8, Aarhus: Aarhus School of Business.

Immervoll, H. and Pearson, M. (2009) *A good time for making work pay? Taking stock of in-work benefits and related measures across the OECD*, OECD Social, Employment and Migration Working Papers, No 81, Paris: Directorate for Employment, Labour and Social Affairs.

Kangas, O. and Palme, J. (eds) (2005) *Social Policy and Economic Development in the Nordic Countries*, Houndsmills: Palgrave.

Kangas, O. and Ritakallio, V.-M. (2000) 'Social policy or structure?', in B. Palier and D. Bouget (eds) *Comparing social welfare systems in Nordic Europe and France*, Paris: Mission de la Recherche.

Korpi, W. and Palme, J. (1998) 'The paradox of redistribution and strategies of equality: welfare state institutions, inequalities, and poverty in the western countries', *American Sociological Review*, vol 63, pp 661-87.

Nelson, K. (2004) 'Mechanisms of poverty alleviation: anti-poverty effects of non-means tested and means tested benefits in five welfare states', *Journal of European Social Policy*, vol 14, pp 371-90.

Nolan, B. and Marx, I. (1999) *Low pay and household poverty*, LIS Working Paper 216, Luxembourg: Luxembourg Income Study.

OECD (1996) *OECD Economic Studies, No. 26*. Paris: OECD.

OECD (2002) *OECD Employment Outlook*, Paris: OECD.

OECD (2008) *OECD Employment Outlook*, Paris: OECD.

Nelson, K. (2003) *Fighting Poverty. Comparative studies on social insurance, means-tested benefits and income redistribution*, Dissertation Series no 60, Stockholm: Swedish Institute for Social Research, Stockholm University.

Political Analysis (2005), vol 13.

Rasbash, J., Browne, W., Goldstein, H., Yang, M., Plewis, I., Healy, M., Woodhouse, G., Draper, D., Langford, I. and Lewis, T. (2000) *A user's guide to MLwiN*, London: Centre for Multilevel Modelling, Institute of Education, University of London.

Rifkin, J. (1995) *The end of work: The decline of the global labor force and the dawn of the post-market era*, New York: Putnam Publishing Group.

Ritakallio, V.-M. (2002) 'Trends of poverty and income inequality in cross-national comparison', *European Journal of Social Security*, vol 4, pp 151-77.

Salomäki, A. and Munzi, T. (1999) *Net replacement rates of the unemployed*, Economic Papers 133, Brussels: European Commission.

Sennett, R. (2006) *The culture of new capitalism*, New Haven, CT: Yale University Press.

Smeeding, T.M. (2002) *Globalization, inequality and the rich countries of the G-20. Evidence from the Luxembourg Income Study (LIS)*, LIS Working Paper Series no 320, Syracuse, NY: Syracuse University.

Standing, G. (2009) *Work after globalization. Building occupational citizenship*, Cheltenham: Edward Elgar.

Social Security Programmes Throughout the World (1995) *Social Security Programs Throughout The World*, Washington D.C.: Social Security Administration Office of Policy.

Wolff, P., Montaigne, F. and Gonzales, R.G. (2010), 'Investing in statistics: EU-SILC', in A. Atkinson and E. Marlier (eds) *Income and living conditions in Europe*, Brussels: Eurostat, pp 37-56.

SEVEN

Social inequalities in health: the Nordic welfare state in a comparative context

Clare Bambra

Introduction

It is now widely acknowledged that welfare states are important determinants of health as they mediate the extent, and impact, of socioeconomic position on health (Navarro et al, 2003, 2006; Bambra, 2006a; Chung and Muntaner, 2007; Eikemo et al, 2008a). Welfare state provision varies extensively, but typologies have been put forward to categorise them into three, four or even five distinctive types or welfare state regimes (see Chapter 1). The concept of welfare state regimes has been used to analyse cross-national differences in population health. These studies have almost invariably concluded that population health is enhanced by the relatively generous and universal welfare provision of the Nordic countries, especially when contrasted to the Liberal welfare states of the UK and Ireland (Navarro et al, 2003, 2006; Coburn, 2004; Bambra, 2006a). In contrast to their comparatively strong performance in terms of overall health, data from a number of comparative European research projects suggest that the Nordic welfare states do not have the smallest health inequalities (Lundberg and Lahelma, 2001; Dahl et al, 2006). However, the position of the most vulnerable social groups is often much better in the Nordic welfare states (Zambon et al, 2006; Avendano et al, 2009; Dahl et al, 2010), and health inequalities in the Nordic countries have remained fairly stable (Lahelma et al, 2002) while they have widened in other countries, such as the US (Krieger et al, 2008) and New Zealand (Blakely et al, 2008), during the more volatile economic and political climate since the 1980s and 1990s. There is tentative evidence from the experiences of other countries to suggest that future changes – such as marketisation and individualisation – in the Nordic welfare model may also increase health inequalities and damage the position of the most vulnerable in the medium to long term. This chapter critically overviews the comparative evidence base on health inequalities in order to place the Nordic welfare states within their international context.

Initially, the chapter examines health inequality – definition, measurement and theory. It then examines the role of welfare states in determining overall population health outcomes. The main studies in the comparative epidemiological literature on European health inequalities are then summarised (Mackenbach et al, 1997, 2008; Cavelaars et al, 1998), with a focus on the relative performance of the Nordic welfare states. The effects on health inequalities of changes to the Nordic welfare state are also examined. The chapter then uses the theories of health inequalities to examine why it is that the highly decommodifying Nordic welfare states do not have the smallest health inequalities in Europe. The chapter concludes by reflecting on how any further changes to the Nordic welfare model may have an impact on health inequalities in the future.

Defining, measuring and explaining health inequalities[1]

Health inequality is a complex and multilayered concept and there are various ways in which it can be defined, measured and explained.

Defining health inequality

The term 'health inequality' is usually used to refer to the systematic differences in health that exist between socioeconomic groups (although there are other inequalities, say, by gender or 'race'). Health inequality can be defined in a purely descriptive way. For example, Kawachi and colleagues refer to health inequality as 'a term used to designate differences, variations, and disparities in the health achievements of individuals and groups' (Kawachi et al, 2002, p 1491). More commonly, however, the moral and ethical dimensions of the term are emphasised: inequalities in health are thereby 'systematic differences in health between different socioeconomic groups within a society. As they are socially produced, they are potentially avoidable and widely considered unacceptable in a civilised society' (Whitehead, 2007, p 473). Inequalities in health between socioeconomic groups are not restricted to differences between the most privileged groups and the most disadvantaged; health inequalities exist across the entire social gradient. The social gradient in health is not confined to the poorest in society; it runs from the top to the bottom of society and 'even comfortably off people somewhere in the middle tend to have poorer health than those above them' (Marmot, 2006, p 2). Socioeconomic inequalities in health are universal within capitalist countries and they extend along the whole social ladder: 'the higher the social position, the better the health' (Lundberg and Lahelma, 2001, p 42).

Health inequalities are not 'natural' or 'inevitable'; they are socially distributed and socially determined. For example, high blood pressure is a biological risk factor for cardiovascular disease, it is associated with adverse health behaviours (such as an unhealthy diet), which in turn are connected to particular social circumstances (what Marmot calls the 'causes of the causes'; Marmot, 2006, p 2). Welfare states and the social policies they operate can therefore have an impact on health inequalities by changing the exposure of different socioeconomic groups to the social determinants of health. This has typically been done in one of three ways: by focusing on improving the health of the most disadvantaged groups; by reducing the health gap between the best and worst off; or by reducing the entire socioeconomic gradient in health (Graham and Kelly, 2004). The universal welfare policies associated with the ideal type Nordic welfare state have tended to operationalise the latter approach.

Measuring health inequalities

There are two major measurement issues in terms of health inequalities: measuring socioeconomic status and measuring health. Measures for the former will operationalise the 'inequality' part of the concept, while measures for the latter will define the health aspect.

Socioeconomic status can be measured in a number of different ways, most commonly in terms of social class, income or education. Social class is a multifaceted concept which incorporates ownership (property owner versus worker), skills and credentials (level of education and qualifications) as well as organisational assets (manager versus subordinate) (Wright, 1985). Income is usually measured using a proportional measure such as quartiles or quintiles so groups are formed based on how close to the top or bottom of the income scale they are. Education can be measured in terms of a specific cut-off such as no qualifications versus a higher degree, or it can be used as a scale variable, such as number of years in education. Clearly, the 'real' meaning of socioeconomic indicators will vary by country as, for example, average years of education will vary by country. Novel measurement approaches have therefore been developed in respect to all of these indicators by those involved in cross-national comparisons of health. Most recently, Eikemo and colleagues developed a standardised measure of educational inequalities expressed as the difference in health between people with an average number of years of education and people whose educational years lay one standard deviation below the national average (Eikemo et al, 2008b). Clearly each of these measures captures a different aspect of socioeconomic inequality and data on the magnitude of health inequalities within a particular country can vary depending on which measure is used (Bambra, 2011b). It will also depend on exactly what contrasts are made as, for example, the result of a study using income as a measure of social inequality would depend on whether the health of the most affluent group (the top income quartile) was compared with the least affluent (the bottom income quartile), or whether the population was merely dichotomised by income into two groups.

In terms of measuring health, studies look at either mortality (such as infant mortality rates [IMRs], adult mortality, all cause mortality or cause-specific mortality) or morbidity (illness, disease etc). Mortality data is considered to be better as it is always objectively measured (although there can be problems with how deaths are recorded in some countries, for example, for suicides). Morbidity can also be objectively measured (for example, through medical examination), but more usually it is self-reported. Self-reported health is considered to be a more subjective measure of health and there is some debate over its validity, especially in terms of cross-national comparisons (Esser and Palme, 2010). Some commentators have questioned whether we can compare self-reported measures of illness between countries and cultures especially over time (Mitchell, 2005). In contrast, others have shown that self-reported health is strongly associated with later mortality across all socioeconomic groups (Burstrom and Fredlund, 2001).

One further issue in measuring health inequalities is whether absolute or relative measures are used. Absolute measures of health inequality refer to the difference in the actual numbers of people who get ill or who die. In contrast, relative health inequality compares the percentage difference in ill health or mortality between groups (Bartley, 2004). So, for example, if the life expectancy of population A is 80 years and the life expectancy of population B is 70, then the absolute inequality in health between groups A and B is 10 years. However, the relative difference is 80:70, or put more simply, population A lives 1.14 times longer than population B. The relative index of inequality (RII) is an example of a well-used regression-based measure of relative inequality. It is the ratio between the estimated mortality or morbidity prevalence among the lowest socioeconomic group (rank 1) and the highest level (rank 0) (Mackenbach et al, 2008). A high score on the RII therefore represents large health inequalities. Best practice in cross-national comparisons is to present both absolute and relative measures of health inequalities (Lundberg and Lahelma, 2001).

Theories of health inequalities

The influential British Black report published in 1980 was the first government-commissioned report anywhere to systematically collate data on social inequalities in health (Black et al, 1980). It also outlined several explanatory theories for why health inequalities existed in countries with welfare states. In the years since Black, these theories have been elaborated and expanded. There are now six overlapping theories of health inequalities: artefact, selection, behavioural, materialist, psychosocial and life course (Mackenbach et al, 2002; Bartley, 2004).

- The artefact approach suggests that socioeconomic inequalities do not really exist but are a result of the data used and methods of measurement.
- The health selection approach asserts that health determines socioeconomic status rather than socioeconomic status determining health. People with ill health are downwardly mobile and are therefore concentrated within the lower socioeconomic groups. Indirect selection suggests that it is selection in terms of the social determinants of health (for example, unemployment) rather than health itself.
- The culture-behavioural approach asserts that the link between socioeconomic status and health is differences in health-related behaviour. Such differences in health behaviour are themselves both a consequence of disadvantage and the fact that unhealthy behaviour may be more culturally acceptable among lower socioeconomic groups.
- The materialist explanation cites income and on what income enables in respect to access to goods and services and exposures to material (physical) risk

factors (poor housing, inadequate diet, physical hazards at work, environmental exposures).

- Psychosocial explanations focus on how social inequality makes people feel and the effects of the biological consequences of these feelings on health. The socioeconomic gradient is therefore explained by the unequal social distribution of psychosocial risk factors (such as levels of control).
- The life course approach combines aspects of the other explanations, thereby allowing different causal mechanisms and processes to explain the social gradient in different diseases. Health inequality between social groups is therefore a result of inequalities in the accumulation of social, psychological and biological advantages and disadvantages over time.

Social determinants, welfare states and population health[2]

The welfare state is an important determinant of health as it mediates the extent, and impact, of the social determinants on health. The main social determinants of health are widely considered to be: access to essential goods and services (specifically water and sanitation, and food); housing and the living environment; access to healthcare; unemployment and social security; working conditions; and transport (Dahlgren and Whitehead, 1991). Access to clean water and hygienic sanitation systems are the most basic prerequisites for good public health, as is the quality, quantity, price and availability of food (Dahlgren et al, 1996). Housing is an important material determinant of health, with poor quality housing resulting in higher prevalence of respiratory disease, while housing costs can also indirectly have a negative effect on health as expenditure in other areas (such as diet) is reduced (Stafford and McCarthy, 2006). Access to healthcare is a fundamental determinant of health, particularly in terms of the treatment of pre-existing conditions. Unemployment is associated with an increased likelihood of morbidity and mortality (Bartley et al, 2006), and the physical work environment can have a negative impact on health via exposure to dangerous substances (for example, lead, asbestos, mining, mercury etc) or via physical load and ergonomic problems. Epidemiological research has also found a relationship between the psychosocial work environment, work-related stress and inequalities in health status (Marmot et al, 2006). Transport works as a social determinant of health in three ways: as a source of pollution, as a cause of accidents and as a form of exercise.

Even when a narrow definition of the welfare state (as the state's interventions in education, health, housing, poor relief and social insurance, in developed capitalist countries during the postwar period; Ginsburg, 1979), is taken, then it clearly has *a* major role in shaping these social determinants. If a broader conceptualisation of the welfare state (as a particular form of the capitalist state) (Hay, 1996) is used, then it becomes *the* major determinant of all of these social determinants, and of the varying extent of exposure of different socioeconomic groups to them. The welfare state is thus *a vital macro determinant of public health*, and as welfare states vary internationally, so does the way in which they moderate exposure (particularly of lower socioeconomic status groups) to the social determinants of health. Welfare states in Europe vary extensively in terms of the principles underpinning them, their population coverage and their decommodification outcomes (Esping-Andersen, 1990). The Nordic welfare states of Denmark, Finland, Norway and Sweden are usually considered to be a distinctive group and highly decommodifying as they are characterised by generous replacement rates, high population coverage, universalism and egalitarianism (Bambra, 2007). International research on the social determinants of health has increasingly concluded that population health is enhanced by the relatively generous and universal welfare provision of the Social Democratic Nordic countries, especially in contrast to the Liberal welfare states.

In terms of mortality, studies have consistently shown that IMRs vary significantly by welfare regime type, with rates lowest in the Nordic countries and highest in the Liberal and Southern regimes. In a longitudinal cross-national study of income inequalities and welfare provision between countries, Coburn (2004) concluded those countries that were the least neoliberal in their economic and social policy orientation (that is, the Nordic welfare states) had significantly lower IMRs, lower overall mortality rates and less mortality at younger ages. This study also suggested that the welfare state regime might be the mediating link between gross domestic product (GDP)/capita and mortality. Conley and Springer (2001) examined IMRs from 1960 to 1992 in the developed countries of the Organisation for Economic Co-operation and Development (OECD). They found significant differences by regime type, but that these differences decreased over time with a certain degree of convergence in terms of IMR. Their analysis also identified that public expenditure on healthcare had an important association with IMR, particularly in the Conservative welfare state regimes. Similarly, Bambra's analysis (2006a) found significant differences in IMRs between the three worlds of welfare: weighted IMRs for the Liberal, Conservative and Social Democratic (Nordic) regimes were 6.7, 4.5 and 4.0 respectively. This study also found a moderate correlation between decommodification levels and IMRs (r=–0.585, p=0.018). Navarro et al (2003, 2006) found that those countries that have had long periods of government by redistributive political parties (most notably the Nordic countries) have experienced lower IMRs and, to a lesser extent, increased life expectancy at birth. These findings were reinforced by Chung and Muntaneer's (2007) multilevel longitudinal analysis of welfare state regimes in which they found that around 20 per cent of the difference in IMR among countries, and 10 per cent for low birth weight, could be explained by the type of welfare state. The Nordic countries had significantly lower IMRs and low birth weight rates, compared to the other welfare state regimes. A wider sample study by Karim et al (2010) examined differences in IMR and life expectancy in 30 welfare states including those in Eastern European and East Asia (see Table 7.1). The analysis found that only life expectancy (R^2=0.58, adjusted R^2=0.47, p<0.05) differed significantly by welfare state regime. The study found that 47 per cent of the variation was explained by welfare state regime type. The Nordic welfare states had the lowest IMRs but not the highest life expectancy (Karim et al, 2010). An innovative study by Lundberg and colleagues (2008) examined the influence of two key Social Democratic Nordic welfare state policies – support for dual earners (1970-2000) and generous basic pensions (1950-2000) – on IMRs

Table 7.1: Infant mortality rates (IMRs) and life expectancy at birth for 30 countries and six welfare state regimes in 2003[a]

	IMR (deaths per 1,000 live births)	Life expectancy at birth (in years)
Scandinavian (Social Democratic)	**3.98**	**78.52**
Denmark	4.90	77.10
Finland	3.73	77.92
Norway	3.87	79.09
Sweden	3.42	79.97
Liberal (Anglo-Saxon)	**5.53**	**78.49**
Australia	4.83	80.13
Canada	4.88	79.83
Ireland	5.34	77.35
New Zealand	6.07	78.32
United Kingdom	5.28	78.16
United States	6.75	77.14
Conservative (Bismarckian)	**4.40**	**78.65**
Austria	4.33	78.17
Belgium	4.57	78.29
France	4.37	79.28
Germany	4.23	78.42
Luxembourg	4.65	77.66
Netherlands	4.26	78.74
Switzerland	4.36	79.99
Southern	**5.65**	**78.47**
Greece	6.12	78.89
Italy	6.19	79.40
Portugal	5.73	76.35
Spain	4.54	79.23
Eastern	**6.83**	**74.19**
Hungary	8.58	72.17
Czech Republic	5.37	75.18
Poland	8.95	73.91
Slovenia	4.42	75.51
East Asian	**5.29**	**78.70**
Japan	3.30	80.93
Korea	7.31	75.36
Hong Kong	5.63	79.93
Singapore	3.57	80.42
Taiwan	6.65	76.87

Note: [a] Reproduced from Karim et al (2010), with permission from Elsevier.

and old age excess mortality in 18 developed countries. They found that every 1 per cent increase in support for the dual-earner family model decreased the IMR by 0.04 per 1,000 births. This was not the case for expenditure in support of the traditional male breadwinner family model (associated particularly with the Conservative regime). Similarly, for every 1 per cent increase in the generosity of basic old age pensions, there was a decrease in old age excess mortality by 0.02 for both men and women. Generosity in earnings-related pensions (a defining characteristic of the Conservative regime) did not decrease mortality.

The studies thus universally suggest that the Nordic countries have the best population health outcomes in Europe. Commentators have chosen to privilege particular explanations for this Nordic supremacy. For example, Coburn (2004) and Bambra (2006a) have both suggested that the key characteristics of the Nordic welfare state package (universalism, generous replacement rates, extensive welfare services) result in narrower income inequalities and higher levels of decommodification, both of which are associated with better population health (Wilkinson, 1996). Coburn (2004), along with Navarro and colleagues (2003, 2006), also highlighted the importance of the accumulative positive effect on income inequalities of governance by pro-redistribution political parties in the Nordic countries. Other commentators have also suggested that increased gender equality and defamilisation within the Nordic countries may be another incremental factor behind their better health outcomes (Stanistreet et al, 2005; Bambra et al, 2009). Furthermore, proponents of the social capital approach have highlighted the high levels of social cohesion and integration within Nordic societies, something which has also been associated with better population health (Kawachi et al, 1997).

Nordic health inequalities in a European context

Health inequalities are universal within capitalist societies. However, given the extensive nature of the Nordic welfare state model and its high performance in terms of improving overall population health, it would be expected that health inequalities would be smallest in the Nordic countries. Evidence from studies conducted in the 1970s and 1980s largely supported this view. However, as detailed below, more recent studies have suggested that health inequalities are not the smallest in the Nordic countries.

Early comparative studies of health inequalities

The British Black report of 1980 contained some comparative data from the 1970s about health inequalities. It showed that Norway and Sweden had the smallest (and reducing) socioeconomic inequalities in mortality, particularly in comparison to France, West Germany and the UK (Black et al, 1980). This was reinforced by subsequent studies which just compared Sweden and the UK (Lundberg, 1986; Vagero and Lundberg, 1989). Other comparative studies of mortality conducted in the 1980s came to similar conclusions. For example, a study by Valkonen examined educational inequalities in mortality in six European countries in the 1970s. It found that relative inequalities were largest in France, then the UK and Finland, while they were smallest in Denmark, Norway and Sweden (Valkonen, 1989). In contrast, a cross-national study of limiting long-standing illness in four countries found that in the mid-1980s, relative inequalities were larger in Finland, Norway and Sweden than in the UK (Lahelma and Arber, 1994).

The first large-scale European study

In the 1990s, a large-scale European Union (EU) funded comparative study of health inequalities was set up. This was a response to criticisms of existing studies which only covered a few countries, differing time periods, used different methods of analysis and different variables. The study was therefore designed to systematically compare as many European countries as possible over similar time periods and using comparable measures of health and inequality (Lundberg and Lahelma, 2001). Both mortality (1975-90, nationally representative linked or unlinked studies, people aged 30-59) and morbidity (1986-92, using nationally representative survey data of people aged 25-69) were examined, and inequality was measured using education (quartiles of no or only primary, lower, upper, post-secondary), income (deciles of household income, adjusted for household size) and, for men only, occupational class (manual, non-manual, farmers) (Mackenbach et al, 1997).

Educational inequalities in morbidity (largely measured using self-reported health: very good or good versus less than good) were examined for eleven Western European countries: Denmark, Finland, France, Italy, the Netherlands, Norway, Spain, Sweden, Switzerland, the UK and West Germany. The study found that using RII, health inequalities between the least and most educated were present in all the countries studied, and ranged from 2.25 to 6.98 (Cavelaars et al, 1998). The Nordic countries had relatively larger educational inequalities in self-reported health than the other European countries, with Norway exhibiting the largest relative inequalities among men (RII = 6.98, 95% CI 4.55-10.7) and Sweden among women (RII = 7.27, 95% CI 4.55-11.6). The Conservative welfare country of West Germany had the smallest inequalities for both men (RII = 2.25, 95% CI 1.81-2.79) and women (RII = 2.5, 95% CI 1.99-3.17).

In terms of income inequalities in self-reported health, data was only available for six countries: Finland, France, Netherlands, Sweden, the UK and West Germany (Lundberg and Lahelma, 2001). Income inequalities in health were again present in all the countries, ranging from 2.25 to 6.98 (measured using the RII). In contrast to the education results, the two Nordic countries, Finland (men RII = 3.74, 95% CI 2.90-4.81) and Sweden (men RII = 3.21, 95% CI 2.16-4.68), had smaller relative income inequalities in self-reported health for men than all the other countries except West Germany, which again had the smallest inequalities (men RII = 2.72, 95% CI 2.21-3.34). For women, the Nordic countries did less well, with Finland mid-table behind the Conservative countries of Germany and the Netherlands, and Sweden second from bottom, out-performing only the Liberal UK. Another 1990s comparative study of income inequalities in health in eight countries reinforced these findings with the two Nordic countries in the sample (Sweden and Finland) having the lowest inequalities in health by income (van Doorslaer et al, 1997).

In terms of inequalities in mortality, the published results focus on occupational inequalities among men in nine countries: Denmark, Finland, France, Italy, Norway, Spain, Sweden, Switzerland and the UK. Mortality was lower for non-manual occupations in all the countries studied with rate ratios ranging from 1.33 to 1.76 (Mackenbach et al, 1997). However, there were little differences in the sizes of relative inequalities in mortality by country. Among Nordic men aged 45 to 59, Denmark had a relative rate ratio of 1.33 (95% CI 1.30-1.36), Finland 1.53 (95% CI 1.49-1.56), Norway 1.34 (95% CI 1.30-1.39) and Sweden 1.41 (95% CI 1.38-1.44). However, in terms of absolute differences, Norway (risk difference of 5.2, 95% CI 4.6-6.0) and Sweden (5.6, 95% CI 5.2-6.0) had the lowest inequalities, with the exception of Switzerland.

Taken as a whole, the results of this groundbreaking study showed that health inequalities were not smaller in the Nordic countries, but also that in the case of self-perceived health, that they were larger. The differences in findings, however, by measure of inequality (particularly education compared to income), the large and overlapping confidence intervals between countries or the differences between relative and absolute measures should not be overlooked (Lundberg and Lahelma, 2001).

The second European study

In 2004 a second comparative study of health inequalities was commissioned by the EU. This study was an update of the earlier study and like its predecessor, both mortality (1990-2002, nationally representative linked or unlinked studies, people aged 30-74) and morbidity (1994-2004, using nationally representative survey data of people aged 30-69) were examined, and inequality was measured using education (quartiles of no or only primary, lower, upper, post-secondary), income (quintiles of household income, adjusted for household size) and, again for men only, occupational class (manual, non-manual) (Mackenbach et al, 2008). The major differences with the first study were that a larger sample of countries was examined which included the former Communist countries of Eastern Europe, and it also looked at differences by country in the social determinants of health inequalities.

In terms of relative educational inequalities in mortality, the findings were very similar to the earlier study (Mackenbach et al, 2008). There was a lot of variability between countries as the RIIs ranged from 1.4 to 4.5 among men and from 1.1 to 3.1 among women. For both men and women, educational inequalities in mortality were smallest in the Southern countries of Spain and Italy (RII <1.5) and largest in the countries of Eastern Europe (RII >4). The Nordic countries held intermediate positions with a mortality rate of people with the least education at about double that of those with the most education. These were similar size inequalities to those of England or Belgium. Finland had slightly larger relative educational inequalities among men than the other Nordic countries, although this was not the case for women. The findings were similar for absolute educational inequalities in mortality. In terms of relative occupational inequalities in mortality among men, Finland had the highest inequalities followed by France, Sweden and Norway (no data for Denmark; only eight countries in the analysis).

In terms of morbidity, there was less variability across Europe and generally the inequalities were smaller (Mackenbach et al, 2008). In respect to educational inequalities, the RIIs ranged from 1.2 to 1.7 with Germany having the smallest inequalities. Spain and Italy still exhibited lower than average inequalities and the Eastern European countries had much smaller inequalities in self-reported health than in mortality (RII <1.6). As with educational inequalities in mortality, the Nordic countries again held an intermediate position. In terms of income inequalities in morbidity the RIIs ranged from 1.2 to 2 among men and 1.2 to 1.8 among women. However, unlike the earlier study, relative inequalities in self-reported health were not smaller in the Nordic countries: Denmark had higher income inequalities in self-reported health than all countries except England, with Norway and Sweden not far behind (no data for Finland; only 13 countries in the analysis). These results were disputed by another extensive comparative study conducted in the same period by Eikemo and colleagues using self-reported health data from European Social Survey (ESS). This cross-sectional study of 23 European countries found that the Nordic countries had intermediate income inequalities in health (Eikemo et al, 2008c).

Taken as a whole, these results reinforce the findings of the first survey in regards to the comparative size of health inequalities in the Nordic countries: there was no evidence of systematically smaller relative inequalities in mortality in the Nordic countries (Mackenbach et al, 2008). Indeed, most subsequent comparative European studies have suggested that overall health inequalities are smallest among the Conservative regime countries. This is demonstrated in Table 7.2, which summarises the findings of three comparative studies of self-reported health by welfare state regime. This data shows that relative inequalities in morbidity (self-reported health) are smallest in the Continental welfare states, not the Nordic welfare states. However, it is important to note that while the epidemiological evidence base suggests that relative and absolute health inequalities are not the smallest in the Nordic welfare states, there is emerging evidence to suggest that the health of the most vulnerable social groups – the old (Avendano et al, 2009), the sick (Dahl et al, 2010) and children (Zambon et al, 2006) – is substantially better in the Nordic welfare states. This raises important normative political questions about the role of the Nordic welfare state in terms of health inequalities, such as whether the state should promote equality among all social groups, or focus on protecting the weakest (Bambra, 2011b).

Table 7.2: Summary findings of three welfare state studies of absolute and relative socioeconomic inequalities in self-reported health (bad/poor versus fair/good/very good)[a]

Study	Measure of inequality	Typology		Summary of results[b]			
				Men		Women	
				Absolute prevalence rate difference	*Relative prevalence OR (95% CI)*	*Absolute prevalence rate difference*	*Relative prevalence OR (95% CI)*
Eikemo et al (2008b)	Education	Ferrera (1996)	Bismarckian	6.4	1.19 (1.14-1.24)	5.7	1.25 (1.20-1.30)
			Anglo-Saxon	9.6	1.35 (1.23-1.48)	8.2	1.29 (1.18-1.41)
			Scandinavian	10.5	1.44 (1.35-1.53)	12.1	1.54 (1.44-1.64)
			Eastern	11.0	1.39 (1.32-1.47)	12.8	1.54 (1.46-1.63)
			Southern	14.8	1.57 (1.47-1.69)	17.3	1.69 (1.58-1.81)
Eikemo et al (2008c)	Income	Ferrera (1996)	Bismarckian	9.8	1.68 (1.50-1.89)	11.6	1.81 (1.62-2.03)
			Southern	10.9	1.79 (1.46-2.19)	14.8	2.14 (1.77-2.57)
			Scandinavian	13.0	1.97 (1.70-2.27)	15.8	2.14 (1.84-2.49)
			Eastern	17.1	2.31 (1.99-2.68)	14.9	2.07 (1.79-2.39)
			Anglo-Saxon	17.4	2.86 (2.12-3.70)	17.4	2.73 (2.17-3.44)
Espelt et al (2008)	Social class	Navarro and Shi (2001)	Christian Democratic	11.2	1.24 (1.12-1.37)	12.7	1.31 (1.19-1.45)
			Social Democratic	13.3	1.43 (1.26-1.63)	13.7	1.36 (1.21-1.52)
			Late Democracies	18.9	1.87 (1.45-2.42)	24.2	1.75 (1.39-2.21)

Notes: [a] This table is reproduced from Bambra (2011b) with permission of BMJ Publishers.
[b] Age-standardised differences between the top and bottom socioeconomic groups in each analysis.

Welfare state change and health inequalities

The central role of the Nordic welfare state in protecting the health of vulnerable groups is also to some extent evident in studies of health inequalities during periods of welfare reform and macro-economic changes. Studies of the effects of welfare state reforms on inequalities in mortality and morbidity in the Liberal regime countries (specifically the US and New Zealand) in the 1980s and 1990s shows that periods of welfare state reform in which labour was substantially recommodified, income inequalities increased and access to welfare services were restricted (such as under the Reagan administration in the US), resulted in increases in socioeconomic inequalities in both mortality and morbidity. However, in comparison, empirical studies of the health effects of welfare reforms in the Nordic countries in the 1990s are less conclusive, as while inequalities in mortality increased, inequalities in morbidity did not change. This may be because the welfare reforms were more extensive in the Liberal welfare states or because they were conducted in a welfare state that was already less generous and offered a lower level of decommodification. Indeed, the post-reform Nordic welfare states were still arguably more decommodifying than the pre-reform Liberal welfare states (Bambra, 2006b).

One longitudinal study examined pre-mature mortality rates (deaths of those aged under 65) and IMRs by income quintiles and ethnicity across the counties of the US from 1960 to 2002 (Krieger et al, 2008). It found that while premature mortality and IMRs declined overall in all income quintiles from 1960 to 2002, relative inequalities by income and ethnicity in premature mortality and IMRs decreased between 1966 and 1980, but increased in the period 1980 to 2002. The improvements in inequalities during 1966-80 was during a period of welfare expansion in the US (the 'War on Poverty'), and the enactment of civil rights legislation which increased access for the lowest socioeconomic groups and minority ethnic groups to welfare state services. The increases in relative health inequalities occurred during the Reagan–Bush period of welfare state retrenchment when public welfare services (including healthcare insurance coverage) were cut, funding of social assistance was reduced, the minimum wage was frozen and the tax base was shifted from the rich to the poor, leading to increased income polarisation in the US.

These findings were mirrored in a study of welfare reform in New Zealand from 1981 to 2004 (Blakely et al, 2008). This study examined income inequalities in all cause mortality rates among adults. In general, mortality rates declined but relative inequalities among men and women increased in the 1980s and 1990s and then stabilised in the early 2000s. Increased inequalities in deaths from cardiovascular disease were the major cause of the overall increase in income inequalities in mortality. A related study found similar findings for childhood mortality (Shaw et al, 2005). The increases in relative inequalities occurred during the period in which New Zealand underwent major structural reform (including a less redistributive tax system, targeted social benefits, a regressive tax on consumption introduced, privatisation of major utilities and public housing, user charges for welfare services and a flexible post–Fordist labour market). In the1980s and 1990s, poverty rates (percentage of households below the European poverty line of 60 per cent median income increased from 12.3 to 26.5 per cent) and income inequality also increased (there was an increase of more that 12 per cent in the New Zealand Gini coefficient). The stabilisation of income inequalities in mortality in the late 1990s and early 2000s was during a period in which welfare reform also stabilised, employment increased and there were some minor improvements in services (for example, better access to social housing, more generous social assistance and a decrease in healthcare costs). A study of oral health inequalities in children found similar increases during the period of neoliberal welfare state reform in New Zealand (Thomson et al, 2002).

In contrast, albeit using a different measure of health, a comparative study of morbidity conducted in Denmark, Finland, Norway and Sweden found that both relative and absolute educational inequalities in self-reported health remained stable during the 1980s and 1990s (Lahelma et al, 2002) despite significant economic and social upheaval. For example, the 1990s was a period in which Finland and Sweden in particular experienced significant recession and welfare state reform (including tax increases, cuts in public spending per capita on welfare services and decreased value of benefits). The authors of the study conclude that health inequalities in the Nordic countries were not strongly influenced by changes in income and labour market inequalities. They argue that the institutional arrangements in the Nordic welfare states, although subject to reform in the 1990s, were still comparatively generous and buffered against the structural pressures towards widening health inequalities (Lahelma et al, 2002). This finding was also supported by the authors of a study of the educational gradient in preterm births in the Nordic countries, which also remained broadly stable from 1981 to 2000 despite structural changes (Petersen et al, 2009).

Explaining Nordic health inequalities[3]

Given the high levels of decommodification provided by the Nordic welfare states, the smaller income inequalities and the commitment to equality underpinning the Social Democratic Nordic model, it has long been a puzzle as to why the Nordic countries do not have the smallest health inequalities (Huijts and Eikemo, 2009; Dahl et al, 2006; Bambra, 2011b). This section draws on the theories of health inequalities (presented earlier) to generate some possible explanations for why health inequalities in the Nordic countries are not the smallest in Europe.

Artefact: the 'puzzle' is not real but merely artefact. It is a result of the measures and analysis used in the studies. Certainly, there are differences between the results of the studies depending on which measure of socioeconomic inequality is used or how it is calculated (particularly income or education) or by health outcome or by age group. There are also more general issues in terms of making cross-national comparisons of health inequalities as it is not clear whether the bottom groups are the same in each regime or in each country (Dibben and Popham, 2010) or over time (for example, there have been reductions in the proportion of the population that are manual or least educated; see Lundberg and Lahelma, 2001). Relative inequalities are also inversely related to overall prevalence (Eikemo et al, 2009).

Health selection: it is possible that the social consequences of ill health are greater in the Nordic countries and that people who have ill health are more likely to be concentrated in the lower socioeconomic classes. There is little empirical support for this explanation and selection is considered to be more influential in respect to income-related inequalities than educational ones and so it is unlikely to explain the results of the comparative studies of educational inequalities in health (Mackenbach and Bakker, 2002).

Culture and behaviour: socioeconomic inequalities in smoking are much higher in the Nordic countries than in the other welfare state regimes (Dahl et al, 2006). Mackenbach and colleagues (2008) found that cardiovascular disease (strongly associated with smoking and obesity, but also psychosocial stress) accounted for 35 per cent of educational inequalities in death rates among men in England, 22 per cent in France but 42 per cent in Finland, 44 per cent in Norway and 49 per cent in Sweden (Denmark is the Nordic exception with only 28 per cent of educational inequalities in death rates accounted for by differences in cardiovascular disease). This is because the majority of smoking behaviour is concentrated in the least educated groups (Cavelaars et al, 2000).

Materialist: the Social Democratic countries have the smallest income inequalities (Ritakallio and Fritzell, 2004) but lower levels of income inequality do not negate inequalities in exposure to the other material determinants of health (Diderichsen, 2002). Further, as has consistently been shown, social inequalities in access to services remain even within universal systems, and there is certainly tentative evidence to suggest that inequalities in total avoidable mortality (as a result of diseases amenable to medical intervention) are higher in the Nordic countries than elsewhere (Stirbu, 2008).

Psychosocial: relative deprivation occurs in all unequal societies, including the Nordic welfare states. Dahl and colleagues (2006) speculated that the effects of relative deprivation may be more extensive in the Social Democratic welfare states because of the high levels of expectation of upward social mobility and prosperity that they generate among the less privileged, expectations that are seldom met (Huijts and Eikemo, 2009). This may increase health inequalities, especially in stress-related conditions, such as heart disease or self-assessed health (Yngwe et al, 2003).

Life course: life course epidemiology has highlighted how different causal mechanisms and processes may be behind the social gradient in different diseases (Bartley, 2004). This may also be the case in terms of the inequalities in different welfare state regimes as it is possible that the same outcomes (socioeconomic health inequalities) may be present in different welfare state regimes, but as a result of differing causal mechanisms.

Empirically, the most well supported arguments to date are that it is an issue of measurement, or that unhealthy behaviours are more stratified by socioeconomic class in the Nordic welfare states than elsewhere. However, it needs to be kept in mind that while inequalities in health are not necessarily smaller in the Nordic welfare states, in absolute terms everyone does better in the Nordic countries. Taking the case of mortality among middle-aged men in Sweden, Lundberg and Lahelma (2001, p 64) comment that:

> On the basis of relative risk it would be possible to draw the conclusion that more than half a century of egalitarian policies have failed, since inequalities in mortality among middle-aged men are as large in Sweden as elsewhere in Europe. This sort of simplistic conclusion would ignore the fact that Swedish working class men have extremely good survival rates compared to similar men in other European countries, which in turn may very well result the wide range of welfare state policies implemented since the 1930s.

The life expectancy of all socioeconomic classes is relatively higher than the equivalent groups in other developed countries, and premature mortality risks are also lower (especially in Norway and Sweden) (Lundberg and Lahelma, 2001; Fritzell and Lundberg, 2005). Further, studies have shown that the most vulnerable social groups – the old (Avendano et al, 2009), the sick (Dahl et al, 2010) and children (Zambon et al, 2006) – fair better in the Nordic countries, and that the negative health effects of macro-economic change, including economic recession, are mitigated by the Nordic welfare model.

Conclusion

This chapter has examined Nordic health inequalities within a comparative welfare state context. It has particularly highlighted the debate about the surprisingly poor performance of the Nordic welfare states in terms of health inequalities. While the Nordic countries have some of the best overall population health outcomes, the lowest levels of income inequality and the most decommodifying welfare states, this has not translated into lower relative health inequalities. This is the basis of considerable debate in social epidemiology as most of the existing theories of health inequalities are unable to explain this apparent anomaly. It therefore remains something of a public health puzzle (Bambra, 2011b). However, this chapter has also drawn attention to the comparatively high performance of the Nordic welfare states in terms of the health status of vulnerable groups – particularly children, the sick and the old. This has given rise to normative questions about the role of the welfare state in regards to health and equality. The research presented in this chapter, as well as the wider debate about health inequalities, is also problematised by how health inequalities are measured (absolute inequalities, relative inequalities or the situation of the poorest), which health outcomes are examined (mortality or morbidity and their various indicators), how inequality is calculated (income, class or education), as well as the effects of welfare state changes on health inequalities. These issues are important in terms of trying to interpret any changes over time in health inequalities in the Nordic welfare states. However, the empirical research presented in this chapter suggests that, despite increased income inequalities, the Nordic welfare states were able to protect the health of vulnerable citizens and minimise the effects of labour market and economic changes on health inequalities during the 1980s and 1990s. However, a warning as to the effects on health inequalities of future welfare reforms within the Nordic model, particularly the further marketisation of health and social care provision, is provided by the data on the effects of reforms to the Liberal welfare states in the 1980s. If public expenditure continues to be cut in the Nordic welfare states to the extent that they become less decommodifying, with their services more subject to market discipline, and their citizens increasingly held responsible for their own health risk and economic status, then in all likelihood, health inequalities will increase in the Nordic welfare states as they have elsewhere. Other potential issues for health inequalities in the Nordic welfare states over the coming years include the effects of increased migration, and a more ethnically heterogeneous population: without access to adequate welfare state safety nets, then the health of these potentially vulnerable groups may well be the first causality of any long-term state retrenchment.

Notes
[1] This section is reproduced from Bambra (2011a), with the permission of Oxford University Press.
[2] See note 1.
[3] This section is reproduced from Bambra (2011b), with the permission of BMJ Publishers.

References

Avendano, M., Jürges, H. and Mackenbach, J.P. (2009) 'Educational level and changes in health across Europe: longitudnal results from SHARE', *Journal of European Social Policy*, vol 19, pp 301-16.

Bambra, C. (2006a) 'Health status and the worlds of welfare', *Social Policy and Society*, vol 5, pp 53-62.

Bambra, C. (2006b) 'Decommodification and the worlds of welfare revisited', *Journal of European Social Policy*, vol 16, pp 73-80.

Bambra, C. (2007) 'Sifting the wheat from the chaff: a two-dimensional discriminant analysis of welfare state regime theory', *Social Policy & Administration*, vol 41, pp 1-28.

Bambra, C. (2011a) *Work, Worklessness and the Political Economy of Health*. Oxford, Oxford University Press.

Bambra, C. (2011b) 'Health inequalities and welfare state regimes: Theoretical insights on a public health "puzzle"', *Journal of Epidemiology and Community Health*, 65, pp 740-45.

Bambra, C., Pope, D., Swami, V., Stanistreet, D.,Roskam, A., Kunst, A. and Scott-Samuel, A. (2009) 'Gender, health inequality and welfare state regimes: a cross-national study of twelve European countries', *Journal of Epidemiology and Community Health*, vol 63, pp 38-44.

Bartley, M. (2004) *Health inequality: An introduction to theories, concepts and methods*, Cambridge: Polity Press.

Bartley, M., Ferrie, J. and Montgomery, S.M. (2006) 'Health and labour market disadvantage: unemployment, non-employment, and job insecurity', in M. Marmot and R.G.Wilkinson (eds) *Social determinants of health*, Oxford: Oxford University Press, pp 78-96.

Black, D., Morris, J.N., Smith, C. and Townsend, P. (1980) *Inequalities in health: The Black Report*, London: Pelican.

Blakely, T., Tobias, M. and Atkinson, J. (2008) 'Inequalities in mortality during and after restructuring of the New Zealand economy: repeated cohort studies', *British Medical Journal*, vol 336, pp 371-5.

Burstrom, B. and Fredlund, P. (2001) 'Self rated health: is it as good a predictor of subsequent mortality among adults in lower as well as in higher social classes?', *Journal of Epidemiology and Community Health*, vol 55, no 11, pp 836-40.

Cavelaars, A., Kunst, A.E. et al (1998) 'Differences in self reported morbidity by educational level: a comparison of 11 Western European countries', *Journal of Epidemiology and Community Health*, vol 52, no 4, pp 219-27.

Cavelaars, A., Kunst, A.E., Geurts, K. et al (2000) 'Educational differences in smoking: international comparison', *British Medical Journal*, vol 320, no 7242, pp 1102-7.

Chung, H. and Muntaner, C. (2007) 'Welfare state matters: a typological multilevel analysis of wealthy countries', *Health Policy*, vol 80, pp 328-39.

Coburn, D. (2004) 'Beyond the income inequality hypothesis: class, neo-liberalism, and health inequalities', *Social Science & Medicine*, vol 58, no 1, pp 41-56.

Conley, D. and Springer, K. (2001) 'Welfare state and infant mortality', *American Journal of Sociology*, vol 107, pp 768-807.

Dahl, E., Fritzell, J., Lahelma, E., Martikainen, P., Kunst, A. and Mackenbach, J.P. (2006) 'Welfare state regimes and health inequalities', in J. Siegrist and M. Marmot (eds) *Social inequalities in health*, Oxford: Oxford University Press, pp 193-222.

Dahl, E., Thielens, K. and van der Wel, K. (2010) 'Health inequalities and work in a comparative perspective: a multilevel analysis of EU SILC', 13th Biennial Congress of the European Society for Health and Medical Sociology; 26–28 August 2010, Ghent, Belgium.

Dahlgren, G. and Whitehead, M. (1991) *Policies and strategies to promote social equity in health*, Stockholm: Institute for Futures Studies.

Dahlgren, G., Nordgren, P. et al (1996) *Health impact assessment of the EU Common Agricultural Policy*, Stockholm: Swedish National Institute of Public Health.

Dibben, C. and Popham, F. (2010) 'Are socio-economic groupings the most appropriate method for judging health equity between countries?', *Journal of Epidemiology and Community Health*, vol 65, pp 4-5.

Diderichsen, F. (2002) 'Impact of income maintenance policies', in J.P. Mackenbach and M. Bakker (eds) *Reducing inequalities in health: A European perspective*, London: Routledge, pp 53-66.

Eikemo, T.A., Bambra, C. et al (2008a) 'Welfare state regimes and differences in self-perceived health in Europe: a multi-level analysis', *Social Science & Medicine*, vol 66, pp 2281-95.

Eikemo, T.A., Huisman, M. et al (2008b) 'Health inequalities according to educational level under different welfare regimes: a comparison of 23 European countries', *Sociology of Health and Illness*, vol 30, pp 565-82.

Eikemo, T.A., Bambra, C. et al (2008c) 'Welfare state regimes and income related health inequalities: a comparison of 23 European countries', *European Journal of Public Health*, vol 18, pp 593-9.

Eikemo, T.A., Skalická, V. and Avendano, M. (2009) 'Variations in relative health inequalities: are they a mathematical artefact?', *International Journal for Equity in Health*, vol 8, p 32.

Espelt, A., Borrell, C., Rodríguez-Sanz, M., et al. (2008) 'Inequalities in health by social class dimensions in European countries of different political traditions', *International Journal of Epidemiology*, 37, pp 1095-1105.

Esping-Andersen, G. (1990) *Three worlds of welfare capitalism*, London: Polity Press.

Esser, I. and Palme, J. (2010) 'Do public pensions matter for health and wellbeing among retired persons? Basic and income security pensions across 13 Western European countries', *International Journal of Social Welfare*, vol 19, pp 103-20.

Ferrera, M. (1996) 'The southern model of welfare in social Europe', *Journal of European Social Policy*, 6, pp 17-37.

Fritzell, J. and Lundberg, O. (2005) 'Fighting inequalities in health and income: one important road to welfare and social development', in O. Kangas and J. Palme (eds) *Social policy and economic development in the Nordic countries*, New York: Palgrave Macmillan, pp 164-85.

Ginsburg, N. (1979) *Class, capital and social policy*, London: Macmillan.

Graham, H. and Kelly, M.P. (2004) *Health inequalities: Concepts, frameworks and policy*, London: Health Development Agency.

Hay, C. (1996) *Re-stating social and political change*, Milton Keynes: Open University Press.

Huijts, T. and Eikemo, T.A. (2009) 'Causality, selectivity or artefacts? Why socioeconomic inequalities in health are not smallest in the Nordic countries', *European Journal of Public Health*, vol 19, no 5, pp 452-3.

Karim, S.A., Eikemo, T.A. and Bambra, C. (2010) 'Welfare state regimes and population health: integrating the East Asian welfare states', *Health Policy*, vol 94, pp 45-53.

Kawachi, I., Kennedy, B.P. et al (1997) 'Social capital, income inequality, and mortality', *American Journal of Public Health*, vol 87, no 9, pp 1491-8.

Kawachi, I., Subramanian, S.V. and Almeida-Filho, N. (2002) 'A glossary for health inequalities', *Journal of Epidemiology and Community Health*, vol 56, pp 647-52.

Krieger, N., Rehkopf, D.H. et al (2008) 'The fall and rise of US inequities in premature mortality: 1960–2002', *PLoS Medicine*, vol 5, pp 227-41.

Lahelma, E. and Arber, S. (1994) 'Health inequalities among men and women in contrasting welfare states: Britain and three Nordic countries compared', *European Journal of Public Health*, vol 4, pp 213-26.

Lahelma, E., Kivela, K. et al (2002) 'Analysing changes of health inequalities in the Nordic welfare states', *Social Science & Medicine*, vol 55, pp 609-25.

Lundberg, O. (1986) 'Class and health: comparing Britain and Sweden', *Social Science & Medicine*, vol 26, pp 511-17.

Lundberg, O. and Lahelma, E. (2001) 'Nordic health inequalities in the European context', in M. Kautto, J. Fritzell, B. Hvinden, J. Kvist and H. Uusitalo (eds) *Nordic welfare states in the European context*, London: Routledge, pp 42-65.

Lundberg, O., Yngwe, M., Kölegård Stjärne, M., Elstad, J., Ferrarini, T., Kangas, O. et al. (2008) 'The role of welfare state principles and generosity in social policy programmes for public health: an international comparative study', *Lancet*, 372, pp 1633-40.

Mackenbach, J.P. and Bakker, M. (2002) *Reducing inequalities in health: A European perspective*, London: Routledge.

Mackenbach, J.P., Bakker, M. et al (2002) 'Socio-economic inequalities in health in Europe: an overview', in J. Mackenbach and M. Bakker (eds) *Reducing inequalities in health: A European perspective*, London: Routledge, pp 3-24.

Mackenbach, J.P., Kunst, A. et al (1997) 'Socioeconomic inequalities in morbidity and mortality in Western Europe', *Lancet*, vol 349, pp 1655-9.

Mackenbach, J.P., Stirbu, I. et al (2008) 'Socioeconomic inequalities in health in 22 European countries', *New England Journal of Medicine*, vol 358, pp 2468-81.

Marmot, M. (2006) 'Introduction', in M. Marmot and R.G. Wilkinson (eds) *Social determinants of health*, Oxford: Oxford University Press, pp 1-5.

Marmot, M., Siegrist, J. et al (2006) 'Health and the psychosocial environment at work', in M. Marmot and R.G. Wilkinson (eds) *Social determinants of health*, Oxford: Oxford University Press, pp 97-130.

Mitchell, R. (2005) 'The decline of death – how do we measure and interpret changes in self-reported health across cultures and time?', *International Journal of Epidemiology*, vol 34, pp 306-8.

Navarro, V., Borrell, C. et al (2003) 'The importance of the political and the social in explaining mortality differentials among the countries of the OECD, 1950-1998', *International Journal of Health Services Research*, vol 33, pp 419-94.

Navarro, V. and Shi, L. (2001) 'The political context of social inequalities and health', *International Journal of Health Services Research*, 31, pp 1-21.

Navarro, V., Muntaner, C. et al (2006) 'Politics and health outcomes', *Lancet*, vol 368, pp 1033-7.

Petersen, C., Mortensen, L. et al (2009) 'Socio-economic inequality in preterm birth: a comparative study of the Nordic countries from 1981 to 2000', *Paediatric and Perinatal Epidemiology*, vol 23, pp 66-75.

Ritakallio, V.M. and Fritzell, J. (2004) *Societal Shifts and Changed Patterns of Poverty*, Luxembourg, Luxembourg Income Study Working Paper Series.

Shaw, C., Blakely, T. et al (2005) 'Do social and economic reforms change socioeconomic inequalities in child mortality? A case study: New Zealand 1981-1999', *Journal of Epidemiology & Community Health*, vol 59, pp 638-44.

Stafford, M. and McCarthy, M. (2006) 'Neighbourhoods, housing and health', in M. Marmot and R.G. Wilkinson (eds) *Social determinants of health*, Oxford: Oxford University Press, pp 297-317.

Stanistreet, D., Bambra, C. and Scott-Samuel, A. (2005) 'Is patriarchy the source of male mortality?', *Journal of Epidemiology and Community Health*, vol 59, pp 873-6.

Stirbu, I. (2008) *Inequalities in health: Does health care matter?*, Rotterdam: Erasmus MC.

Thomson, W.M., Williams, S.M. et al (2002) 'Were New Zealand's structural changes to the welfare state in the early 1990s associated with a measurable increase in oral health inequalities among children?', *The Australian and New Zealand Journal of Public Health*, vol 26, pp 525-30.

Vagero, D. and Lundberg, O. (1989) 'Health inequalities in Britain and Sweden', *Lancet*, vol ii, pp 35-36.

Valkonen, T. (1989) 'Adult mortality and level of education: a comparison of six countries', in A.J. Fox (ed) *Health inequalities in European countries*, Aldershot: Gower, pp 142-60.

van Doorslaer, E., Wagstaff, A. et al (1997) 'Income related inequalities in health: some international comparisons', *Journal of Health Economics*, vol 16, pp 93-112.

Whitehead, M. (2007) 'A typology of actions to tackle social inequalities in health', *Journal of Epidemiology and Community Health*, vol 61, no 6, pp 473-8.

Wilkinson, R.G. (1996) *Unhealthy societies*, London: Routledge.

Wright, E.O. (1985) *Classes*, London: Verso.

Yngwe, M., Fritzell, J. et al (2003) 'Exploring relative deprivation: is social comparison a mechanism in the relation between income and health?', *Social Science & Medicine*, vol 57, pp 1463-73.

Zambon, A., Boyce, W. et al (2006) 'Do welfare regimes medicate the effect of socioeconomic position on health in adolescence? A cross-national comparison InEurope, North America and Israel', *International Journal of Health Services*, vol 36, pp 309-29.

EIGHT

Income inequality and poverty: do the Nordic countries still constitute a family of their own?

Johan Fritzell, Olof Bäckman and Veli-Matti Ritakallio

Introduction

The comparatively low degrees of income inequalities and relative poverty rates have long been a salient feature of the Nordic countries. Low inequality and low poverty rates are commonly viewed as key ingredients of what constitutes the Nordic welfare model (see, for example, Kautto et al, 1999), with strong influences from institutional characteristics and welfare state redistribution systems (see, for example, Brandolini and Smeeding, 2007; Bäckman, 2009; Fritzell and Ritakallio, 2010). A fundamental dimension of these social schemes – and of the Nordic model in general – is universalism (Kildal and Kuhnle, 2005). No doubt, there is abundant evidence that the Nordic countries have been at the top of the equality league and that they actually form a family of their own when it comes to poverty and income inequality. As one of us concluded in an earlier study of income inequality in a number of European countries, analysing whether the Nordic countries were becoming more like other European countries: '*Yes*, the Nordic countries ... still have a low degree of inequality in the distribution of income and *No*, we find no support for a convergence' (Fritzell, 2001, p 39).

Moreover, more recent publications by supranational organisations suggest that the Nordic countries are among those with the lowest income inequality and relatively low poverty rates (OECD, 2008; Eurostat, 2010). The thorough OECD (Organisation for Economic Co-operation and Development) report *Growing unequal* (2008) concludes that the countries with the most compressed income distributions are Denmark and Sweden, placing Finland, Iceland and Norway in a group of European countries with similar degrees of income inequality. Most national Nordic reports and official statistics have, however, shown that income inequality has widened. Thus the fundamental question in this chapter is whether the Nordic countries are different in terms of income inequality and poverty. In other words, do they still constitute a family of their own?

Welfare regimes and poverty and inequality

The concept of welfare regimes provides the broad framework for this volume. Given the three types of welfare capitalism – Liberal, Conservative-Corporatist and Social Democratic (Esping-Andersen, 1990) – we see that basic principles differ among regimes. Although the examination of welfare state typologies can certainly be seen as obsessive (Abrahamson, 1999), we nonetheless must understand welfare state variation not as a one-dimensional element but as differences in kind (and not merely degrees) (Titmuss, 1974).

From the perspective of the outcomes highlighted in this chapter, we see that regime theory expects countries to follow certain patterns. Poverty and income inequality are probably the two outcome measures that have lent the most support to the idea that countries tend to cluster along certain dimensions. Hence, Nordic countries have welfare state schemes with institutional characteristics that in turn appear to support low poverty rates and fairly compressed income distributions. In contrast, Anglo-Saxon countries, following the logic of the Liberal regime type, with more emphasis on market solutions and residual schemes, tend to have much higher poverty rates and higher income inequality. Many Continental European countries have for historical reasons followed another logic, in which social policies often constitute insurance relationships formed on the basis of employment contracts. Such a country cluster also puts more emphasis on the family as a welfare provider. Esping-Andersen (1990), in his welfare state typology, views Germany as an archetype of this Conservative-Corporatist model.

However, as Esping-Andersen (1990) paid little attention to the welfare regimes of Southern Europe, whether these countries have another specific model or whether they are simply at an earlier stage of developing a model that Esping-Andersen identified is a subject of much discussion. Whatever the final answer, Southern European countries tend towards an even higher degree of familialism and less developed social security programmes than, for example, Continental European and Nordic countries (Ferrera, 1996).

While our analyses obviously emphasise the Nordic countries, to answer our research questions we need comparisons. We chiefly use Germany, Italy, the Netherlands and the UK as our primary comparison countries, because earlier research has identified them as belonging to welfare regimes different from those of the Nordic countries. Germany and Italy are often described as belonging to the Conservative-Corporatist regime type, whereas the UK belongs to the Liberal regime. The Netherlands is often regarded as a special hybrid case, with certain characteristics following the logic of the Nordic model. In addition, to discover whether the Nordic countries still differ from the Western average, we also present averages using data from other Western countries. To present a comprehensive picture of change, we study change from different angles and with different data.

Our empirical analyses and results are divided into four subsections. The first shows time trends in overall income inequality, concentrating on all the Nordic countries, including Iceland, and giving yearly estimates covering around 20 years. We use national data sources that most likely give the most accurate time trends within each country but perhaps have less comparability across countries.

As such an approach cannot answer the question of whether the Nordic countries have become more or less similar to non-Nordic countries, we therefore shift our focus in the second section to a comparison with other European countries – and the US. We present data not only on inequality but also on overall poverty rates. Although our time perspective is about the same as in the first empirical section, we rely here on the most reliable comparative source for income and poverty analysis, the Luxembourg Income Study (LIS) database. We present three time snapshots: from around the mid-1980s, the mid-1990s and the mid-2000s. We focus both on changes and levels for the question of convergence versus divergence.

The third section considers change from a different angle, relying on cross-sectional, cross-national micro-data for the study of poverty rates and poverty profiles in a number of European countries. Focusing on risk categories rather than on the overall levels and their differences, we contrast 'new' and 'old' social risk groups. The discussion of new and old social risks is often framed within a discussion of societal transformation from industrialism to post-industrialism (Taylor-Gooby, 2004), and earlier research has shown that the Nordic universalistic, service-oriented welfare states are especially well suited to handle some of these risks (Timonen, 2004).

In terms of poverty, although what one should regard as new social risk categories is not totally clear-cut, certain population groups, such as immigrants, are obviously more central to the social policy discussion today than in the golden age of welfare capitalism. When the first comprehensive studies were performed over 100 years ago (Rowntree, 1901), they showed that older people were at particular risk for poverty. They are a good example of an 'old' social risk category that was in focus during the early period of welfare state reforms, and Kangas and Palme (2000) show that the Nordic countries have been particularly successful in mitigating the classical life cycle of poverty that Rowntree outlined. Our analysis here aims at revealing whether the comprehensive Nordic welfare model, which is well-suited for dealing with old social risks, might have more difficulties handling some of the newer ones, particularly that of immigrants.

The fourth section focuses on income variation or, more specifically, the persistence of poverty. As we have good reason to expect that the persistence of poverty is particularly harmful for people's living conditions and life chances, preventing longer spells of poverty and creating possibilities for exiting poverty constitute crucial aspects of any political attempt to combat poverty. When the European Union (EU) in 2001 decided to put a stronger emphasis on developing common European indicators on social inclusion and poverty, a key product was the 2002 recommendations of Atkinson et al (2002). They state that the longer an individual lives in poverty, the greater the risk of his or her permanently remaining there. We use one of their suggested indicators of persistent poverty risk: the proportion below the 'at risk of poverty' rate in one year and in at least one of the two preceding years. Thus when looking at poverty from a dynamic perspective, we investigate whether the Nordic welfare states are successful in mitigating long-term poverty or not.

Poverty, income and income inequality: definitions and measurements

Out of the ongoing discussions of and extensive literature on how poverty should be theoretically defined and empirically measured, we use an income poverty approach (Jäntti and Danziger, 2000). In line with EU definitions, we set the poverty threshold at 60 per cent of current median income. This income measurement is equivalent to disposable income and, unless otherwise stated, we use the modified OECD scale, which sets a weight of 1.0 for the first adult, of 0.5 for any additional person aged 14 or older and of 0.3 for children under the age of 14. In other words, to reach the equivalent disposable income of one adult, a household consisting of two adults and two children needs to have a disposable income 2.1 times higher. As it is well known that poverty measures are sensitive to both the choice of poverty threshold and the equivalence scale (Jäntti and Danziger, 2000; Ruggeri Laderchi et al, 2003), we therefore conduct sensitivity analyses with alternative definitions. We report these results only when they deviate from earlier findings.

Our inequality measure is most often the traditional Gini coefficient. Because the Gini coefficient is more sensitive to differences in the middle of the income distribution (see, for example, Atkinson, 1970), we sometimes supplement it with measures better suited for capturing change and differences in the bottom and top of the income distribution, such as the relation between the top and bottom 10 per cent.

That the 60 per cent of median income poverty threshold is merely a proxy for a more profound poverty concept is common knowledge. That the EU has chosen the term 'at risk of poverty rate' indicates that people with incomes below this threshold should be treated as being *at risk of* poverty rather than being *in* poverty. Several indicators have been suggested for capturing a deeper or more serious poverty risk. The EU standard definition of persistent poverty is the equivalent disposable income below 60 per cent of median income in the current year and in at least two out of the three preceding years. This definition – one of the Laeken indicators set by the European Council in 2001 as part of the Lisbon agenda – was developed from the recommendations of Atkinson et al (2002).

While Atkinson and colleagues stress the importance of a persistency indicator, they also discuss the limitations of using panel data. One such limitation occurs when panels suffer from attrition, as the character of the attrition can bias results in various directions. Thus researchers have to find a balance between the number of panel waves necessary for achieving an appropriate persistency measure and the need for minimising attrition. Atkinson et al suggest either a three or four-year indicator. In the three-year indicator those who are poor and have been so for at least one of the two preceding years are considered permanently poor. The four-year indicator constitutes the Laeken indicator just described. The reason for allowing for one year above the poverty threshold is to minimise the effect of measurement errors. An occasional year out of poverty (according to data) may be the result of measurement error. But even in cases when a measurement error is not involved, one could argue that such temporal transitions should not be treated as true transitions out of poverty.

For our analysis of poverty persistency rates, we use the 2008 EU–SILC (EU Statistics on Income and Living Conditions) longitudinal dataset. To construct the Laeken indicator, we need to go as far back as 2005 for the necessary four years. Unfortunately, the 2005 dataset contains much smaller samples for most countries, thereby producing some peculiarities in outcomes. For this reason we have chosen to use the three-year indicator suggested by Atkinson et al (2002). We calculate the poverty thresholds from the cross-sectional datasets, using the conventional weight variables.

Data

The first empirical part is based on *national* data sources from within the Nordic countries. The data come from national statistical offices, material either presented in earlier national reports or acquired from national statistical agencies (for details, see Figure 8.1). We see a four-fold reason for our choice of using national data in this section: first, by using national sources we can use yearly data points. Second, we are able to include the most recent estimates. Third, we are able to more fully include realised capital gains, capital income and taxation of capital income, which, according to some, have been the main drivers of inequality, especially at the top of the income distribution (Riihelä et al, 2008). Fourth, we focus on the time trends, and the within-country trends have a high degree of reliability in the annual national sources.

The second part uses the LIS data. We mainly use waves two, four and six, corresponding approximately to the years 1985, 1995 and 2005 (for a thorough presentation of the database, see Atkinson et al, 1995). LIS is commonly regarded as the best source for cross-national comparisons of poverty and income inequality. Countries to be analysed in this section are Denmark, Finland, Norway, Sweden, Germany, Italy, the Netherlands, the UK and the US. Moreover, we present the average for thirteen EU15 countries, plus Norway and the US, as they have available data in LIS ($n=15$).

The third and fourth empirical parts are based on data from the EU–SILC. This is the main source for the compilation of comparable indicators on social cohesion used for policy monitoring at the EU level in the framework of the Open Method of Coordination (OMC). Every year the EU–SILC collects comparable multidimensional micro-data on income, poverty, social exclusion and living conditions – both cross-sectionally and longitudinally. The EU–SILC was launched in 2003 with six EU15 countries plus Norway, and re-launched in 2004 with 12 of the EU15 countries. In 2005 the rest of the EU25 countries joined the EU–SILC (Eurostat, 2010). While our study primarily uses the 2007 cross-section, we also use longitudinal data from 2006 to 2008. For our purposes EU–SILC is unique because it contains pre-harmonised data from all five Nordic countries. Another strength of the EU–SILC is its extensive sample size, as it allows detailed analysis even at rather small subpopulation levels. The main drawbacks of using these data for cross-national comparative welfare research are that the EU–SILC does not cover non-European countries and covers only relatively short periods.

Results

Income inequality trends in the Nordic countries

Figure 8.1 shows the trends of inequality in the distribution of disposable household income for the Nordic countries between the mid–1980s and 2008 (or the latest possible time point). Our inequality measure is the Gini coefficient. As mentioned earlier we have deliberately chosen to report the changes as reflected in national sources. The drawback of this choice is that these trends are based on

Figure 8.1: Relative changes of income inequality according to the Gini coefficient in the Nordic countries from around 1985-2008

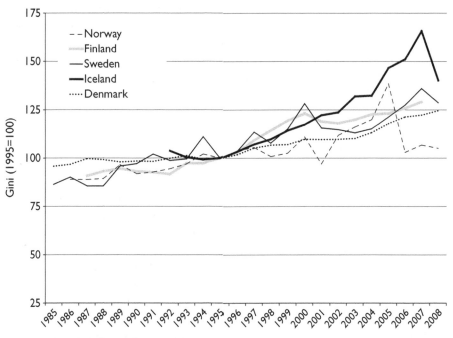

Note: The value of the Gini coefficient has been set to 100 in 1995 for each country.

Sources: Own calculations of Statistics Finland Income distribution survey and of Statistics Denmark Income distribution statistics; NOU (2009: 10); Olafsson and Kristjansson (2010); Statistics Sweden (2010)

less comparable measurements of income across countries. Within each country, however, the trends are more reliable than in any cross-national source.

For these methodological reasons we present the trends in relatives. For each country we have set the inequality to 100 in 1995. Our series also have slightly different start and end points.[1]

Figure 8.1 makes some patterns immediately obvious. The trends of increasing inequalities are more evident in the later period than in the earlier period. The trends in Finland and Sweden are roughly similar throughout the observed period (1985-2008). These trends relate to macro-economic circumstances, as in the early 1990s both countries experienced a severe economic recession in which unemployment skyrocketed to figures totally unthinkable before the crisis, and with negative growth for three consecutive years (see Kautto, 2000, for a thorough comparison of Sweden and Finland during the 1990s). However, while the median income fell dramatically during the crisis years, income inequality hardly changed at all (Palme et al, 2002). If, for example, one considers the changes of the Gini in the series in Figure 8.1, comparing the changes from 1991-95 with the changes from 1995-99, one sees that it is both in the aftermath of the recession and during the economic recovery that income inequality grew. Whereas the changes were small in the first of these two periods, the Gini grew by more than four percentage points in Finland and close to four percentage points in Sweden. Such marked increases of the Gini coefficient in a four-year period are indeed uncommon, including from an international perspective.

Danish data also suggest a similar trend, with only minor changes between the mid-1980s and the mid-1990s, but a steady increase thereafter. Norway has a much more volatile income distribution in the 2000s, driven mostly by taxation changes but perhaps also by more households having much higher incomes than in the other Nordic countries. The overall increase in Norway is very modest, given the sharp decline since 2005. Even though Norway appears remarkably volatile, it is stable indeed by comparison with Iceland. Income inequality in Iceland skyrocketed from 1995 to 2007. Between those years it increased by an astonishing 65 per cent, followed by a dramatic drop in 2008, and it appears most likely that this drop continued in 2009, when the Icelandic crisis reached its peak.

Thus income inequality in the Nordic countries is higher today than in the mid-1980s or mid-1990s. In percentages, instead of percentage points, the increase between 1995 and the latest time point is the same in Finland and Sweden – 29 per cent – and in Denmark 24 per cent. In Norway the increase was above 38 per cent until 2006 but dropped remarkably thereafter, so that it is only 5 per cent higher in 2008 than in the mid-1990s. In contrast, the increase in Iceland from 1995 to 2008 is 40 per cent. Thus we find a considerable widening of income distributions in the Nordic countries.

Explaining the widening income distributions in the Nordic countries: capital and top incomes

The trends just described have many similarities, and Nordic national reports and publications on income distribution trends reveal even more. First, a substantial part of the increase is due to realised capital gains and capital income; second, the changes are driven by what is happening in the upper part of the distribution. A decomposition analysis of the changes of the income distribution in Finland shows that these changes were almost completely the result of capital income (Riihelä et al, 2008): Finland, in line with the other Nordic countries, introduced a dual-income tax model in its 1993 tax reform, which gave strong incentives for high-income earners to shift earnings to capital incomes. In Denmark the tax reforms took place in 1994, in Norway in 1992 and in Sweden in 1991. The dual-income tax model was a key topic in these reforms (Sørensen, 1994).

Analyses of top income have lately become a key issue in distributional research (see in particular Atkinson and Piketty, 2007), where changes are most marked among the highest earners. In Sweden the top 1 per cent had a total income share of 4 per cent in 1995, more than doubling in 2007 and nearly doubling in 2008 to 7 per cent (Statistics Sweden, 2010). This trend of sharply increasing income shares among the top earners since the mid-1990s is also evident in Finland (Riihelä et al, 2008) and Norway (NOU 2009: 10; Aaberge and Atkinson, 2008), with the magnitude appearing roughly similar to that of Sweden.

In Iceland, the change at the top is even more dramatic. For example, Olafsson and Kristjansson (2010) show that among the top decile, which had a marked increase of their total income share, the increase is almost totally driven by the top 1 per cent. This share of the population gradually increased their total income share from around 4 per cent in 1995 to almost 20 per cent in 2007, then decreasing to around 11 per cent in 2008. Consequently, if one measures the change of inequality by the coefficient of variation, which is very sensitive to the top of the distribution, it indicates almost a four-fold Icelandic increase between the mid-1990s and 2007 – a much steeper increase than what the Gini coefficients in Figure 8.1 show. Nonetheless, although the top is the key driver of the inequality increases, we should not make the mistake of arguing that nothing of importance is happening at the bottom. For example, a substantial erosion of the purchasing power of minimum social benefits in the Nordic countries has taken place over this same period (see Chapter Four, this volume). These changes at the lower end of the income distribution constitute an issue to which we shall return.

More like others?

Although income inequality in the Nordic countries has grown, national trends clearly cannot answer the question of whether the Nordic countries have become more similar to other Western countries. It is to this issue we now turn, using data from the LIS to study income inequality and relative poverty rates in nine countries. As Iceland is not part of the LIS, we have four Nordic countries that we compare with Germany, Italy, the Netherlands, the UK and the US.

Figure 8.2 gives income inequality at three different time points for the nine countries at around the mid-1980s, mid-1990s and mid-2000s. Grand means in addition to these nine countries also include Austria, Belgium, France, Ireland, Luxembourg and Spain. A look at the changes over the first 10 years clearly shows that the difference between the Nordic countries and the other countries becomes more marked. In one country, Denmark, the distribution of income first becomes more compressed and then increases only slightly, thereby reaching about the same level of inequality of the other Nordic countries.[2] In three countries – Italy, the UK and the US – we see a clear change towards higher inequality, and the average Gini for all the 15 countries increases.

A somewhat different picture emerges when we focus on changes over the second 10-year period. Here, partly echoing the changes that appear in Figure 8.1,

Figure 8.2: Income inequality (Gini coefficient) around 1985, 1995 and 2005, and cross-national variation of these inequality estimates

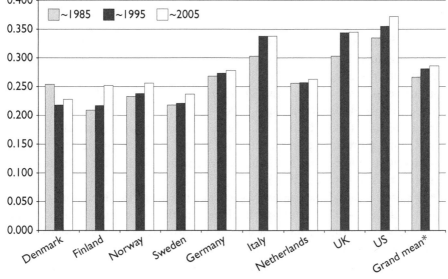

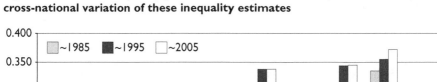

	Cross-national variation: coefficient of variation				
Nordic countries			All 15* countries		
1985	1995	2005	1985	1995	2005
0.086	0.044	0.054	0.156	0.184	0.145

Note: * Grand mean includes the following countries: Austria, Belgium, Denmark, Finland, France, Germany, Ireland, Italy, Luxembourg, the Netherlands, Norway, Spain, Sweden, the UK and the US.
Source: LIS

we find increases of inequality in all four Nordic countries but not in all of the comparison countries. While we find a continuation of the trend in the US, the degree of inequality is unchanged, for example, in the UK; in both instances this result confirms findings from national studies (Hills et al, 2010; US Census Bureau, 2010). During the second period, which largely coincides with the Blair Labour governments, we find that the widening of income differential stopped but not reversed the earlier trend. In the Netherlands we find almost no changes over the two decades. A comparison of the inequality increases from the mid-1990s in the Nordic countries to our 'grand mean' of 15 countries shows clearly that the Nordic countries deviate. On average the Gini coefficient among these 15 countries hardly changes at all, while it increases substantially in the Nordic countries.

The overall inequality increases in the Nordic countries are more modest in Figure 8.2 than in Figure 8.1. The major reason for this discrepancy is the treatment of capital income in particular, realised capital gains. Realised capital gains are not included in the LIS data and, as discussed earlier, capital income is a major drive of the inequality increase in the Nordic countries.

Poverty trends

Figure 8.3 shows relative poverty rates from the LIS for the Nordic countries (excluding Iceland) and the same five other countries (Germany, Italy, the Netherlands, the UK and the US). The poverty trends in the LIS data differ slightly from those in other national and international sources. The drop in Denmark between the mid-1980s and mid-1990s is not evident in the OECD report *Growing unequal* (2008, pp 127-9), which instead reports a relatively flat time trend. Although relative poverty rates in Finland and Sweden increase between the two latter time periods in Figure 8.3, this increase is greater in national data sources (Statistics Sweden, 2010).

As Figure 8.3 shows, the relative poverty rate in Finland declined from the mid-1980s to the mid-1990s. For those familiar with the great depression in Finland in the early 1990s, this decline may appear paradoxical, but the explanation is the strong decline of median incomes during the recession years. Many beneficiaries of social benefits, typically pensioners, were suddenly no longer 'poor', despite no change in their absolute income. This peculiarity of the relative poverty approach also supports the necessity for developing complementary methods for measuring poverty, especially during economic crises (Kangas and Ritakallio, 1998).

On average the Nordic poverty rates are lower than in most other countries at almost all time points. The exceptions are Germany and the Netherlands in 1985. In an earlier study, Ritakallio (2002) found that from 1980 to 1995 cross-national variation in poverty more clearly began corresponding with the respective models of social policy. But now, comparing the trends in the Nordic countries with those in the others, we find that between 1995 and 2005 the Nordic countries became slightly less of a family of their own. The increase in poverty rates that

Figure 8.3: Relative poverty rates (%) (60% of median equivalent disposable income) and cross-national variation in these rates, by coefficient of variation around 1985, 1995 and 2005

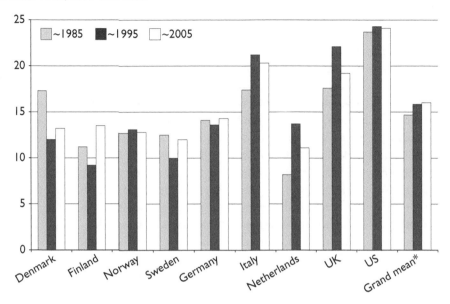

	Cross-national variation: coefficient of variation					
	Nordic countries			All 14* countries		
1985	1995	2005	1985	1995	2005
0.199	0.162	0.050	0.284	0.306	0.259

Note: * Grand mean includes the following countries: Austria, Belgium, Denmark, Finland, France, Germany, Ireland, Italy, Luxembourg, the Netherlands, Norway, Spain, Sweden, the UK and the US.
Source: LIS

we find in the Nordic countries, except for Norway, is not totally followed by the non-Nordic countries. In the UK the rate declines slightly between 1995 and 2005 while remaining stable in the US. Altogether this result means that the difference between the Nordic countries and these other countries was reduced between 1995 and 2005.

However, according to the coefficient of variation, the cross-national variation within the Nordic countries is nearly eradicated during this second period, indicating that the Nordic countries have become more equal to one another in this respect. However, calculating the coefficient of variation on four countries is open to question and must therefore be interpreted with caution.

Poverty in new and old risk groups

Poverty rates

Although the overall income inequality and poverty estimates presented thus far indicate that the Nordic countries are less unique in the midst of the first decade of the 2000s than in the final decades of the 20th century, inequality and poverty rates nonetheless remain lower than in the comparison countries. We now turn to a more in-depth, up-to-date analysis of cross-national differences in poverty. We use two approaches: first, we analyse poverty among both old and new social risk categories. While the Nordic countries appear especially successful at combating poverty among the old risk categories (Kangas and Palme, 2000; Fritzell and Ritakallio, 2010), whether this success also applies to newer social risk categories is less certain. Second, we analyse poverty dynamics, presenting cross-national differences in the persistence of poverty. For both these analyses we use data from the EU-SILC.[3]

Table 8.1 shows poverty rates among certain old and new risk groups of poverty in the Nordic countries, in four other selected European countries and in the unweighted EU17[4] country mean in 2007. In line with our earlier analysis of the LIS data the Nordic average rate is much lower than the EU average, and the variation between the Nordic countries is rather small. Thus the Nordic countries in that sense constitute a family. From the standpoint of overall poverty the Netherlands appear to belong to the Nordic group, while the German rate is above the Nordic but clearly below the British and Italian groups (whose figures are almost twice the Nordic ones). Nonetheless, 11.5 per cent of the population in the Nordic countries are living 'at risk of' poverty according to the EU definition given earlier.

Table 8.1: Poverty rates of old and new risk groups in Europe in 2007 (%)

	Children[a]	Large families	Single parents	Elderly[b]	Young single adults[c]	Immigrants born inside EU	Immigrants born outside EU	Total population
Denmark	9.4	14.6	16.6	17.0	50.0	23.9	24.7	11.7
Finland	9.8	11.3	22.5	21.1	38.2	15.0	34.8	12.9
Iceland	12.4	10.6	17.6	14.5	29.7	–	–	9.9
Norway	11.3	7.1	26.2	14.2	43.3	13.9	27.4	12.4
Sweden	11.3	12.8	22.6	11.2	38.3	14.2	28.1	10.8
Nordic mean	10.8	11.3	21.1	15.6	39.9	16.8	28.8	11.5
Germany	13.7	10.6	31.6	16.9	39.8	–[d]	–[d]	15.2
Italy	25.4	40.8	29.2	21.7	24.5	27.0	29.5	19.8
Netherlands	14.2	17.7	22.8	10.1	24.7	9.8	23.0	10.2
UK	23.3	30.0	40.7	30.0	18.0	26.0	24.8	19.1
EU17 mean	16.7	28.1	28.1	18.8	26.9	18.3	27.9	14.8

Notes: [a] 16 years of age and younger; [b] 65 years of age and older; [c] 18-34 years of age; [d] data not available.
Source: EU-SILC

We defined seven population categories for our analysis of the prevalence of poverty. Children, large families and the elderly constituted traditional social risk groups of poverty at high risk in the 19th and early 20th centuries before the evolution of welfare state systems (Rowntree, 1901). We analyse families and children in more detail – we separately count children (all children, no adults), large families (at least three children in a family) and single parents (mostly mothers, because the numbers of single fathers are very small). Our 'elderly' category comprises those whose age at the time of data collection is at least 65.

One new social risk is immigration. The nature and volume of immigration in the past three decades justifies our examining it here, even though comparing immigrant populations cross-nationally is notoriously difficult. Altogether, the country of origin, the reason for migration and time spent in the new country vary (see Chapter Nine, this volume). Although we cannot control for all these factors, we separate immigrants into those born inside and outside the EU. We assume that people born in EU countries (more often labour migrants) are on average in a better economic and social position than those born outside the EU (more often refugees).

Another new social risk group in our analysis is young single adults (16-34 years old). The transition to adulthood and the possibility for young single adults to obtain a secure livelihood has declined (Danziger and Ratner, 2010). The nature of the interdependence between life course and living conditions has changed comprehensively in many Western countries, as a result of what Airio (2008) argues is a change of norms: one income is no longer enough for a family to make ends meet. As a dual-earner family model now defines the norm, including the housing price level, by definition single people, single parents and male breadwinner families are disadvantaged. Moreover, prolonged years in education and the increased difficulty of labour market entry also deteriorate the relative position of young adults.

Our table clearly shows that the Nordic countries succeed much better at handling the old social risks than the new ones. Children on average and large families have a below-average poverty rate in the Nordic countries while the opposite applies to the other EU17 members. Germany is the one exception, with its Nordic-level low poverty rate for large families. Single parents have a relatively high poverty risk both inside and outside the Nordic countries, with a poverty rate that is on average twice that of the respective population as a whole. For single parents the Nordic countries are much like the others.

While poverty among older people still exists, the poverty rates typically deviate only slightly from the population average figures – a finding common to all the countries we studied. Moreover, we have made sensitivity analyses using 50 per cent of median income as the poverty threshold in parallel to the mainstream 60 per cent operationalisation in all the analyses. The results are about the same except for older people: both inside and outside the Nordic countries their poverty rate is slightly higher than the population average (see Table 8.1). With a less generous poverty line (50 per cent of median) poverty among older people is no longer a key social issue in either the Nordic countries or Western Europe. Except for the UK, the poverty rate of older people is now below the national average in all the countries in this study. While in the Nordic countries poverty rates tend to be much higher among the new risk groups than among the traditional ones, this difference is not as pronounced in the other countries. Young single adults have more than three times the risk of being poor relative to the population average in the Nordic countries, and immigrants born outside the EU have between two and three times the risk. The absolute poverty risk for immigrants born outside the EU is about the same in the Nordic countries and the EU17.

Poverty profiles

What is the composition of the poor population in each country? To what extent is poverty occupied by new or old social risk groups? Table 8.2 shows these poverty profiles, with the same categories as earlier. These poverty profiles constitute the share of old and new social risk population categories of the total poverty in a country.

In Table 8.2 these categories clearly overlap. For that reason the rows do not add up to 100 per cent. In all the countries about 20 per cent of the poor are children. For older people the result again very much depends on the poverty threshold. When we use the 60 per cent poverty threshold, around 25 per cent of the poor are elderly in all the studied countries. However, when we use a 50 per cent poverty threshold, we find that the share of older people in total poverty notably diminishes to around 17 per cent in the Nordic countries, while remaining the same or even increasing in the other European countries. When we divide the poverty population into the old and new risk groups, the old risk groups now comprise less than half of the total poverty population in the European countries.

Table 8.2: Poverty profiles of old and new risk groups in Europe in 2007 (%)

	Children[a]	Large families	Single parents	Elderly[b]	Young single adults[c]	Immigrants born inside EU	Immigrants born outside EU
Denmark	16.1	6.5	6.1	28.6	25.4	2.7	6.6
Finland	14.2	5.5	5.5	32.9	12.5	1.3	3.9
Iceland	29.2	10.3	8.8	24.6	7.6	–	–
Norway	19.2	3.7	11.5	21.9	24.5	2.5	8.0
Sweden	21.3	6.8	9.5	23.2	17.5	4.9	14.9
Nordic mean	20.0	6.6	8.3	26.2	17.5	2.9	8.4
Germany	13.7	2.6	8.4	26.6	8.0	–[d]	–[d]
Italy	20.2	6.8	3.2	28.4	0.8	1.2	6.3
Netherlands	27.9	13.3	6.7	20.2	9.1	1.2	7.9
UK	24.2	6.7	8.6	32.6	1.4	1.4	10.2
EU17 mean	21.2	7.5	7.3	26.1	7.5	4.8	8.7

Notes: [a] 16 years of age and younger; [b] 65 years of age and older; [c] 18-34 years of age; [d] data not available.
Source: EU-SILC

The role of our new social risk groups in the total picture of poverty should not be exaggerated. Again, for young single adults and immigrants the selection of poverty indicator crucially affects the research outcome. A 60 per cent poverty threshold puts their combined share at around 33 per cent in the Nordic countries and 10 to 20 per cent in the non-Nordic countries. Finland, with much lower shares, clearly deviates from the other Nordic countries – not (as seen earlier) from lower risks but primarily from the smaller size of its immigrant population. In contrast, a 50 per cent poverty threshold places the new social risk groups in a more central position. In particular, the share of young single adults now increases profoundly, as about 50 per cent of the poor in Denmark and Norway are young single adults. In Sweden their share is also high, as is the role of immigrants, as 25 per cent of the poor in Sweden are immigrants, most of them born outside Europe. In all the other countries the role of immigrant poverty is smaller than in Sweden.

In analyses of poverty among immigrants, different factors (for example, illegal migration) may weaken the comparability across countries. Likewise, patterns of childhood home-leaving behaviour also differ from country to country, with the differences possibly influencing our results on young single adults. In the Nordic countries children tend to leave the parental home earlier (Isoniemi, 2009), many when starting vocational education. Comparatively generous study allowances makes this home-leaving possible. As a further sensitivity test we therefore analysed young single adults, separating students from others, but the result did not change. Both groups had poor positions in the Nordic countries.

Poverty persistency

This section examines the persistence of poverty, defining those with incomes below 60 per cent of median income in 2008 and in at least one of the two preceding years as persistently poor (Atkinson et al, 2002). To calculate this measure, we use the panel in the EU-SILC.

As we need longitudinal data for three consecutive years, we must use the EU-SILC 2008 longitudinal dataset, which unfortunately entails some restrictions on both which countries we can include and which risk groups we are able to construct. In comparison with our earlier cross-sectional analysis of the EU-SILC, we are forced to exclude Denmark, Germany and Iceland from this analysis, as they are not included in the longitudinal part of the 2008 wave of the EU-SILC. Moreover, as the analysis is restricted to the following subgroups – children, young adults and elderly – the only 'new' risk group included is young adults.

Table 8.3 reports the persistence of poverty both aggregately and separately among these groups. The Nordic countries show a distinct pattern of comparatively low rates for the persistence of poverty among children, with slightly higher rates in Finland than in Norway and Sweden. However, the Netherlands is the most successful at combating persistent child poverty, while the Italian child poverty

Table 8.3: Poverty persistency, 2008[a]

	Children[b]	Old age[c]	Young adults[d]	Total
Finland	5.7	14.3	8.6	7.5
Norway	3.9	6.2	11.0	5.0
Sweden	4.2	4.7	5.3	3.8
Italy	17.6	18.0	14.3	14.5
Netherlands	2.8	4.0	3.1	2.4
UK	15.2	21.1	9.6	12.6
EU10[e]	13.1	13.8	10.2	11.0

Notes: [a] Below 60% of median disposable income in 2008 and in at least one of the two preceding years.
[b] ≤16 years of age in 2008.
[c] ≥68 years of age in 2008.
[d] 18-34 years of age in 2008.
[e] Finland, Norway, Ireland, Italy, Luxembourg, the Netherlands, Portugal, Spain, Sweden, the UK.
Source: EU-SILC

persistency rate is more than four times greater than that of Norway and Sweden. The UK rate is also markedly higher than those for the Nordic countries.

Poverty persistency rates among older people are also lowest in the Netherlands, followed closely by Sweden and Norway. The Finnish rate is higher, and the highest rates are in Italy and the UK. The exception of Finland in the Nordic cluster reported in Table 8.1 with regard to the risk of poverty among older people is thus repeated here.

For young adults, Sweden and the Netherlands have comparably low rates, with slightly higher rates in Finland and Norway. The UK has about the same rate as those of Finland and Norway, while Italy's is much higher. Thus the high poverty rates among young single adults in the Nordic countries (see Table 8.1) are not repeated here. Even though young people in the Nordic countries run a higher risk for low income in one single year (Table 8.1), the chance of their escaping that situation appears greater, especially in Sweden. However, the Dutch situation, with low risks both for entering and for remaining in poverty, is clearly a better achievement. In contrast, Italy shows a comparably low risk rate among young single adults while showing the highest persistency rates for young adults. While this finding could indicate that a high risk of being *trapped* in poverty is higher in Italy, the groups are not perfectly comparable, in that unlike Table 8.1, Table 8.3 cannot identify young *single* adults. Because young Italians in general tend to remain at home longer than young adults in most other countries (see, for example, Rossi, 1997), the groups of young adults and young single adults might differ significantly in Italy.

The far right column of Table 8.3 presents the overall poverty persistence rates. We find a low risk cluster for Norway, Sweden, the Netherlands and (to some extent) Finland, while the UK and Italy lag behind.

When we use the 50 per cent poverty threshold, the pattern remains fairly stable, although of course at a lower level. The only substantial deviation from the results in Table 8.3 is that the poverty persistency rate among older people in Finland comes closer to that in Norway, the Netherlands and Sweden.

The overall impression from Table 8.3 as compared to Table 8.1 is that the Nordic countries fare much better than the other countries in terms of a more severe state of poverty. Again the Finnish poverty rate among older people deviates from the Nordic cluster, and the Netherlands stands out as the most successful at combating poverty among both old and new risk groups. The Nordic countries do not appear as a family of their own when it comes to poverty among young adults, as the UK fares as well as Finland and Norway. The Netherlands and Sweden do better, with Italy standing out as the worst performing country in this respect among those in Table 8.3. For the old risk groups, children and the elderly, the Nordic countries appear more as a family of their own, but only if the Netherlands is included.

Conclusion

Discussions of the Nordic model and its differences from other countries or welfare state types often focus on historical similarities and institutional arrangements (in relation to either social or labour market policies). This chapter instead examined *outcomes* both in terms of distributions of income and in terms of poverty. Although welfare state schemes at best fulfil many needs, the issue of poverty has always been at the root of welfare state activities.

A relatively equal distribution of income and comparatively low poverty has long been regarded as central dimensions of the Nordic model. Therefore, our research questions were embedded in the overall topic of whether the Nordic countries constitute a family of their own in terms of income inequality and poverty. To answer such a question, we needed an eclectic approach that allowed us to study income inequality and particularly poverty from several different angles and perspectives. Our findings, which we discuss here, are as follows.

The Nordic countries have definitely not been immune to the overall surge in income inequality in many countries around the globe. Not only do the Nordic income inequality trends have some commonalities with other Western countries, but in particular we note a marked increase of income inequality from around the mid-1990s in all five Nordic countries. Nonetheless, our comparison of income distribution statistics across the Western world in the mid-2000s shows that the Nordic countries still have lower income inequality, albeit less distinctly so than in earlier decades.

In our title to this chapter we framed the study in terms of whether or not the Nordic countries belong to one family of nations. Looking at both income inequality and relative poverty rates, we find no evidence to refute such a claim. Some of our admittedly crude indicators on cross-national variation suggest a greater similarity within the Nordic family of nations than earlier.

For poverty trends in the Nordic countries, a clear increase is evident in Finland. Finland also deviates from the Nordic cluster in the cross-sectional case because the poverty risk among older people in Finland is significantly higher. Otherwise, the cross-sectional analysis shows that the Nordic countries manage well at combating poverty risks among the traditional risk groups. However, when we look at the new risk groups – immigrants and young single adults – a completely different picture emerges. Poverty risks among immigrants born outside the EU are fairly similar in all the countries we study, that is, the Nordic countries fare neither better nor worse for this subgroup. For young single adults the Nordic countries perform even worse than the others, and in Denmark the poverty risk for this group is particularly high. In all the countries the new risks challenge social policies, a finding particularly evident in the Nordic countries.

In contrast, our analysis of poverty persistency – defined as being poor in the latest year and in at least one of the two preceding years – showed that the Nordic countries overall perform better than most countries, especially for young adults. Nonetheless, the Netherlands out-performs the Nordic countries in that the rate of poverty persistency is lower.

But what about our results relative to the overall issue of the 'Nordic family'? In so far as Iceland is concerned, it belongs to the Nordic region but not to the Nordic model. As Ólafsson (2005) states, while Iceland shared some commonalities with the other Nordic countries in the early postwar period, it then began deviating in many respects. Thus while the Icelandic experience is of great interest in its own right, we cannot take its experience as proof of whether or not the Nordic model is falling apart.

Our three questions were, first, whether our analysis supports the belief that the Nordic countries are a family of their own through being very similar in terms of poverty and income inequality. Second, we asked whether the Nordic countries deviate – for the dimensions we study – from other relatively wealthy Western countries to a higher or lower degree than in earlier decades. Third, we asked whether the results are congruent with the usual characteristics of the Nordic model, that is, basically low income inequality and low poverty rates.

As to the first question ('family' or not?), the outcomes show a high degree of similarity. Thus income inequality has increased in the Nordic countries, especially from the mid-1990s, a difference from many other countries. Poverty rates according to the LIS are very similar, even more so than earlier, and persistent poverty rates are largely low. Moreover, our analyses of new and old social risk categories also show many similarities. The Nordic countries are largely good performers in alleviating poverty risks among old social risks, but they perform equally poorly or even worse when it comes to new social risks.

For the second question (more or less like other Western countries?) the Nordic countries still out-perform most of the other countries in our analysis. Nonetheless, a look at recent trends and new social risks clearly shows that the Nordic countries are less distinct than they were 10 to 15 years ago. The high 'at risk of poverty' rates among young single adults and immigrants in the Nordic countries are particularly discouraging for advocates of the Nordic model.

The real challenge, however, lies in answering the third question (congruence of results with usual characteristics of the Nordic model?). Income inequality has obviously increased, especially in Finland and Sweden, a result that in itself is at odds with the Nordic model. Moreover, poverty risks have increased, and that more than 10 per cent of the Nordic populations are living at risk of poverty does not mesh well with the classic features of the Nordic welfare model. Obviously, the fruits of the economic growth of the last two decades have not been as evenly distributed as during the golden age of the welfare state. Perhaps even more troublesome is the situation for the new social risk categories of immigrants and single young adults. Although we can offer many caveats for our admittedly crude analysis of poverty risks, our notable findings about young adults and immigrants definitely differ from – and are indeed at odds with – the characteristics of the universal Nordic model. Such differences, in addition to any continuation of the overall widening of income differentials, will ultimately erode the legitimacy of the Nordic model.

Notes

[1] We thank Stefán Ólafsson, Axel West Pedersen, Niels Ploug and Jarl Quitzau for help in constructing these series.

[2] A rather different time trend in Denmark can be observed when comparing national data (see Figure 8.1) to the data in the LIS.

[3] We thank Saara Hämäläinen for excellent research assistance in the analyses of the EU-SILC.

[4] Countries included in the EU17 mean are Austria, Belgium, Denmark, Finland, France, Germany, Greece, Iceland, Ireland, Italy, Luxembourg, the Netherlands, Norway, Portugal, Spain, Sweden and the UK.

References

Aaberge, R. and Atkinson, A.B. (2008) *Top incomes in Norway*, Discussion Paper 552, Oslo: Statistics Norway.

Abrahamson, P. (1999) 'The welfare modelling business', *Social Policy & Administration*, vol 33, pp 394-415.

Airio, I. (2008) *Change of norm? In-work poverty in a comparative perspective*, Studies in Social Security and Health No 92, Helsinki: Kela – The Social Insurance Institution of Finland.

Atkinson, A.B. (1970) 'On the measurement of inequality', *Journal of Economic Theory*, vol 2, pp 244-63.

Atkinson, A.B. and Piketty, T. (eds) (2007) *Top incomes over the twentieth century: A contrast between Continental European and English-speaking countries*, Oxford: Oxford University Press.

Atkinson, A.B., Rainwater, L. and Smeeding, T.M. (1995) *Income distribution in OECD countries*, OECD Social Policy Studies No 18, Paris: OECD.

Atkinson, A.B., Cantillon, B., Marlier, E. and Nolan, B. (2002) *Social indicators. The EU and social inclusion*, Oxford: Oxford University Press.

Bäckman, O. (2009) 'Institutions, structures and poverty. A comparative study of 16 countries, 1980-2000', *European Sociological Review*, vol 25, pp 251-64.

Brandolini, A. and Smeeding, T.M. (2007) *Inequality patterns in western-type democracies: Cross-country differences and time changes*, Luxembourg Income Study, Working Papers, No 458.

Danziger, S. and Ratner, D. (2010). 'Labour market outcomes and the transition to adulthood', *The Future of Children*, vol 20, pp 133-58.

Esping-Andersen, G. (1990) *Three worlds of welfare capitalism*, Cambridge: Polity Press.

Eurostat (2010) *Statistics in focus 9/2010, Population and social conditions*, Eurostat: Luxembourg.

Ferrera, M. (1996) 'The "southern model" of welfare in social Europe', *Journal of European Social Policy*, vol 6, pp 17-37.

Fritzell, J. (2001) 'Still different? Income distribution in the Nordic countries in a European comparison', in M. Kautto, J. Fritzell, B. Hvinden, J. Kvist and H. Uusitalo (eds) *Nordic welfare states in the European context*, London: Routledge, pp 18-41.

Fritzell, J. and Ritakallio, V.-M. (2010) 'Societal shifts and changed patterns of poverty', *International Journal of Social Welfare*, vol 19, pp S25-S41.

Hills, J., Brewer, M., Jenkins, S., Lister, R., Lupton, R., Machin, S. et al (2010) *An anatomy of economic inequality in the UK*, Report of the National Equality Panel, London: CASE, London School of Economics and Political Science.

Isoniemi, H. (2009) 'The role of economic factors in young adults home leaving process. A comparative longitudinal analysis of ECHP data', in P. Koistinen, L. Mosesdottier and A. Serrano Pascual (eds) *Emerging systems of work and welfare*, Brussels: Peter Lang, pp 255-73.

Jäntti, M. and Danziger, S. (2000) 'Income poverty in advanced countries', in A.B. Atkinson and F. Bourguignon (eds) *Handbook of income distribution*, North Holland: Elsevier, pp 309-78.

Kangas, O. and Palme, J (2000) 'Does social policy matter? Poverty cycles in the OECD countries', *International Journal of Health Services*, vol 30, pp 335-52.

Kangas, O. and Ritakallio, V.-M. (1998) 'Different methods – different results. Approaches to multidimensional poverty', in H.-J. Andress (ed) *Empirical poverty research in a comparative perspective*, Aldershot: Ashgate, pp 167-203.

Kautto, M. (2000) *Two of a kind? Economic crises, policy responses and well-being during the 1990s in Sweden and Finland*, Report to the Swedish Welfare Commission (Kommitté Välfärdsbokslut), SOU 2000: 83, Stockholm: Fritzes.

Kautto, M., Heikkilä, M., Hvinden, B., Marklund, S. and Ploug, N. (eds) (1999) *Nordic social policy: Changing welfare states*, London: Routledge.

Kildal, N. and Kuhnle, S. (eds) (2005) *Normative foundations of the welfare state: The Nordic experience*, London: Routledge.

NOU (2009:10) *Fordelningsutvalget*, Oslo: Departementenes Servicesenter.

OECD (Organisation for Economic Co-operation and Development) (2008) *Growing unequal? Income distribution and poverty in OECD countries*, Paris: OECD.

Ólafsson, S. (2005) 'Normative foundations of the Icelandic welfare state: on the gradual erosion of citizenship-based welfare rights', in N. Kildal and S. Kuhnle (eds) *Normative foundations of the welfare state: The Nordic experience*, London: Routledge, pp 214-36.

Ólafsson, S. and Kristjansson, A.S. (2010) 'Income inequality in a bubble economy – the case of Iceland 1992-2008', Presented at the Luxembourg Income Study Conference 2010, University of Iceland.

Palme, J., Bergmark, Å., Bäckman, O., Estrada, F., Fritzell, J., Lundberg O. et al (2002) 'Welfare trends in Sweden: balancing the books for the 1990s', *Journal of European Social Policy*, vol 12, pp 329-34.

Riihelä, M., Sullström, R. and Suoniemi, I. (2008) *Tax progressivity and recent evolution of the Finnish income inequality*, Working Papers, 264, Helsinki: Labour Institute for Economic Research.

Ritakallio, V.-M. (2002) 'Trends of poverty and income inequality in cross-national comparison', *European Journal of Social Security*, vol 4, pp 151-77.

Rossi, G. (1997) 'The nestlings. Why young adults stay at home longer: the Italian case', *Journal of Family Issues*, vol 18, pp 627-44.

Rowntree, S. (1901) *Poverty: A study of town life*, London: Macmillan. Centennial Edition (2000). Bristol: Policy Press.

Ruggeri Laderchi, C., Saith, R. and Stewart, F. (2003) *Does it matter that we don't agree on the definition of poverty? A comparison of four approaches*, Queen Elizabeth House Working Paper Series 107, Oxford: University of Oxford.

Statistics Sweden (2010) *Inkomstfördelningsundersökningen 2008*, Statistiska meddelanden HE21SM1001, Örebro: Statistics Sweden.

Sørensen, P.B. (1994) 'From the global income tax to the dual income tax', *International Tax and Public Finance*, vol 1, pp 57-80.

Taylor-Gooby, P. (2004) 'New risks and social change', in P. Taylor-Gooby (ed) *New risks, new welfare: The transformation of the European welfare state*, Oxford: Oxford University Press, pp 1-28.

Timonen, V. (2004) 'New risks – are they still new for the Nordic welfare states?', in P. Taylor-Gooby (ed) *New risks, new welfare: The transformation of the European welfare state*, Oxford: Oxford University Press, pp 83-110.

Titmuss, R.M. (1974) *Social policy: An introduction*, New York: Pantheon Books.

US Census Bureau (2010) *Income, poverty, and health insurance coverage in the United States: 2009*, Current Population Reports, P60-238, Washington: US Government Printing Office.

NINE

Is immigration challenging the economic sustainability of the Nordic welfare model?

Christer Gerdes and Eskil Wadensjö

Introduction

The idea that substantial immigration, especially from countries outside the rich West, is incompatible with a Nordic kind of welfare state, has been put forward in the debate on immigration. This chapter asks under what conditions immigration from countries outside the rich West is – or might become – a real and significant challenge to the economic sustainability of the Nordic welfare model. Immigration might, for instance, have an effect on wages and employment. More specifically, this chapter examines if immigration might lead to a financial weakening of the Nordic welfare state.

We ask to what extent immigration leads to net transfers from the welfare state to the immigrant population. If such net transfers were substantial, they could undermine public finances in the long term and through this, the sustainability of the Nordic welfare state. Given that immigration might influence public sector finances, the effects are likely to depend on the composition of the immigrant population, for example, in terms of origin, ethnicity, reason for migration, age and skills; the situation in the labour market; and the design of the welfare state.

The first part of this chapter explores a simplified account of the immigration story of the Nordic countries from the first decades after the Second World War up to the present day. The second part presents research on factors that might determine the actual effects of immigration on public financing, primarily the results of studies of Scandinavian countries, but for comparative purposes also the results for some other receiving countries. In the final part we build on the results of this research to summarise the economic effects of immigration and the possible responses to such effects related to the institutional design of Nordic welfare states.

Immigration to Western Europe in the first decades after the Second World War was mainly labour migration either from neighbouring countries or from Mediterranean countries (Greece, Italy, Portugal, Spain, Yugoslavia and Turkey). Many also came from former colonies such as India, Pakistan, Bangladesh, Indonesia, Algeria and the West Indies. It was a period of high economic growth with an unlimited supply of labour due to the large supply of immigrant labour (Kindleberger, 1967). The labour migration policy was primarily designed as a guest worker policy characterised by high labour force participation, tax revenues, few income transfers to the immigrants and low additional costs for public consumption (schools, health, childcare and care of older people). However, many of the labour immigrants remained in the receiving countries, and their offspring grew up in these countries.

The economic crisis of the early 1970s led to a large decline in labour migration, partly because of the lower availability of jobs in the destination countries, and partly as a result of the adoption of more restrictive immigration policies. Additionally, governments adopted restrictions or embargos on labour immigration as a response to criticism of the liberal labour migration policy. Competition in the labour market between immigrants and the native-born had become national issues.

The decline in labour migration did not mean that the migration discontinued, but it took other forms. Most importantly refugee immigration came to dominate. In the 1970s many refugees came from Chile and other South American countries; in the 1980s, from Iran and the Middle East; in the 1990s, from the former Yugoslavia; and in the 2000s, from the Middle East, especially Iraq, Afghanistan and the African countries of Eritrea, Somalia and Sudan.

Moreover, family-related migration had a growing role, both in the Nordic countries and other European countries. Many of the immigrants arriving in the 1990s and the 2000s were family members of earlier labour migrants and refugees. Some of this migration was due to family members joining migrants who had arrived earlier; another reason was as a result of marriage.

In the same way as governments of the receiving countries had expected that most of the early labour immigrants would eventually return to their home countries, governments expected refugees to return 'home' as soon as political changes in their countries of origin made such return possible. However, large proportions of both labour immigrants and refugees settled in the receiving country. In some cases, the immigrants and their descendents did not became fully integrated but rather established their own ethnic or religious groups within the receiving countries and formed new institutions and networks. As a result, the population of the Nordic countries – especially of the three Scandinavian countries (Denmark, Norway and Sweden) – has become considerably more ethnically heterogeneous and diverse along several dimensions such as country of origin, language and religion.

The consequent increased diversity of the population has led to various concerns and political polarisation between groups in favour of or against immigration. Chapter two by Finseraas in this book deals with how increased ethnic heterogeneity has affected popular support for redistributive welfare policies in the Nordic countries. In this chapter we focus on the concerns related to how immigration and greater ethnic diversity have had an impact on the labour market and public finances in the receiving countries. At the centre of these concerns is the issue of whether immigrants and their offspring will have lower labour market participation and employment rates than the native population. First, we clarify some general effects of immigration on the functioning of the labour market of the receiving countries.

Effects of immigration on the labour markets of receiving countries

Much of the discussion on immigration and its effects centres on the labour market. Those who are against immigration and who wish to reduce it often use arguments related to the labour market situation of immigrants or the labour market effects of immigration. While the specific arguments against labour migration and refugee or family-related immigration are different, in many cases they too relate to the labour market situation. Those who are critical of labour migration primarily stress job competition between immigrants and the native-born and the presumed negative wage effects of immigration on the native-born. The critics of refugee immigration mainly stress the low labour force participation among immigrant groups and the unemployment-related public sector costs. We first discuss whether immigration leads to pressure on wages and higher unemployment, and second, what effects immigration has on the labour market situation, followed by a discussion of the low labour force participation among some immigrant groups.

In general, an increased supply of a commodity in a market leads to a lower price for the product, with everything else kept constant. Correspondingly, an increased supply of labour leads to a lower price for labour (a lower wage rate), if nothing else changes as a result of the increased labour supply. As immigration involves an increase in the supply of labour, one should expect lower wages. However, in many cases – to which we shall return – researchers have not found such wage effects (see, for example, Borjas, 2003; Card, 2005; Longhi et al, 2005a; Nickell and Saleheen, 2008; Ottaviano and Peri, 2008, for studies on the wage effects of immigration, and Hanson (2008) for a survey).

How can the absence of negative wage effects be explained? The 'negative effect on native-born wages' hypothesis builds on an economic model with one type of labour and one production factor (capital) used in the production of commodities and services. In such a model of the production process, immigrant and native-born labour are perfect substitutes; hence, an increased supply of either group leads to a lowering of the wage level (or a lower wage increase in the economy). Labour, however, constitutes more than one factor in the production process (besides capital). It may be divided into different skill groups, so that native-born labour and immigrant labour are not necessarily substitutes but complement each other in the production of commodities and services. If two types of labour are complementary in the production process, an increase in the supply of one type of labour and a corresponding wage decline lead to increased demand for the other type of labour and a correspondingly higher wage for that group. For example, the immigration of unskilled labour may lead to a wage increase for skilled native-born labour. By contrast, unskilled immigrant labour and unskilled native-born labour may be substitutes. Since labour immigration often comprises mainly unskilled labour (or skilled labour that cannot make use of those skills), concerns about the negative wage effects of immigration apply mainly to the unskilled native-born.

However, the negative effects of immigration on the wages of unskilled native-born workers are in most studies not found – and when they are, the effects are mostly small. While some studies find a negative wage effect of immigration, these findings apply to earlier immigrants from the same country of origin as the newly arrived ones (see Longhi et al, 2005a, for a meta-analysis). For instance, Bratsberg and Raaum (2009) find a negative effect in construction work in Norway, but these effects are small in some areas and non-existent in others.

Another explanation for the problematic issue of the absence of negative wage effects is that the amount of capital used in an economy may change as a result of immigration. On recognising the opportunity to recruit cheaper labour from outside the country, firms may be more inclined to invest in building and machinery. A parallel import of capital and labour was typical for the expansion of the US economy in the 19th century (Thomas, 1954), and the 1960s expansion of the manufacturing industry in Western Europe was greatly facilitated and stimulated by the unlimited supply of labour during this period (Kindleberger, 1967). Such an induced increase of investments may make the increase in labour demand equal to or larger than the increase of labour supply. In such a setting, immigration may induce wage increases. More recently, the 1990s expansion of the Irish economy exemplifies this combination of immigration and capital import – but the continued Irish expansion in the 2000s (mainly in housing and construction) has subsequently led to serious economic problems.

In earlier research we estimated the influence on wages in Denmark of the share of Western and non-Western immigrants in a municipality and the change in that share (Wadensjö and Gerdes, 2004b). We included controls for age, gender, family status, country of origin, education and the unemployment rate in the municipality in all estimations. When we did not include controls for the degree of municipality urbanisation, the wage effect was positive, but when we included controls for urbanisation, the effect (small in all cases) was negative for male and female non-Western immigrants and for female Western immigrants, but positive for male Western immigrants.

The main conclusion on the basis of this and other research is that the wage effects of immigration are small and sensitive to other variables (Barrett et al, 2009). Yet, to the extent that we find the belief among the native-born population that consequences of immigration include increased job competition and pressure towards reduced wages, this may trigger a popular demand for more restrictive immigration policies, as was – at least partially – the case in the Nordic countries of the 1970s.

Another issue is whether immigration increases the overall unemployment rate. A general answer is that the size of a population is not the key factor: larger countries do not have higher unemployment rates than smaller countries. Instead, according to Say's law, an increase in the supply of labour leads to an increase in the demand for labour. More specifically, the NAIRU (the non-accelerating inflation rate of unemployment) is determined by frictions (cost of mobility) in the labour market. Such frictions may increase if immigrants are less mobile than the native-born if they have greater difficulties finding work in other firms, occupations or regions. On the other hand, frictions may decrease if immigrants are more mobile if they are searching harder for jobs outside the local labour market (Blanchflower and Shadforth, 2009). A tentative conclusion is that the effects of immigration on the overall unemployment level are small, and that the sign of the effect is undetermined.

A slightly different question is whether immigration influences the unemployment rate of the native-born. If the general unemployment rate is more or less fixed as a share of the labour force, independent of the immigrants' share, and the immigrant unemployment rate is higher than that of the native-born, a higher immigrant share of the labour force means a lower unemployment rate for the native-born. In such a case the immigrants take up a larger part of the burden of unemployment than their share of the labour force should warrant. This result may be attributable, for example, to immigrants having less seniority or being objects of discrimination. However, if immigrants experience lower unemployment than the native-born, the effect is the opposite. The results of most studies are that there are no or only small (positive or negative) effects on the native unemployment rate (see Longhi et al, 2005b, for a meta-analysis).

One idea is that international migration may act as an automatic stabiliser of the business cycle in the countries of destination, but the effect could also be higher amplitude of the business cycle variations. The result depends on whether immigration leads to larger capital investments in the private and public sectors and, if so, on the timing of those investments.

When we estimated the effects of the share of immigrants in the municipality in Denmark and of the changes in this share on the unemployment rates of native-born Danes, we found that unemployment increased with an increase of the Western share but decreased with an increase of the non-Western share (Wadensjö and Gerdes, 2004b). The interpretation is that while Western immigrants and native-born Danes were substitutes in the production process, non-Western immigrants and native-born Danes complemented each other.

Immigrants' labour force participation and earnings

In general, *labour migrants* were often recruited for specific jobs or they immigrated when they found a job. At first their labour force participation was high and in some cases, very high. However, some of those who stayed in the receiving country for a longer period have lost their job, for example, due to structural changes in the economy, and have had difficulties in finding a new one. These issues, however, have differed greatly between countries and over time.

Refugees generally have a much more difficult labour market situation than labour migrants, primarily because their reason for immigrating has not been job-related. However, not all refugees have had difficulty in establishing themselves in the labour market of the receiving country. For instance, those who came to Sweden from different countries during the Second World War, from Hungary in 1956, and from Poland and Czechoslovakia in the late 1960s, exemplify groups of refugees who found work soon after arrival. But other refugee groups have had much greater difficulties in establishing themselves in the labour markets of their countries of destination. They have arrived in periods with high unemployment and few job vacancies and often had skills not in demand. The labour market experience of immigrants who have come to the Nordic countries for family-related reasons is in several respects similar to that of refugees.

For various reasons immigrants' labour market integration has tended to improve with years of residence in the receiving country. For instance, many have needed some time to acquire language skills and to gain familiarity with other aspects of the country's culture or to establish the necessary network to get a job. Refugees who arrived as asylum seekers have often not been allowed to work before receiving a residence permit. As the employment rates of immigrants from African and Asian countries have been lower in the Nordic countries than in a number of other countries, differences in the composition of the immigrant population have probably again been one of the major explanations.

More generally, not only differences in employment rates but also differences in wages and incomes in a population depend on the composition of human capital (education, job experience), and on the demand for people with different qualifications. If the immigration is mainly low skilled and if this inflow does not lead to the upgrading of the qualifications of the native-born population, the result may be larger wage and income differences within the population (Card, 2009). Even if both the low and high-skilled among the native-born benefit from immigration (either because the immigrants and natives complement each other in the production process or because capital investments accompany immigration), the result could nonetheless be a less equal society. The extent of the effects on income equality thus depends on the policies in other areas than those directly related to the labour market. Furthermore, even if the wages of the native-born do not decline as a result of immigration, the inflow of immigrants may cause the average wage, including that of the immigrants, to decline.

Take-up of cash transfers among the native-born and immigrants

In general, the take-up of cash transfers among both the native-born and immigrants is largely dependent on whether they are in gainful employment (or being provided for by somebody who is) and the availability of cash benefits and rules determining eligibility to such benefits. We have already discussed factors related to immigrants' prospects of being in the labour force and finding employment. How accessible cash benefits are for immigrants are to a great extent determined by whether eligibility for benefits are based on currently having legal residence in the receiving country or conditioned on having a certain record of employment and earnings (or contributions) or a certain number of years of residence in the country. For newly arrived immigrants, the most relevant benefits are means-tested minimum income protection, family benefits and targeted introduction support (if such exists). Immigrants who have lived a number of years in the country may also have established eligibility for social insurance benefits related to illness, disability, unemployment or loss of provider.

Immigration and public sector finances

Immigration, as all other demographic changes, affects public sector finances (see Rowthorn, 2008, for a survey). As immigrants pay both income taxes and sales taxes, immigration leads to an increase in public sector revenue. But as we have seen, public sector expenditures also increase as a result of immigration as immigrants receive income transfers. It also leads to increased public consumption and investments. Some of these costs relate to individuals – for example, education, daycare for children, healthcare and old age care – while other costs relate more to the size of the population, increasing more or less proportionally with either the population or the number of dwellings, for example, improvements in city streets. Yet other forms of public consumption and investment may be independent of changes in the population due to immigration, such as the cost of national defence.

Net transfers through the public sector – the sum of paid taxes, received public transfers and in-kind benefits – mainly constitute a distribution of resources over the life cycle. Those who are employed pay more than they receive, and children, young people and older people receive more than they pay. Among those of working age, net transfers also go from those who are employed to those who are not. The net transfers from those who are employed are larger, that is, more positive, from those with high wages and incomes than from those with low wages and incomes.

As labour migrants are usually employed, they therefore pay more in taxes than they receive from the public sector. Few labour migrants (including their family members) are elderly, and at least at the start, few immigrant household members are children or young people (who are mostly students). Over two or three generations, the age and employment distribution of a cohort of labour migrants and their family members increasingly resembles the native-born population, and the net transfers decline.

As for refugees, when they arrive they are younger on average than the native-born population. If, as in many cases, a large share of the refugee population is not integrated into the labour market, the net transfers go from the public sector to the refugee immigrants. Or, the net transfer account becomes negative from the perspective of the immigrant. Beyond the size of the refugee problem, the extent of such transfers depends not only on the institutions and rules of the welfare state (for example, how accessible and generous the income transfer systems are) but also – and most importantly – on their labour market integration. The more successful this integration is, the smaller the net transfer for that group will be.

A number of studies of the fiscal effects of immigration, based on cross-sectional analyses, have been carried out in different countries. We will now discuss studies from the Nordic countries (Denmark, Norway and Sweden), another European country (Germany) and three countries outside Europe (the US, Australia and Canada).

In earlier work we studied the net transfers to the public sector from immigrants in Denmark and Germany by using information on population cross-sections to examine the effects of a number of variables. In the case of Denmark, we were able to study more issues because the data covered samples of the total population (natives and immigrants) over several years (1991, 1995-2001), (Wadensjö and Orrje, 2002; Wadensjö and Gerdes, 2004a). In the case of Germany we had information on five major immigrant groups from non-Western countries for one year, 2002 (Wadensjö and Gerdes, 2004a; Gerdes, 2007; Gerdes 2011b).

For *Denmark*, the data allowed us to follow the development over time. These data showed that the net transfer in all the years studied went from Western immigrants to the public sector and from the public sector to immigrants from non-Western countries. The volume of the transfers was considerable. The transfers per person varied with the business cycle (and the employment rate), while the size of the immigrant population influenced the total volume. Somewhat surprisingly, the reduction in amounts (both individual and total) between 1996 and 1998 did not continue in 1998-2000, especially as the labour market situation improved in the latter period.

In *Germany*, we found that the net transfer went from the public sector to the immigrants, that is, in the same direction as in Denmark for non-Western immigrants. The net transfers per person were smaller on average in Germany than in Denmark, and varied considerably between different non-Western immigrant groups. Gerdes (2011a) found that the legal migration status granted on arrival in Germany had a significant impact on net transfer outcomes, irrespective of country of origin.

For both countries we were able to study the effects of individual characteristics and the employment situation (and income from employment) on the individual net transfer to the public sector. In both countries, when the employment/income variables were left out, the net transfers from the public sector were greater to women than to men, and greater to the young, older people and those with children (especially single parents). While some of these effects disappeared when variables representing employment/income were included, the effect of having children was still very strong. For other variables the effects became smaller and to some extent changed signs for the two countries, a result possibly attributable to differences in the tax and transfer systems between the countries.

The employment/income variables were highly significant, with large effects that were larger in Denmark than in Germany. These differences might be explained by differences in the tax systems and profile of the public sector expenditure between the two countries.

Larsen and Bruce (1998) carried out a study of public sector redistribution in *Norway*. Their results indicated a significant redistribution to refugee immigrants, with a smaller transfer from other immigrants to the public sector. The one factor that greatly determined these results was the poor labour market situation for refugees. If refugees had been employed to the same extent as native-born citizens of the same age, the net transfer to refugees would fall significantly, and the net fiscal transfer from other immigrants would rise sharply.

We have a number of cross-sectional analyses of the fiscal effects of immigration in *Sweden*. The results of the analyses have changed over time, as immigration itself has changed from mainly labour migration to primarily refugee immigration. Moreover, the Swedish economy has undergone considerable transformations over the last five decades. The main results are presented below.

- A study of labour immigration during the 1960s from four European countries (Finland, Germany, Italy and Yugoslavia) indicated net transfers from the immigrants to the rest of the population (Wadensjö, 1973). Of decisive importance for the results was that the immigrants showed a very high level of labour force participation.
- A study covering the 1970s suggested that there was still a net transfer from the immigrants, but that this transfer was considerably smaller (Ekberg, 1983).
- By contrast, later studies have shown a fairly substantial net transfer to immigrants. According to Gustafsson and Österberg (2001), this reversal occurred in the early 1990s, during which time unemployment rose quickly in Sweden. Ekberg (1999) found that the net transfer to immigrants amounted to 0.9 per cent of the gross domestic product (GDP) in 1991 and 2.0 per cent in 1994, explaining the large difference between the two years mainly by the downturn of the Swedish economy in this period and by the large influx of Bosnian refugees unable to find jobs in the recession.
- Several studies have found that the age at which immigrants arrive, their country of origin, education, family status, length of stay and employment while being in Sweden are important (see, for example, Storesletten, 1998; Gustafsson and Österberg, 2001; Ekberg, 2011).

By comparison, a review of studies carried out in *the United States* by MaCurdy, Nechyba and Bhattacharya (1998) found the fiscal effects of immigration to be negative in all cases. However, as these studies lack important details that account precisely for expenditure and income, interpreting them is difficult. Studies carried out within the framework of the US National Research Council's comprehensive report on the effects of immigration were considerably more thorough as regards the system of accounting for expenditure and income, but have still produced similar results (see the various studies in Smith and Edmonston, 1998).

Ablett (1999) analysed the effects of immigration on the public sector in *Australia* in a generational framework. The main conclusion was that immigration was likely to make a substantial net positive contribution to the Australian public sector.

Akbari (1991) studied the fiscal effects of immigrants who arrived in *Canada* in 1979 or earlier, based on the 1981 Canadian census of population, and calculated the fiscal effects for four different groups of origin: the US; the UK; Western Europe; and Asia, Africa and South and Central America. The net present value for the public sector was calculated for a representative immigrant household arriving in 1980. The net contribution was positive for all four immigrant groups – highest for those from the UK and lowest for those from Western Europe. Canadian migration policy favours highly skilled and highly educated migrants.

All in all, we have seen that the fiscal impact of immigration varied not only among the countries studied but also within each country, depending on the period covered and the method of calculation used. Common to all studies was that the immigrants had an age structure with a positive fiscal impact. Nonetheless, in most cases the employment rate and earnings were lower for immigrants than for the native-born, leading to lower tax payments and higher income transfers to immigrants of working age. Hence in most countries, one factor, the age structure, had a positive fiscal impact, and one factor, the employment situation, had a negative impact. In some cases the first factor was the most important; in other cases, the second factor.

Conclusion

While international migration has enlarged the production of the world economy, migration is still highly regulated by the countries of destination, much more so than trade in goods and services or capital mobility. Immigration policies of many countries have become more restrictive over time (Facchini and Mayda, 2009; Hanson, 2009). The political establishment in many countries is much more critical of immigration in the 2000s than in the 1990s, and the general public is overall more critical of immigration than their governments.

As discussed in this chapter, the arguments against immigration have taken different shapes. Some of the arguments have been of an economic nature, for instance, when some have argued that labour immigration leads to lower wages and higher unemployment for the native-born. We have referred to research that has largely refuted this assumption, showing that in general the effects of immigration are small, and in many cases even positive for the native-born's wages and employment. Admittedly, some negative effects might have occurred, especially for groups in sectors and occupations that have attracted many migrants. Yet fears about possible effects of immigration have probably had a greater impact than any negative effects that have been experienced.

Another economic argument has been that fiscal effects for welfare states of the Nordic or Scandinavian type have generally been positive for labour immigration but negative for refugee immigration. Arguably, in countries with more selective welfare states of the Liberal type and larger wage differentials (and therefore more working poor), the fiscal effects might be negative not only for refugee immigrants but also for low-skilled labour immigrants. The skill composition of the migrants has influenced the size of the welfare state (Cohen et al, 2009). We have also argued that the attitudes towards immigration among different groups of the native-born may depend on how a financial deficit is financed – whether by tax increases, reduction in public expenditures, or a combination thereof.

If immigration leads to a negative fiscal effect, the money can come from either higher taxes or a combination of lower compensation levels in income transfer schemes and fewer resources to publicly financed services such as healthcare and education (see Facchini and Mayda, 2009). Assuming a progressive tax system, higher taxes would most likely mean that those with high incomes were the main contributors, whereas lower compensation levels in income transfer schemes, such as unemployment insurance and sickness benefits, most likely would make those with low incomes contribute most to the savings.

The total effects on public sector finances of the Nordic countries have been fairly small compared to the size of GDP or total public expenditures. In this sense, the fiscal effects of immigration are hardly a threat to the sustainability of the Nordic welfare model. The strong public opinion against immigration and immigrants in many European welfare states, including some of the Nordic countries, juxtaposed against the relatively small economic effects of immigration, lead us to conclude that factors other than economic ones are most important in explaining negative attitudes towards immigrants and differences in attitudes between countries.

References

Ablett, J. (1999) 'Generational accounting in Australia', in A.J. Auerbach, L.J. Kotlikoff and W. Leibfritz (eds) *Generational accounting around the world*, Chicago, IL: The University of Chicago Press.

Akbari, A.H. (1991) 'The public finance impact of immigrant population on host nations: some Canadian evidence', *Social Science Quarterly*, vol 2, pp 334-46.

Barrett, A., Bergin, A. and Kelly, E. (2009) *Estimating the impact of immigration on wages in Ireland*, IZA Discussion Paper No 4472, Bonn: Institute for the Study of Labour.

Blanchflower, D.G. and Shadforth, C. (2009) 'Fear, unemployment and migration', *Economic Journal*, vol 119 (February), F136-F182.

Borjas, G. (2003) 'The labor demand curve is downward sloping: re-examining the impact of immigration on the labor market', *Quarterly Journal of Economics*, vol 118, no 4, pp 1335-74.

Bratsberg, B. and Raaum, O. (2009) *Immigration and wages: Evidence from construction,* CReAM Discussion Paper Series No 06/10, London: Centre for Research and Analysis of Migration, Department of Economics, University College London.

Card, D. (2005) 'Is the new immigration really so bad?', *Economic Journal,* vol 115 (November), F300-F323.

Card, D. (2009) *Immigration and inequality,* NBER Working Paper 14683, Cambridge, MA: The National Bureau of Economic Research.

Cohen, A., Razin, A. and Sadka, E. (2009) *The skill composition of migration and the generosity of the welfare state,* NBER Working Paper 14738, Cambridge, MA: The National Bureau of Economic Research.

Ekberg, J. (1983) *Inkomsteffekter av invandring* [*Income effects of immigration*], Acta Wexionensia, Serie 2, Economy & Politics, Växjö: Väsjö University College.

Ekberg, J. (1999) 'Immigration and the public sector: income effects for the native population in Sweden', *Journal of Population Economics,* vol 12, pp 278-97.

Ekberg, J. (2011) 'Will future immigration to Sweden make it easier to finance the welfare system?', *European Journal of Population Economics,* vol 27, pp 103-24.

Facchini, G. and Mayda, A.M. (2009) *The political economy of immigration policy,* Human Development Research Paper 2009/03, New York: United Nations Development Programme.

Gerdes, C. (2007) *Determination of net transfers for immigrants in Germany,* Study Paper No 16, Copenhagen: The Rockwool Foundation Research Unit.

Gerdes, C. (2011a) 'A comparative study of net transfers for different immigrant groups: Evidence from Germany', *International Migration,* doi: 10.1111/j.1468-2435.2009.00573.x.

Gerdes, C. (2011b) 'The impact of immigration on the size of government: empirical evidence from Danish municipalities', *Scandinavian Journal of Economics,* vol 113, pp 74-92.

Gustafsson, B. and Österberg, T. (2001) 'Immigrants and the public sector budget – accounting exercises for Sweden', *Journal of Population Economics,* vol 14, pp 689-708.

Hanson, G.H. (2008) *The economic consequences of the international migration of labor,* NBER Working Paper 14490, Cambridge, MA: The National Bureau of Economic Research.

Hanson, G.H. (2009) *The governance of migration policy,* Human Development Research Paper 2009/02, New York: United Nations Development Programme.

Kindleberger, C.P. (1967) *Europe's postwar growth. The role of labor supply,* Cambridge, MA: Harvard University Press.

Larsen, K.A. and Bruce, E. (1998) 'Virkninger av innvandringpå de offentlige finanser i Norge', in T. Bager and S. Rezaei (eds) *Indvandringens økonomiske konskvenseri Skandinavien* [*Effects of immigration on public finances in Norway*], Esbjerg: Sydjysk Universitetsforlag, pp 87-96.

Longhi, S., Nijkamp, P. and Poot, J. (2005a) 'A meta-analytic assessment of the effect of immigration on wages', *Journal of Economic Surveys,* vol 19, pp 451-77.

Longhi, S., Nijkamp, P. and Poot, J. (2005b) 'The Fallacy of "job robbing": a meta-analysis of estimates of the effect of immigration on employment', *Journal of Migration and Refugee Issues*, vol 1, no 4, pp 131-52.

MaCurdy, T., Nechyba, T. and Bhattacharya, J. (1998) 'An economic framework for assessing the fiscal impacts of immigration', in J.P. Smith and B. Edmonston (eds) *The immigration debate. Studies on the economic, demographic and fiscal effects of immigration*, Washington, DC: National Academy Press, pp 13-65.

Nickell, S. and Saleheen, J. (2008) *The impact of immigration on occupational wages: evidence from Britain*, Working Paper, No 08-6, Boston, MA: Federal Reserve Bank of Boston.

Ottaviano, G.I.P. and Peri, G. (2008) *Immigration and national wages: Clarifying the theory and the empirics*, CEPR Discussion Paper Series No 6916, London: Centre for Economic Policy Research.

Rowthorn, R. (2008) 'The fiscal impact of immigration on the advanced economies', *Oxford Review of Economic Policy*, vol 24, pp 560-80.

Smith, J.P. and Edmonston, B. (eds) (1998) *The immigration debate. Studies on the economic, demographic and fiscal effects of immigration*, Washington, DC: National Academy Press.

Storesletten, K. (2000) 'Sustaining fiscal policy through immigration', *Journal of Political Economy*, vol 108, pp 300-23.

Thomas, B. (1954) *Migration and economic growth: A study of Great Britain and the Atlantic economy*, Cambridge: Cambridge University Press.

Wadensjö, E. (1973) *Immigration och samhällsekonomi* [*Immigration and the Swedish economy*], Lund: Studentlitteratur.

Wadensjö, E. and Gerdes, C. (2004a) 'Immigrants and the public sector in Denmark and Germany', in T. Tranæs and K. Zimmerman (eds) *Migrants, work and the welfare state*, Odense: University Press of Southern Denmark, chapter 10.

Wadensjö, E. and Gerdes, C. (2004b) 'Some socioeconomic consequences of immigration', in T. Tranæs and K. Zimmerman (eds) *Migrants, work and the welfare state*, Odense: University Press of Southern Denmark, chapter 11.

Wadensjö, E. and Orrje, H. (2002) *Immigration and the public sector in Denmark*, Aarhus: Aarhus University Press.

TEN

Nordic responses to rising inequalities: still pursuing a distinct path or joining the rest?

Jon Kvist, Johan Fritzell, Bjørn Hvinden and Olli Kangas

In the introductory chapter to this volume (Chapter One) we identified a number of key issues related to current changes in social inequality in the Nordic countries. In these concluding remarks we first summarise the main factors contributing to the changes, based on the analyses presented in the individual chapters. Second, we discuss whether the Nordic welfare states have been able to prevent or mitigate increasing inequalities. Finally, we seek to give some answers to the critical question raised in the introductory chapter: are the Nordic countries managing to stem the international tide of inequality better, worse or perhaps just differently than other countries?

Consequences of immigration and ethnic diversity

Several chapters give considerable attention to the role of immigration, especially from outside the richer part of the world, as a new challenge for the Nordic welfare states and as a potential source of increased inequalities. Henning Finseraas (Chapter Two) takes issue with the growing international literature claiming that immigration-driven ethnic diversity is diminishing the electoral support for redistributive public provisions and, through reduced backing of parties favouring redistribution, creating greater social inequalities. While he refutes the simple hypothesis that immigration-driven ethnic diversity in itself decreases support for redistribution, he finds that comparatively low employment rates among immigrants tend to weaken support for the main parties in favour of redistribution.

Comparatively low employment rates among immigrants are also an important factor when in Chapter Eight, Johan Fritzell, Olof Bäckman and Veli-Matti Ritakallio find that immigrants from outside the European Union (EU) are one of the major groups at risk of poverty, in both the Nordic and other European countries. To the extent that newly arrived immigrants without work are particularly dependent on means-tested minimum income benefits, the situation appears no better, as Susan Kuivalainen and Kenneth Nelson (Chapter Four) show that such benefits in most countries provide decreasing protection against poverty.

In Chapter Five Gabrielle Meagher and Marta Szebehely emphasise how the home childcare allowance (HCA) provided by several Nordic countries may reinforce traditional gendered divisions of labour, under-use of childcare services and low female employment among immigrants from non-Western countries. More generally, Christer Gerdes and Eskil Wadensjö (Chapter Nine) identify three main factors determining the effects of immigration on public finances: the composition of the immigrant population, the situation in the labour market and the design of the welfare state. Their conclusion is that the effects of immigration on public sector finances are small, varying according to the immigrant population's composition, and that these effects do not constitute a threat to the Nordic model's sustainability. However, the Nordic welfare state model does not perform well when it comes to integrating immigrants in the labour market or preventing poverty among immigrants. The poor performance of the Nordic welfare states towards living conditions among immigrants thus stand in contrast to the major universalistic principles of the Nordic welfare model. This situation, in turn, is also likely to have an impact on the support for the welfare state along the lines that Finseraas discusses in Chapter Two. In sum, the findings in this book show not immigration in itself but rather the links with labour market integration, poverty risks and subsequent welfare state support as being problematic.

Consequences of changes in gendered family and employment patterns

Two chapters point to the significance of the growing prominence of dual-earner families and the way in which two earners are better positioned than single providers to protect their household against economic hardship. M. Azhar Hussain, Olli Kangas and Jon Kvist (Chapter Six) demonstrate that families with two earners tend to be less severely affected by unemployment than families with only one. When one spouse in a dual earner couple becomes unemployed the partner's income cushions the most harmful effects of unemployment; one earner families lack such a cushion. Two of the main findings of Fritzell, Bäckman and Ritakallio (Chapter Eight) are that young single adults and single parents are at particular risk of poverty.

Fritzell, Bäckman and Ritakallio examine the issue of whether dual-earner households have become the normative standard or framework in the Nordic countries, with potential effects on wage levels, housing prices and dominant consumption patterns and expectations. To the extent that such a normative framework has emerged, we may interpret the shift towards a dual-earner household as a paradoxical and unintended consequence of an otherwise largely desirable development of the Nordic welfare model. Certainly this shift from single- to dual-earner families has been an important aspect of the change towards greater gender equality in many countries.

At the same time some would say that having two earners in families or households cannot be an ideal in all circumstances or at all stages of the life course of family members. As already illustrated, some of the minority ethnic groups in the Nordic countries may hold other ideals. Meagher and Szebehely (Chapter Five) show that even within a Nordic majority population we find diverse preferences and adjustments, although these may not be completely independent of the situation in the labour market and other factors. Meagher and Szebehely also hint at the more general issue of what role variation in preferences and choice should have in relation to the pursuit of social equality. Traditionally, the Nordic countries have tried to promote end-state equality that perhaps has led to a limited set of preferences. The increasing diversification of individuals' preferences, along with changing family and employment patterns, may create some tension in the traditional social democratic way of thinking. Whether social democratic policy may change as a result of these tensions is beyond the scope of our book; however, in terms of consequences for the Nordic model, social democrats appear to have lost their previous leading – and in some cases, hegemonic – role, and liberal, conservative and more populist parties now have a stronger position in politics. These parties do not necessarily pursue the same goals as the social democrats did.

Writing about social inequalities in health, Clare Bambra (Chapter Seven) notes that one of the factors behind such inequalities in the Nordic countries may be differences in lifestyles and health-related behaviour (for example, smoking, diet and physical activity) between social strata. Compared to many other European countries, such health-related behaviours appear particularly socially structured in the Nordic countries.

The entire issue of whether the Nordic welfare states should respond to or accommodate diversity in preferences related to differences in lifestyles, cultures, ideologies and political positions is beyond the scope of this book, however. The two chapters dealing with public opinion related to the ambitions for redistribution and scope of welfare states (by Finseraas and Jæger, Chapters Two and Three, respectively) suggest that we would probably find considerable internal variation on these issues in the Nordic and other countries. Here we clearly see a potential for political pressures for other welfare state arrangements and divisions of responsibilities between public and private spheres, with likely impacts not only on the scope for individual choice but also on the degree of social inequality in society.

Consequences of changes in public welfare provision

We have already referred to Meagher and Szebehely's discussion of how the introduction of HCA has reproduced or created social inequalities (for example, in children's use of childcare centres and mothers' participation in the labour market), albeit to a different extent in the Nordic countries. Meagher and Szebehely also touch on the growing strand of research studying the long-term effects of having been enrolled in childcare centres on future educational and work-related achievements.

In their chapter on the development in different countries' means-tested minimum income arrangements, Kuivalainen and Nelson (Chapter Four) show that the capacity of such arrangements to protect recipients against poverty has been weakened, because of insufficient upgrading for keeping pace with general increases in earnings. Similarly, the findings of Hussain, Kangas and Kvist (Chapter Six) indicate that the replacement rates of unemployment insurance benefits generally declined from the mid-1990s to the mid-2000s.

Again, it is beyond the scope of this book to fully explain why the redistributive or protective capacity of Nordic welfare states in some respects appears to have been diminished. As in other areas of welfare reform, we are probably faced with a mix of causes and motivations. Some reductions in generosity of benefits – or lack of adjustment of benefit levels in relation to the general development in earnings – may be dictated by a perceived need for reducing public expenditure. The Nordic welfare states have always put a great deal of emphasis on work ethics. Given the costs for public expenditure, both high employment rates and high tax revenues are prerequisites for the model. Less generous benefit systems are now becoming part of the Nordic governments' attempts to improve incentives to work and to hasten the flow of potential workers into or back to employment.

Are the Nordic responses to social inequalities better, worse or different from those of other countries?

One answer to this question is that as a rule the Nordic countries are doing better than most other European countries at limiting income inequality and poverty. The one important exception is the Netherlands, which actually appears to do better in combating poverty – both generally and in relation to several risk groups – than most of the Nordic countries. (The Netherlands is also more successful than the Nordic countries at preventing persistent poverty.) Despite the Nordic successes in stemming the tide of income inequality better than most countries, income inequality in the Nordic countries has also clearly increased, making the region less distinct in this respect today. Put differently, the Nordic countries have become 'more European' with regard to income inequalities and poverty risks.

The picture is slightly different when we consider protection against economic hardship in the context of transition into and out of unemployment. While the Nordic countries have maintained high employment levels, other European countries have increased their employment levels through higher female labour market participation. The level of income protection offered by unemployment insurance has decreased in the Nordic countries (as it has in Central Europe), while it has increased in the UK, Ireland and the Southern European countries. Even if Nordic poverty rates related to transitions have increased, the rates are still lower than for the Central, Liberal and Southern European groups of countries.

When it comes to formal childcare systems, the Nordic countries as a group are again performing better than most other countries in defamilisation and equality-promoting potential, albeit with some overlap with the Netherlands and France on defamilisation.

Overall, the Nordic countries are still fairly distinct as a group and different from most other countries in terms of maintaining small income inequalities and low poverty rates, and providing formal childcare services, although the Netherlands is more successful at combating poverty. While the Nordic countries have retained the lead in high overall employment levels (thanks to high female employment rates), the differences between the Nordic and the other groups of countries are smaller than before. The reason is that the other countries have been able to catch up to the Nordic countries, thereby diminishing the gap – the other countries are becoming 'more Nordic'. When it comes to poverty figures, the gap has likewise diminished because poverty and inequality are also expanding in the Nordic region. Thus in this respect the Nordic countries are gradually losing one of the central hallmarks of their welfare model.

The transformation of the Nordic welfare model is complex. The overall aims of motivating individuals and helping them find work, form families and excel in society may be intact. However, the mix of policies has become ambiguous in relation to the aims of promoting individuals' agency and protecting their level of living outside work. At the same time rewarding employment is becoming more dominant. The Nordic countries seem to be on a track that will eventually lead to a welfare model where 'some are more equal than others'.

Index

Note: The letter 'f' following a page number indicates a figure, 't' a table and 'n' a note.

A

APWs (average production workers) 127
Ablett, J. 196
ageing *see* older people
Airio, I. 121, 177
Akaike Information Criterion (AIC) 53
Akbari, A.H. 196
Alesina, A. 23, 24, 25, 37
Allardt, E. 2
Andreß, H.-J. 121
anti-solidarity hypothesis 27–30
Arts, W. 59, 62n2
asylum seekers *see* refugees
Atkinson, A.B. 167

B

babies *see* infant mortality
Bambra, C. 148, 150
Bayesian Information Criterion (BIC) 53
Bean, C. 62n2
Benoit, K. 35, 37
Bhattacharya, J. 195
Bismarck, Otto von 10
Black Report (1980) 146, 150
Bratsberg, B. 190
Bruce, E. 195

C

care provision 90
cash-for-care 105
cash transfers 192–3
Causa, O. 38
childcare
  benefits 91, 92
  class inequality 90, 102–3, 116t
  defamilialisation 90–91, 97–100, 102, 103, 104t, 107, 204–5
  gender equality 98–102
  home childcare allowances (HCA) 92, 94, 95, 96–7, 107–8, 109–10, 203
  participation 92–3
  private sector 107
  systems 104t, 204–5
childminders 96, 98, 99t, 101f, 102, 108
children
  benefits 8

poverty 105, 110, 176f, 177, 179–80
Chung, H. 148
class
  and childcare 90, 102–3, 116t
  and health 144–5, 158
Coburn, D. 148, 150
conflict theory 25
Conley, D. 148
corporatism 77
Crepaz, M. 25–6

D

Dahl, E. 157
De La O, A.L. 26
decommodification 7, 148
deprivation 157 *see also* poverty
deservingness 48
distraction hypothesis 24, 30–8
Duvander, A.-Z. 110

E

ECHP User Data Base 122
ESS *see* European Social Survey
EU *see* European Union
EU-SILC *see* European Union Statistics on Income and Living Conditions
'educare' 109
education
  and morbidity 151, 153
  and mortality 152–3
  parental 117t
  and socioeconomic status 145
  welfare state, support for 117t
egalitarianism 32, 71
Eikemo, T.A. 145, 153, 154t
Ekberg, J. 195
elderly people *see* older people
employment 71
  and health 147
  immigrants and 25
  incentives for 131
  and labour market 124–6
  and poverty 120–1, 129, 130t
  strategies for 72
  see also labour market; work
equality

childcare 89–110
  definitions 3
  gender 6
  impacts of 9
  'passion for' 6, 45, 47, 61–2
Espelt, A. 154t
Esping-Andersen, G. 7, 166
  Three worlds of welfare capitalism 119
ethnic diversity 23, 188
European Community Household Panel Survey
    (ECHP) 121, 132, 138
European Social Survey (ESS) 27, 63n3
European Union (EU)
  'at risk of poverty' threshold 77, 168
  inequalities 2
  Statistics on Income and Living Conditions
    (EU-SILC) 89, 98, 105, 122–3, 126, 132, 138,
    169–70, 176, 179
European Values Study 62n2, 63n3
Evans, G. 62n2

F

familialism 95–6
families
  benefits 73
  childcare 90–1
  migrant 188
  poverty 176f, 177
  single-parent 105, 107
family allowances, Continental European welfare
    model 10
Ferrarini, T. 90, 110
Ferrera, M. 154t
Finseraas, H. 25, 26
Fleckenstein, T. 107
fractionalisation
  ethnic 26, 28–9, 37, 38–9
  racial 29, 30t, 34t, 37, 39
freedom of choice 2–3, 13

G

Gelissen, J. 59, 62n2
Gelman, A. 26–7
gender equality 6
  and childcare 90, 98–103, 109
  and employment 124
Gerdes, C. 194
Gini coefficient 168, 170–1
Glaeser, E. 23, 24, 25, 37
Gough, I. 70, 71
grandparents 98, 100, 103, 108
Growing unequal (OECD) 165, 174
Gustafsson, B. 195

H

Hägglund, G. 97
health inequalities 143–59
  comparative studies 150–4
  defining 144–5
  measuring 145–6
  Nordic countries 156–9
  theories 146–7, 156–7
healthcare 9, 147
heterogeneity, racial 24–5
home childcare allowances (HCA) 92, 94–7,
    107–10, 203
homogeneity 5 *see also* ethnic diversity
horizontal redistribution 8
housing 147
Huber, J.D. 26

I

ISEI *see* International Socio-Economic Index
    [ISEI] of Occupational Status
ISSP *see* International Social Survey Programme
immigrants/immigration
  benefits 25
  cash transfers 192–3
  childcare 91
  economic sustainability 183–97
  employment 25
  labour market 38, 187–92
  policies 28, 30, 31, 33f, 35–8, 188, 193–7,
    201–2
  poverty 12, 110, 167, 176f, 177–8, 182–3
  public sector finances 193–6
income
  inequalities in 1, 154t, 169–74, 192
  and labour market 120–2
  and poverty 131
  redistribution of 48–9
  replacement rates of 128t
  social 6, 7, 8–9
  see also wages
inequalities
  changes 4–5
  framing 5
  health 143–59
  income 1, 154t, 169–74, 192
  and poverty 165–83, 204
  welfare regimes 5–9, 9–10, 204–5
infant mortality 148–50, 155
insurance
  social 7, 10
  unemployment 127–8, 131–2, 133, 137–8
International Social Survey Programme (ISSP)
    'Role of Government' (RoG) modules 46,
    48, 51–2, 62n2, 63n3
International Socio-Economic Index [ISEI] of
    Occupational Status 52, 66

J

Jean, S. 38
Johansson, S. 2, 3

K

Kangas, O. 167
Karim, S.A. 148
Kawachi, I. 144
Korpi, W. 6, 90
Kristjansson, A.S. 172

L

LIS *see* Luxembourg Income Study
labour markets 8
  changes 129–31
  immigration 38, 189–92
  and income 120–2
  inequalities 10
  policies (ALMPs) 122, 126
  women 6, 90, 96, 105–6, 108–9, 120, 122, 137
  see also employment
Laeken indicators 168, 169
Lahelma, E. 157
Larsen, K.A. 195
latent class analysis (LCA) 52–3, 55
latent class regression (LCR) models 53, 55–6, 66
Laver, M. 35, 37
Leftist parties
  and redistribution 26, 30–2
  voters' preferences 32–8
  welfare state policies 39
Leibfried, S. 69
Level of Living Surveys 2
life chances 4
life-course epidemiology 157
living conditions 3
Lødemel, I. 72
Lohmann, H.121
low-income groups 6 *see also* poverty
Lundberg, O. 149, 157
Luxembourg Income Study (LIS) database 74–5, 167, 169, 174

M

Mackenbach, J.P. 157
MaCurdy, T. 195
Mahon, R. 97
Marshall, T.H. 69
means testing 8, 10, 69–71, 73, 75, 79–80, 82
MEANSI income variable 75
middle class 6, 7
morbidity 145–6, 151, 155–6
mortality 145–6, 151–2, 155

  infants 148–50, 155
  old people 150
multicultural societies 12
Muntaner, C. 148

N

Navarro, V. 148, 150, 154t
Nechyba, T. 195

O

OECD (Organisation for Economic Co-operation and Development)
  Growing unequal 165, 174
  immigration data 29
  infant mortality 148
  poverty scale 168
  social assistance 70–1
Ólafsson, S. 172, 182
older people 11
  mortality 150
  poverty 167, 176f, 177–8, 180–2
Open Method of Coordination (OMC) 169
Österberg, T. 195

P

Palme, J. 6, 167
Papadakis, E. 62n2
parents
  childcare 91–3, 95–7, 100, 101f, 102, 107
  educational background 102–3
  single 105, 107, 176f
pensions 8, 150
Pontusson, J. 25
poverty
  children 105, 110, 176f, 177, 179–80
  data 74, 169–70
  definitions 168
  and employment 120–1, 129, 130t, 167
  families 176f, 177
  immigrants 12, 110, 167, 176f, 177, 182
  indicators 167–8
  and inequality 165–83, 204
  Laeken indicators 9, 168
  measuring 168–9
  older people 167, 176f, 177–8, 180–2
  persistency 179–82
  threshold of 168, 178–9
  profiles 178–9
  and redistribution 81–3
  risk groups 176–8
  single-parents 176f
  social assistance and 70–1
  trends 174–5
  and unemployment 120, 131, 137–8

young single adults 177–81
see also deprivation; low-income groups
preschools 92, 108
public sector 49, 56, 61, 193–6

R

Raaum, O. 190
racism 23–4
Rawls, J. 69
redistribution
  paradox of 6, 7
  and poverty 81–3
  vertical 8
  and xenophobia 24–7
refugees 188, 192
Rightist parties 26, 37
Ritakallio, V.-M. 174
Rodden, J.A. 26
Roemer, J.E. 24, 26
Rothstein, Bo 6
Rowntree, S. 167

S

SaMip *see* Social Assistance and Minimum
  Income Protection Interim Dataset
self-reporting 145–6, 151
Sen, A. 2–3
Senik, C. 25
Shi, L. 154t
single-parents 105, 107, 176f
Sipilä, J. 89, 105
Slovenia, infant mortality/life expectancy 149t
smoking 157
social assistance 69–84
  benefit generosity 75–9
  extent of 79–80
  poverty and redistribution 81–3
Social Assistance and Minimum Income
  Protection Interim Dataset (SaMip) 74
social insurance schemes 7, 69
social services 9–10
social trust 26
Springer, K. 148
Stanig, P. 26

T

tax
  childcare 89, 92, 95
  health inequalities 155
  immigrants 193, 197
  income inequalities 169, 172
Three worlds of welfare capitalism (Esping-
  Andersen) 119
Titmuss, R. 2

transport 147
Trickey, H. 72

U

unemployment 6, 7, 38, 72, 84, 96, 124, 126,
  130t, 137, 204
  and health 147
  and immigration 191
  insurance 127–8, 131–2, 133, 137–8, 204
  and poverty 119–39, 129, 131
universalism 165

V

Valkonen, T. 151
Vernby, K. 26
voters
  immigration 25–6
  party preferences 26, 30–8
  xenophobia 39

W

wages 189–90 *see also* income
water 147
welfare regimes 48–50
  Anglo-Saxon 10
  Continental European (Conservative) 10, 49,
    50, 119, 166
  equality 166–8
  inequality 9–13
  Liberal (Anglo-Saxon) 49, 50, 119, 166
  poverty 166–8
  Social Democratic (Nordic) 5–9, 49–50, 119,
    122, 166
  Southern (Latin Rim) 49–50, 119–20, 166
  variables 131–3, 134f, 135f, 136f
  see also welfare states
welfare states
  health regimes 143, 144–5, 147–50, 154–6
  redistribution paradox 6, 7
  Anglo-Saxon countries 47
  changes in 50, 59–61
  conditional supporters of 50–1, 54–5, 56, 58,
    60, 62, 63n3, 67f, 68f
  Continental Europe 47
  cross-national patterns 47, 51, 56–9
  dimensionality 50
  and education 67f
  and income 67f
  Nordic countries 46–7
  principles 47
  programmes 47–8
  sceptics 55–6, 59, 63n3, 67f, 68f
  socioeconomic correlates 55–6, 66, 68f
  Southern Europe 47

unconditional supporters of 54–6, 58–61, 63n3, 67f, 68f

trade-offs 7, 10–11, 44t

see also welfare regimes

women

childcare 89–91, 93, 95

health inequalities 154t

labour market 6, 90, 96, 105–6, 108–9, 120, 137

welfare state, support for 56, 61

work, passion for 6–8

The working poor in Europe: Employment, poverty and globalization (Andreß and Lohmann) 121

World Values Survey 25

X

xenophobia 24–7, 39

Y

young single adults

benefits 8

poverty 177–82, 187